W9-BBB-279

# HOLLYWOOD RAJAH

# Hollywood Rajah

## THE LIFE AND TIMES OF
## LOUIS B. MAYER

BY

BOSLEY CROWTHER

*New York*
*Henry Holt and Company*

ABIGAIL E. WEEKS MEMORIAL LIBRARY

791.43
M468

Copyright © 1960 by Bosley Crowther
All rights reserved, including the right to reproduce
this book or portions thereof in any form.

FIRST EDITION

Library of Congress Catalog Card Number: 60–6435

81623–0110
Printed in the United States of America

FOR FLORENCE

"We have deep psychic hungers, all of us, hungers for money or power or dazzling beauty or acclaim."

—MAX LERNER

# Illustrations

A celebrity luncheon in the Marion Davies "bungalow."

following page 180

Mayer presents a make-up box to Miss Davies.
Mayer, Charles A. Lindbergh, Edgar Hatrick, and W.R. Hearst.
Mayer in a fireman's cap to promote *The Fire Brigade*.
Mayer in baseball uniform.
Mayer and Irving Thalberg at a studio picnic.
Herbert Hoover on his first visit to a motion picture studio.
Former President Coolidge and his wife on the Metro lot.
Mayer and Jeanette MacDonald.
Jean Howard.
Ginny Simms.
Mayer and Jean Harlow.
Mayer and Judy Garland.
Mayer and Elizabeth Taylor.
Mayer and Margaret O'Brien.
Proud Grandpa with Judith Goetz.
The budding horseman with his famous sire, Beau Pere.
Mayer escorts Mrs. Franklin Roosevelt around the Culver City lot.
Edsel Ford, Henry Ford, Mickey Rooney, and Mayer visit Detroit where *Young Tom Edison* opened.
Dore Schary with Mayer.
Mayer, Nicholas Schenck, Greer Garson, and Mrs. Schenck.
Mayer with his new wife, Lorena.
Mayer receives an LL.D. from the University of New Brunswick.

# HOLLYWOOD RAJAH

# Prologue

*It is the* Book of Genesis *which says, "There were giants in those days. . . ."*

The words came, barely audible, from the curiously tightened lips of actor Spencer Tracy. He stood with head lowered and his eyes, shaded behind dark glasses, were fixed on the unfolded page of typewritten manuscript before him, searching to read the words that others had written for him to say about Louis B. Mayer.

Mayer was dead now. His stocky body, wasted by the violent disease that had ironically come upon him in the last bruising clash of his career, lay in a flower-covered coffin before the rostrum at which the actor stood. It had looked strangely small and ungiantlike to those who viewed it in its cold, embalmed repose.

*Another book tells us . . .*

The actor read, then uncomfortably paused and threw a quick glance at the mourners who sat stoically in pews beneath the high-domed ceiling of the handsome temple on Wilshire Boulevard in Los Angeles.

*. . . that a giant is a man of great stature . . .*

Tracy painfully picked up the words, as though they were stones that he must carry to the construction of a mortared monument, and passed them along in the somber relay of service to the dead. . . .

And so it had come to this last ritual, the long and stormy career of Hollywood's most dynamic and momentous film producer, Louis Mayer. Here, in the customary gathering of long-faced movie stars and dark-suited studio executives, ranked in discreetly balanced rows in "Rabbi Magnin's temple," the sanctuary of Hollywood's wealthier souls, Mayer had reached the final station in his passage through that odd community.

How many in the solemn gathering knew the departed man—knew him for the person, as well as the symbol, that he was? How many seated there in mourning or in the appropriate attitudes of soberly civilized tribesmen from whom the show of "last respects" was due had ever really seen beneath the surface of the volatile Louis Mayer and glimpsed the motivating wellsprings and mysteries of this powerful human being?

Had Tracy, the eminent actor and one-time outstanding star of the studio controlled by the Goliath, Metro-Goldwyn-Mayer? Had he seen beneath the surface and scanned the so-called guts of the man?

*Louis B. Mayer knew people better than all the other many things he knew so well. It was because he knew people that he was able to know the other many things . . .*

Smooth words. Yet wasn't it Tracy whom all of the "insiders" knew to be something less than an admirer—indeed, a studious avoider—of Mayer? "I was told he didn't like me because he knew I was onto him," he had said in a moment of candid reflection, a few years before Mayer died. What was it Tracy was "onto"? Or was Mayer "onto" him?

Who else had seen beneath the surface? Perhaps some of those executives, last of the Old Guard at the studio that

Mayer had ruled for twenty-seven years, until a compounding of pressures and his own follies had dumped him from his throne?

Beyond any question, they had known him. They had seen a great deal of him, in all of his operational aspects, which were grandly involved yet uniform. They were cold-bloodedly familiar with his weaknesses as well as his strengths, with his bold and exciting inclinations as well as his pettinesses. And because it was part of the system to have their quidnuncs and spies, they knew all about his private didoes that he himself didn't recklessly reveal.

But had they really seen beneath the surface with cool and comprehending eyes? Had they sensed the psychic whirlpools that spun and spewed in Louis Mayer? Did they know that he had often struggled through sleepless and terrifying nights, lashing himself with black anxieties and piercing himself with doubts and fears? Did they know that he went into tantrums that were something quite different and apart from the bursts of temperament and anger that he often put on to make a point? Did they know that, in the silence of his bedroom, he could sweat and grovel and moan?

And did the odd group of pallbearers, which included his latest chauffeur, a veteran motion picture director, and an ex-Secretary of Defense—did they know the complicated nature of the man they were carrying to his grave? Or did fifty-year-old Jeanette MacDonald, who opened the services by singing "Ah, Sweet Mystery of Life"?

Did Mayer's family truly know him—his daughters and his younger second wife who had been married to him for only ten years, after he had crossed the roughest mountains of his life? Could they perceive him clearly through the inevitable and obfuscating gauze of their own individual psyches, ambitions, and private memories?

What of the elderly lady who sat there to one side? She was Mayer's older sister, older by several years than he, and (as was known by intimates) long estranged from him. She had

been living modestly for years in Los Angeles, seldom seeing
the famous brother who was hailed as the giant of former
days. Yet here she was at his funeral, humbly come to hear
the melancholy *Kadish* said for the little *bruder* of long ago.
What did the eyes of this old lady perceive through the haze
of many years, farther back into the past of the deceased man
than anyone present could see? Was there something back
there in his distant childhood that provided a clarifying clue?

*The story he wanted to tell was the story of America*
(Tracy read)—*the land for which he had an almost furious
love, born of gratitude—and of contrast with the hatreds in
the dark land of his boyhood across the seas. It was this love
for America that made him an authority on America, and his
counsel was sought by men in high places. . . . All the rest is
history. . . .*

In the street outside the temple, a few hundred curious
persons stood, drawn by another opportunity to look at a concentration of movie stars. They were mostly older people, as
were the stars who arrived—people whose interests in movies
were formed and nourished in other days. Their recollections were likely of the great motion pictures that raised the
screen to its highest eminence of abundance and achievement
in the years before World War II—years long before television became the top entertainment device, when Hollywood
was still unique as a sort of Mecca and its prophet was
Louis B. Mayer.

How many of them paused to reckon the morbid significance of his death?

How many of them knew exactly—or cared very much—
who was dead?

It was perhaps to be expected that the nature of Mayer and
the extent of his contributions to the advancement of American films should have been miscalculated and exaggerated, to
one or the other extreme, by those who came within the ra-

dius of his powerful command and sway—and this meant a large swath of the people who worked in his time in Hollywood. For his decisions and instructions carried a stern authority, and upon them the fortunes and the fates of many suppliant people rose or fell.

In Hollywood, such authority was nerve-wracking beyond the ken of anyone whose experience with job security and self-promotion has been in normal fields. For there, in the fantastic business of manufacturing films, the judgment of a person's ability to deliver was largely a matter of guess.

To be sure, there were records of "past performance" on which decisions might be based, and abilities in the managerial areas could be reckoned on fairly conventional grounds. But the major decisions on artists in whom to trust and invest elaborate sums for the making of problematic films had to be arbitrary, determined by intuition and hope.

Furthermore, the rewards to those chosen were likely to be so immense, not alone in financial treasures but in a curious community prestige, that the competition for jobs was wicked and emotional involvements were intense. Those who had the say-so on selections were more than strategically placed. They had, in the Hollywood cosmos, the power of bestowing life or death.

This was a power that Mayer wielded through momentous years in the growth of American motion pictures. It was a pyramided power, exercised with himself at the apex and with subordinates to administer it lower down, so that always there was an awareness that the chain of command descended from him. And this was for many years established upon the richness, resources, and prestige of the great studio he directed, Metro-Goldwyn-Mayer.

Therefore, it is no wonder that Mayer, with this concentration of power and this unassailable position from which to throw weight in the community, was one whose attentions and favors were assiduously sought and whose counsels on over-all matters largely swayed the producing industry. Those whom he generally favored regarded him as a demigod; those whom he did not favor thought him a monster—or worse.

More than that, there were varying tides and currents of interests that flowed through Hollywood, shifting and taking different courses over the changing years. Studios and stars, individuals and companies waxed and waned. Mayer held a strong position over three decades. Naturally, in that virtual lifetime, he himself underwent change, made friends and lost them, made enemies and turned some of them into friends. By the time he had passed through the dark crises that beclouded the end of his career, he had done as much to quicken and shake the business as any man alive.

Naturally, then, he was regarded as something more than a man. He was a force, an emanation, an aura, a monolith. Those who had dealt directly with him or had come within his sway as pieces which he had occasion to move upon the board had their particular ideas of him. David O. Selznick proclaimed that "Louis B. Mayer was the greatest single figure in the history of motion picture production." Danny Kaye warmly said, "He exercised all the passions fiercely. He could love and he could hate. He could help you or hurt you badly. He was full of enthusiasms. He was great!" And Samuel Goldwyn, a rugged individual who never loved him, remarked tersely at the end, "The reason so many people showed up at his funeral was because they wanted to make sure he was dead."

To others, below the levels of dealings or contacts with Mayer but constantly aware of his being and his importance in Hollywood, he was a supernatural presence, a cosmic phenomenon like the jet-stream that pours across the heavens at an altitude of thirty thousand feet.

Of course, there were stories about him. And legends. The whole community had heard of the famous histrionics and subterfuges of Mayer. Some of the stories were accurate, such as that of the time he got down on his knees in his office in front of Jeanette MacDonald and sang "Eli, Eli," the Jewish lament, in order to show the singer how he wanted her to get more *schmaltz* into her voice. Some were inaccurate, yet so vivid in suggesting the tactics of the man that they were regularly recalled and repeated until they almost warranted belief.

One such was the story of Robert Taylor, in the second year of his career at the studio, going to Mayer and politely requesting an increase in his beginner's salary of seventy-five dollars a week.

"Sit down, Bob," Mayer supposedly said to the nervous young man. "Sit down and let me talk to you."

Supposedly the actor sat down.

"Bob," Mayer is quoted as saying in a kindly, wistful way, "God never saw fit to give me the great blessing of a son. He gave me daughters, two beautiful daughters, who have been a great joy to me. They're now married to fine, successful fellows—top producers—Dave Selznick and Billy Goetz. But for some reason, in His infinite wisdom, He never saw fit to give me a son.

"But if He *had* given me a son, Bob—if He had blessed me with such a great and wonderful joy—I can't think of anybody I would rather have wanted than that son to be exactly like you. I would have wanted him to be . . . ," and thereupon Mayer supposedly ran the whole catalogue of physical assets and professional endowments the actor abundantly possessed. So warm was his legendary approval that Taylor supposedly became convinced that he would get not only an increase but the unexpected and unstinting help of Mayer.

He was happily dwelling upon this prospect (according to the legend), when he heard the producer continuing sweetly, "And if that son came to me and said, 'Dad, I am working for a wonderful company, Metro-Goldwyn-Mayer, and for a good man, the head of that company, who has my best interests at heart. But he's only paying me seventy-five dollars a week, Dad. Do you think I should ask him for a raise?' Do you know what I'd say to my son, Bob? I'd say, 'Son, it's a fine company. It is going to do great things for you—greater things than it has already done. It is going to make a great star of you. It is going to give you a wonderful career. You'll be famous! That's more important than a little money. Don't ask for a raise now, son.'"

When Taylor supposedly left the office, in something of a daze, his agent grabbed him in the hallway. "Did you get the raise?" he asked.

"No, but I got a father," the actor is supposed to have beamed.

Taylor says that such a thing did not occur. But a lot of people believed it happened; it was characteristic of Mayer.

Accurate or not, stories contributed to the myth of the man whose soubriquets ran from "Mister Movies" to "that sunnava bitch, L.B."

Certain facts are on record. Mayer did run the full range of experience in the motion picture business from owner and operator of a nickelodeon in the infancy of "flickers" through the office of a film distributor to the exalted station of head of the largest studio in the world. He did pal with "men in high places." He was "big" in politics. He did have the most successful horse farm and racing stable in California. And he was, for a span of eight or nine years, the "highest salaried man in the United States." These are unqualified details entombed in public prints.

However, there is more to know about him—much more than was ever put in print or even talked about by his associates while he was still alive, in more or less position to discourage a thorough estimate. Mayer was the sort who cherished and cultivated his myth. It would not have been to his advantage to have himself too well understood.

But the important consideration, the important illumination now, is what manner of man was this who wielded such arbitrary power over a medium that had so much influence upon the concepts of people throughout the world, a medium that has vastly conditioned the mental processes of many millions in our time? What manner of man was known as the most powerful in Hollywood?

There is a surprisingly meager body of solid literature on Hollywood producers, the motley executives who played roles of clairvoyants and attempted to ride some sort of herd on much more conspicuous and publicized writers, directors, and stars. There has been a lot of gossip written and also fantasy that has oozed from the semi-clitoral styluses of female columnists. There have been some good journalistic pieces, a few bought biographies, and several respectable novels that have helped to distinguish the breed. Best of the lot is Budd Schulberg's *What Makes Sammy Run?* Most elusive and overrated is F. Scott Fitzgerald's unfinished synthesis, *The Last Tycoon.*

It is my hope that this searching observation of the life and times of Louis B. Mayer will help correct this shortcoming in our abundant American literature. And I hope it will serve to help illuminate more than a Hollywood type, more than the monolithic figure of Metro-Goldwyn's many-sided Mayer. For I find that this man is characteristic of a large group of magnates and tycoons who have marched across the landscape of industrial America. With them, he is in that phalanx of men of aggressive bent who seized on the opportunities that an expanding civilization exposed. With them, he ascended to high places along an upwardly spiraling route that was there to be ascended by those who had the necessary stamina and drive. And, with some of them, he was unsettled and rendered dizzy by the heights, so that he could not control his footing when the road itself began to narrow and fall.

I wish to offer this volume as an inspection of one of those "giants." It embraces a long and lusty drama that ends in tragedy.

# 1

A short, chunky, black-haired boy, in scuffed shoes and nondescript clothes which clearly betrayed that their wearer was far from well-to-do, began to become a familiar figure on the pleasant streets of Saint John, a small city in the Canadian province of New Brunswick, toward the close of the last century.

He was a sturdy, energetic youngster, as supple and active as a goat, and he went about his business with a determination gratifying to see. His business was simple. Over his shoulder he carried a large, coarse bag which bulged in odd shapes around the bottom and dragged clumsily on the boy. Scuttling along the sidewalks or through back lanes and alleyways, he was constantly searching the ground before him with small, dark, lively eyes. Now and again, he would be rewarded with the discovery of a scrap of rusted iron, a piece of pipe, a sliver of metal, a worn horseshoe, or a broken tool. Quickly, the lad would grab it and plunge it into his bag, then move on as though he were being pursued.

What he was doing was more familiar and rewarding in those days than it is now. He was collecting junk. He was a ragpicker. His name was Louis Mayer.

At least, that is what he and his parents had decided was to be his name when they made their unobtrusive entrance into the gentle community of Saint John. What it had been back in Russia, where he and his parents were born, in the dank and obscure Minsk district, is not precisely known. His first or given name was probably Lazar, a familiar Hebrew name which was commonly transformed into Louis when migrants came to the western world. But what the old surname of the family was is lost in the shadows of the years.

This seemingly careless disposition to lose a family name, to drop and thankfully forget it, was not uncommon among rootless Jews who poured out of Russia and eastern Europe in great waves of emigration toward the end of the last century. An old name was often a nuisance, a clumsy sound that was difficult to translate from guttural Yiddish into the crisper syllables of the English tongue. Sometimes it might be an embarrassing reminder of an unpleasant past. Occasionally, it could be an undesirable and even dangerous identifying mark. To change one was not difficult.

Likewise, it wasn't unnatural that the ties with a bleak and ugly past that had been a nightmare of pain and anguish, as life in Czarist Russia was, should have been dropped without hesitation. And life for this family had been one of endless poverty and suffering in the unfriendly land of their birth.

The father, Jacob, had been a poor laborer and sometime tradesman in a little town near Minsk, and Mother Sarah (or Chaye, in the Hebraic spelling) was a woman of peasant stock. They were propertyless, hand-to-mouth descendants of long generations stretching back into the dark and nameless ages of the wandering Israelites. What was known of the family background was told from father to son, garbled and twisted in the telling. Crowded ghettos had been their hopeless home. Brutal pogroms of the nineteenth century had been their tragic lot.

Under such circumstances, vital statistics were of slight concern; records were inconvenient and memories were fallible. The date of a person's birth or marriage or death might easily be confused in the muddle of harsher recollections. So it was with the date of Louis' birth.

His mother seemed to remember that he was born in 1885. Or, being a year of famine, it may have been 1882. Louis himself was evidently uncertain. When applying for a marriage license in 1904 he gave the year of his birth as 1882. On his later naturalization petition he gave it as 1885. Eighteen-eighty-two, eighteen-eighty-five—what did it matter? Obviously, he was born.

And on what day? Well, it was in midsummer, his mother also recalled. So Louis later decided it must have been July 4. That was a suitable birthday for a new American.

His own recollections of his early childhood were mercifully meager and dim. They were mainly recollections of being hungry and thirsty for milk. A tiny child, perpetually undernourished after he left his mother's breast—that was the only memory Mayer had of himself as a little boy.

At some time in the late 1880's—again, the date is not sure —that hard-pressed father and mother, both nearly forty years old, heard the call of westward emigration to which so many of their neighbors and friends were now beginning to respond. With everything to gain and little to lose, they gathered their brood of youngsters—Yetta, the eldest, and Lazar and Ida Mae, a second daughter, still an infant—and, with the small means they had, went to a port on the Baltic and took passage for the New World.

To get out of Europe at that time was a blessed liberation for those who had lived with choking restrictions placed upon the freedom of Jews. Yet freedom itself was a condition they could only remotely comprehend, especially those of little education and a single philosophy—to survive. They swarmed across the Atlantic to the New World, now open to them, with little more concept of its nature than that it was a Promised Land, a land of milk and honey and boundless opportunities to get rich.

What they brought with them, in general, was the impulse to get away, to be shed of restraints and threats of slaughter, rather than a passion to be free. Their notions of social organization were mainly those imposed by generations of self-protective living in rigid orthodoxy. And this orthodoxy came with them. In the climate of the New World, which itself had oppressive aspects, they clung to it as an ethnic group.

Probably the Mayers came through England, as most migrants from eastern Europe did, and transshipped in Liverpool or Plymouth for the United States. They landed in New York and attempted to earn a living there, for it was in that teeming center of immigrant traffic that two more sons, Ruben and Jacob, were born.

When and in what circumstances the family moved on to Saint John are further unrecorded details about which memories grew vague. Certain shreds of old gossip hint at some embarrassment over a fire, and there could be a possible connection between this and a change of the family name. For deep in the recollections of a few old-timers in Saint John is the fact that the Mayers never talked much about their origins, and the boys always clammed up coldly whenever questioned about the name.

But such reluctance was heeded and respected in the community where new arrivals—some ship-jumpers—were asked few questions and were often hidden by charitable *lansmen* (kinsmen) for months or years. That's why immigration records for that period are incomplete.

The first concrete record of the presence of the Mayers in Saint John is to be found in a modest notation in the 1896-97 city directory. There Jacob Mayer is listed as a "pedler" with an address on Main Street. Main Street? Don't let that fool you. Main Street, so called, in Saint John—or in Portland, as the section of the city north of the harbor was known—was an unpaved and unimpressive thoroughfare that came up from mucky tidal flats (where railway yards later were constructed) and circled under the hill below Fort Howe. It was lined with ugly frame buildings, carpenter shops, and cheap stores. The streets that went off from it—Acadia, Portland, and Sheriff Streets—running down to the water, were crowded with frame tenements, the homes of sailors, draymen, laborers, peddlers, and the poor. In this working-class section the Mayers had their scanty home.

Saint John was a sturdy little city, prospering by lumber milling and the fabricating of iron. From the time of the American Revolution, when groups of Loyalists fled there from the new republic to continue as subjects of the king, it had thrived as a maritime port on the ice-free Bay of Fundy. It was a conservative community, made up mostly of English and Scots who lived comfortably in their prim houses, with Anglican and Calvinist principles setting the character of their commerce and somewhat starched social life.

Except for three Hebrew families that had arrived in the mid-nineteenth century—cigar manufacturers and tobacconists from Holland and Alsace-Lorraine—there were none of that religion in the community until the last decade of the century. Then the great tide of immigrants from Russia, Poland, and Hungary began to be felt in Saint John. Jacobsons, Boyaners, Komienskys, Myers, and others arrived. It was with this wave of immigrants that the Mayers came.

They were poor when they arrived in the community, agonizingly poor, which means they had practically nothing but the clothes they wore on their backs, perhaps a few chattels, a little money sewed into a coat. Work for them meant doing anything they could find, anything to get themselves started and have pennies to buy food. And food oftentimes consisted of no more than a stale loaf of bread, a few potatoes, or whatever staple could be got the most of for the least expense.

Father Jacob was a short, chunky fellow, somewhat hunched—indeed, almost deformed—who was slow and solemn by nature and talked in a labored, asthmatic way. He took up peddling, the house-to-house vending of small goods —buttons, pins, vegetables, whatever he could secure on which a profit might be turned. This was the starting station for a potential entrepreneur, as well as a way of earning a living, familiar to many immigrants.

The mother, Sarah, was also a toiler. She was a stout, solid woman, round-faced and swarthy, an uneducated peasant who spoke little broken English but was strong and indomitable. She, too, became a peddler, hawking live chickens from door to door. She bought the fowls from New Brunswick farmers and sold them to poor families for butchering in the homes. It was considered a somewhat menial, even degraded enterprise, this handling of "unclean" chickens, but Sarah had a family to feed and she couldn't afford to be dainty, even if she knew the meaning of the word. Her simple pride and satisfaction was the maintenance of her family, keeping her children together and putting a little food into their mouths. For her, it was sufficiently rewarding when she could afford to bring an extra chicken home and make a big pot of soup from it. Compensation was in her children's eyes.

In these circumstances, it is easy to understand why the boy Louis looked upon his mother as the kind and comforting center of his life. She was the gentle sanctuary and somehow-provider of food in a world which was constantly harassing and bewildering a poor boy. Within orthodox Jewish culture, the father, of course, is the head and unquestioned solon of the family. His word is inviolable law, and in the maintenance of his status he is traditionally stern. Apparently Louis disliked his father, feared him and resented him, as a boy, because of his rigid coercion. The mother absorbed the youngster's love.

And so it was that Louis, compelled to help add to family funds, was out on the streets ragpicking and collecting scraps at all hours when not in school.

School for the immigrant youngster was first the old Elm Street grammar school in cheapside Portland and later the Winter Street school in Saint John. There he was pushed and exhorted through elementary grades. He was not a conspicuous scholar. Indeed, he ranked poorly among his contemporaries in the respectable public school. But it hardly would be expected that a boy from a foreign land, whose language was only Yiddish until he was five or six, and who was forced to work all his spare time at fairly exhausting toil, would be an exceptional scholar among the more fortunate youngsters of the town.

It wasn't uncommon for Louis and his brothers, Ruby and little Jake, to have to fight their way home in the evenings through gangs of Irish kids, and some Germans and Scandinavians, that lived in the Sheriff Street slums. "Jew-baiting" was a candid pastime, and Louie came to know all too well the epithets that were flung at him and his brothers by young hooligans of Saint John. It was harsh and infuriating to be bullied and abused because of his background and religion, but the fighting was not too tough. As a matter of fact, Louie rather liked it; it became a cultivated taste. The sharp sting of fists on his tough hide was a goad to the electrifying joy he got from slamming his own fists into the faces and stomachs of other boys. Fighting provided an easy and convenient release for him. He had a lot of natural aggressions that came out in a rough-and-tumble brawl.

Not long after the arrival of the Mayer family in Saint John, Jewish residents formed a congregation for worship in the orthodox faith. By 1896, there were some thirty families in the town, and it was felt by them that they should have their facilities for religious gathering and for obtaining kosher food. The Congregation Ahavath Achim (Brotherly Love) was formed and a rabbi, Moses Topkin, was brought from the United States. For two years, the congregation met in borrowed or rented rooms—in the old Star Theater, the Venetian Gardens, and even the Odd Fellows Hall. In 1898, its first synagogue, a one-room frame structure, was built and blessed, and it was there that Louie and his brothers were instructed in Hebrew and became bar mizvah, in the age-old tradition. It was there, too, that he attended services dutifully on holy days, marking the long and solemn rituals, sitting among the men.

Papa Mayer was considered a Hebrew scholar by his ortho-dox friends, which meant that he probably had attended a yeshiva, or a formal religious school. This was not necessarily an indication that he had acquired any breadth of scholar-ship. The teachings of orthodox yeshivas were generally along rigid parochial lines, devoted to exhaustive study of the *Tal-mud* (the Hebrew laws) and the proper performance of ritu-als. Teaching was not primarily intended to impart intellec-tual scope; on the contrary, it was meant to bulwark the ho-mogeneity and isolation of the Jews. Living, as they did, in communities constantly threatening them, these people de-signed their religion to contain and protect themselves. They sought in their ancient laws and rituals a spiritual wall be-hind which they could survive, and in the old philosophy of the "chosen people" they found a flimsy prop for their mo-rale. It was mainly the strength of Judaism that the old world yeshivas taught.

Because of his exposure to such learning, Jacob Mayer was one of the first to be chosen an elder of the Saint John con-gregation—he, a poor peddler who, by slow degrees, was working to become a junk collector and dealer in metal scrap.

It was, indeed, as junk dealers that the Mayers became established in Saint John, and it was as such that they were respected as hard-working citizens. Long after the family had departed—after the simple, toiling mother had died and the sons and daughters and then the father had left the city where they found roots in the New World—there were those

in Saint John who could look back, across the span of the
years, and still see the father driving a rickety wagon pulled
by an old nag, with son Louie beside him, going out to pick
up metal and haul it back to their junk yard.

How powerful and violent were the urges in the depths of
the growing boy to break out of his immigrant encasement, to
throw off the unmistakable yoke of his Russian-Jewish characteristics and become more like the Canadian boys is interestingly indicated by an incident an old playmate recalls. It is
a seemingly innocent episode that might beguile a disciple of
C.G. Jung.

Louie had taken a strong fancy to the baseball he had seen
the fellows play, and he had made the usual gestures to get
into their games. But he still was a clumsy "foreigner"—and
he didn't possess a glove. He didn't own that shining symbol
that would let him into this game. The very idea of such a
folly would have made his poor parents howl. A glove for the
hand? To play games with? Louie, *du bist a nudnik!* A fool!

But he made up his mind he must own one, and he secretly put pennies away until he had the needed dollars.
When the great day for the purchase came, he went to the
hardware store, with his money, accompanied by a corps of
clattering friends. The word had been passed among his fellows: Louie was going to buy a glove! Louie was going to buy
the best one in the sports shop! His would be the best glove
in town!

His friends couldn't enter the store with him. He made
them wait outside, probably because he didn't want them to
see how much he really paid. He was in the store a long time.
When he came out, the glove was strapped to his belt, in the
proper professional position, bouncing against his thigh, and
his head, although sitting on his shoulders, was obviously up
in the clouds. He didn't even look at his playmates. He
walked down the street, as in a daze, literally transported by
the possession and display of a baseball glove. His friends
thought he was being haughty. Little did they realize what a

psychological experience this represented for the boy, what a long step out of his environment was accomplished by the purchase of that glove.

Another and later experience was in the same pattern of advance, but, alas, it was not so successful in accomplishing a boost to morale. Louie and one of his friends had pushed a cart out to the country to get some crates of live chickens from a farmer and fetch them back for the mother to sell. At Luneville they met a man who confronted them with a glittering idea. Why were they pushing this cart? Why wasn't it being pulled by a horse, and them sitting up on it riding, in proper style? Louie allowed the reason was that they didn't own a horse. Well, that could be remedied, said the fellow; he had a fine horse he would sell them. And cheap.

The rest of the story is familiar. The gullible boy bit on the bait that was dangled in a slick and seductive way. The first thing he knew, he was paying nine dollars for a spavined old nag that could barely support the crude rope harness devised to hitch it to the cart. On the way back to Saint John, it happened. The poor old creature could not endure the ardent encouragement of its new owner. It stumbled, fell down, and died.

Louie's subsequent ordeal with his father, when he futilely tried to explain what he had done, how he'd thrown away nine dollars, can readily be presumed. The poor peddler could not forgive him. "A businessman you'll never be!" he cried.

It is always a question what qualities a growing boy may reveal to give a fair indication of what may be expected from the man. Certainly aggressiveness and ambition were outstanding in Louie Mayer. He was persistent and tireless in his efforts to "get ahead."

In his early career as a ragpicker he met (under circumstances less in the vein of Horatio Alger than some charitable accounts would have you believe) an older man named John E. Wilson. Wilson was a calm and canny Scot with a large and successful tin business and firm notions about diligence and toil. The fiction is that young Louie showed up at his tin yard one day with a sack full of scrap which he unwittingly told the watchman he wanted to sell. Those who remember more clearly say that Louie was hanging around the yard with other less honorable intentions. These may be surmised.

Anyhow, the watchman had nabbed him and was giving him a tough time when Wilson came along and wanted to know what the fuss was all about. The watchman explained. So did Louie, and being of quicker wit, he made a better impression. He said he was in business, too, and gave some interesting reasons why he should be allowed around the yard. Wilson took him into his office, questioned him further, and found the boy worth his interest.

Thereafter, the merchant and the lad became good friends. Wilson was sage and understanding, free with encouragement, and help. He strongly impressed upon the youngster some of the good basic rules of life and gave him a sense of the importance of being able to draw strength from within oneself. One of his favorite maxims, which stuck in the mind of the boy, had to do with behavior in adversity (which Louie naturally did not anticipate). "When you come to the end of your rope," Wilson told him, "tie a knot in it and hang on." He did not explain how to perform this odd maneuver, but Louie considered it wise.

The friendship and help of Wilson were a bright memory of his boyhood, and when he went back to the old home town years later Mayer made a point of placing flowers on the gentleman's grave.

As the family continued in Saint John its fortunes slowly improved. From peddling and then junk dealing, the father eventually moved on to the more ambitious enterprise of salvaging materials from wrecked ships along the coast. Louie participated in these ventures, which required the employment of many men and called for some elementary management and the use of capital. In helping to guard the family's interests, the lad, now well in his 'teens, got his first experience in being a manager. The physical work was hard and heavy, and he developed the muscles of a robust stevedore, along with a disposition to stevedore language and attitudes.

But by the time he was approaching twenty, Louie was growing restless in Saint John. The urge to move on was pressing. Brothers Ruby and Jake, now Rudy and Jerry, were there to help the old man. Louie thought he could do better somewhere else.

Already he had made trips to Boston to arrange for the sale of scrap metal there. These trips were entrusted to him as the most capable representative of the family. However, his mother was always nervous when her boy departed on these trips. She would put him in the care of a railway conductor they knew, a chap named Sandy Brown. With a bag full of food and some money stitched into the pocket of his coat, young Louie would go down to Boston and attend to business affairs.

Now he was ready to go to Boston to live. He would continue to attend to the family business, as necessity arose, but he would be on his own. The decision, no doubt, distressed his mother, who cherished her eldest son. But this was his wish, so who should stop him? He left the day after New Year, 1904.

How tearful or stoic was the parting? Young Louie was probably jittery. He may have grown cocky and self-sufficient in his own community, but down deep were doubts and dreads. Old terrors battled with ambition inside the vigorous young man. Ambition won, of course. It won always—but not without struggle and pain.

Probably his parents and brothers were at the station to see him off. Probably his mother gave him an ample bag of food. Probably his brothers shouted best wishes and clumsy jokes. And most likely his father's last words to him were that he should be sure to go regularly to synagogue.

## 2

As cocky, ambitious, and determined as Louie Mayer may have been, he was still a greenhorn when he arrived in Boston on January 3, 1904. The tag of his foreign background was still on him, his education was slight, he lacked polish, he had little money. All he had was the will to get ahead.

Whether his happy dreams of conquest ranged beyond the prospect set for him by his helpful friend, John Wilson, of becoming an affluent businessman, possibly a merchant, is open to serious doubt. To be a rich junk dealer was a high aim for an immigrant boy.

The lad found cheap lodgings with a family at 17 Rochester Street, in the so-called South End of Boston. It was a family that had been friends of friends of his mother, back in Russia—one of those intertribal deals. Mama Mayer had taken the precaution to make sure her son had a place to live with a respectable and dependable family in that strange and untrustworthy world.

The South End of Boston encompassed the principal Jewish quarter in those days. It was a crowded, conglomerate section, much like New York's lower East Side, noisy and full of the alien babble of Middle European and Russian Jews. Houses and stores were piled together, pushcarts lined the streets, sidewalks teemed with Yiddisher-mamas and old men with beaver hats and mohair coats. This was the aspect of Boston, the Athens of America, that Louie Mayer first knew.

He got odd jobs as a "helper" while he was learning his way around, then he worked his way into a junk yard located in Chelsea. Chelsea was another Jewish section on the north side, beyond Bunker Hill. It was not fashionable, but there, at least, a trader saw the whites of his customers' eyes.

Across the way from Mayer's lodgings, at 14 Rochester Street, was a kosher butcher shop, and above it the butcher and his family lived. The butcher's name was Hyman Shenberg, and in addition to his trade he had the distinction of being cantor of the Emerald Street Synagogue. This was a poor congregation (Knesseth Israel), which was rigidly orthodox and obviously could not provide its cantor, its chief singer, with a living wage. So Cantor Shenberg picked up further small fees by performing the functions of *mole*, the surgeon at the circumcision ritual, and officiating at the poorest marriages.

Since the office of kosher butcher was also religiously ordained and thereby possessed a certain status, Papa Shenberg permitted his wife to attend to money transactions and keep the books of his little shop. This was a prudent arrangement, for Papa was not practical, while Mrs. Shenberg was sharp and thrifty.

So was daughter Margaret, a plump, pretty girl of twenty-one who had a high school education and was bookkeeper for a neighboring grocery store. Maggie, as they called her, had dark hair, a pair of large bright eyes, and a smile that was sweet and engaging. She was popular in the neighborhood. There was also a younger daughter, Lillian, and Victor, a gangling son.

Mayer, as a dutiful attendant at the Emerald Street Synagogue, soon came to know dark-haired Maggie and was evidently smitten by her as she sat piously among the women at orthodox services. A romance quickly developed, a marriage was properly arranged, and on June 14, five months after the arrival of Mayer in Boston, the couple were wed, with Rabbi Abram Shershevsy performing the service. Mayer gave his age as twenty-two.

On the marriage license application he included the initial B. in his name. That was its official acquisition. He later said it stood for Burton—or Burt.

The couple moved in with Maggie's family, in their already crowded home, and the young bridegroom continued in the junk business, barely getting along. The next year, on August 13, 1905, a daughter was born. They named her Edith.

Soon after, Mayer got wind of a chance to do some business in Brooklyn, New York, where he had aunts and an uncle on his mother's side. Thither he moved his wife and baby and took a small flat in the Greenpoint section, at 101 Russell Street. But the scrap metal business wasn't booming, and Mayer skated along its downside edge. On April 2, 1907, a second daughter was born. Irene was the name they gave this one. The father accepted the baby stoically. He had wanted, and confidently expected, the traditional blessing of a son.

The Brooklyn venture was a fiasco, and Mayer began to lose the unqualified expectation of prosperity in the great United States. The one business he knew, the junk business, was not panning out for him. Something was wrong with the prescription; this wasn't what was promised in the books. Furthermore, a financial recession hit the country that year. Mayer finally gathered up his little family and crept back to Boston, to return to the home of his misgiving in-laws and try to start over again. He was close to being a bankrupt, and he told his friends dismally that before he came to that dishonor he would certainly kill himself.

However, it is a truism that suicides are rare among a people who have learned to endure misfortune and have developed a passion to survive. Mayer might be given to hopeless wailing and head-knocking gestures of despair. But he would no more take a knife to his gullet than he would mount the State House roof and try to fly. He would tie that knot in the end of his rope, as John Wilson counseled, but never around his neck. Something was bound to happen. A miracle would occur.

And it did.

In this year of 1907 there was sweeping the United States a new entertainment phenomenon. It was the nickelodeon craze. The nickelodeon was a species of theater, or playhouse, devoted to the showing of the new "moving pictures" at a nickel (or a dime) per customer.

The sudden emergence of these show places, which were usually no more than vacant stores equipped with folding chairs, film projectors, and cotton sheets for screens, had started a few years earlier with the spontaneous outcrop and success of a scattering of tentative ventures in Pittsburgh, New Orleans, and Los Angeles.

Up to this time, the primitive "flickers," which W. K. L. Dickson, the Lathams, and the Lumières had invented in the 1890's, had been confined for commercial exhibition to vaudeville theaters, where they were carelessly offered as novelty items on straight variety bills. For a brief while after the sensation of their first showings in 1895 and 1896, theatergoers were fascinated by them, by the sheer novelty of seeing pictures that moved. But the novelty soon wore off as succeeding items, turned out by the hundreds, showed no change. They remained merely brief presentations of events or comedy gags, lacking continuity or drama. Audiences were bored. Soon, the pictures were used for "chasing" customers at the end of the vaudeville show.

But a series of circumstances which began to develop around 1903 brought on the wave of cheap show places, or

ABIGAIL E. WEEKS MEMORIAL LIBRARY

"nickelodeons," that actually were the cradles of a mechanical entertainment industry and marked the real beginning of the "motion picture age."

First, the new medium was discovered to be effective as a story-telling device with such crude but arresting little dramas as *The Great Train Robbery,* made in 1903, and the succession of brief story-pictures that followed and imitated it. Even though these elementary items had a notable similarity, in that they stuck to the formula of a hold-up and a "chase," they provided the startling demonstration that a public would go for them and would continue to be fascinated by essentially the same dramatic story over and over again. This was a massive public that was untutored and naïve and whose pocketbooks were most congenial to a nickel admission price.

Then the great rush of immigration which reached its climax in the decade from 1900 to 1910 was dumping into the country successive shiploads of potential customers for the brisk little picture entertainments that were cheap and required no language to be understood. The nickelodeons, especially those in larger cities, thrived on the foreign-born.

By 1907, it was calculated there were between 2,500 and 3,000 nickelodeons in the United States, with the number rapidly increasing. A small trade paper, the *Motion Picture World,* noted with innocent humor that they were "multiplying faster than guinea pigs."

Now Mayer, in his hopeful circulating around Boston, had made a friend, a handsome and amiable fellow named Joe Mack who ran a nickelodeon on Dover Street, near Washington. He called his place the Hub. Mack was a former vaudevillian who had started his little theater when the nickelodeon craze was just beginning and he had built it into a tidy thing, the pleasingly successful center of entertainment in a large neighborhood.

Mayer attended Mack's theater and got acquainted with him. He also got acquainted with the show-shop; he liked to pick up knowledge as well as friends. When he was back in town from Brooklyn, with time and despair on his hands, he went often to the Hub for consolation and to talk with Mack. Indeed, he was not above doing occasional jobs for him, such as standing at the door and taking tickets or handling the box-office till. Immediately, this form of commerce attracted and fascinated Mayer. He saw it as something much more likely to return quick profits than buying and selling junk.

In those early days of the picture business the distribution of films from little producers and manufacturers who were located mostly in New York to the increasing number of theaters was done largely by the theater men themselves. They would buy films from the producers at so much—usually ten cents—per foot, and after showing them in their own theaters, would swap them with other theater men. This led to the growth of "exchanges," where theater men met to swap their films. Out of these primitive arrangements grew the distribution system of later days.

Joe Mack was the agent in Boston for the films of Miles Brothers, one of the small pioneer producing outfits that long ago succumbed. He had the franchise for selling their little pictures, brief comedies and scenic films, in the New England area. Naturally it was to his advantage to have as many theaters operating there, buying (or renting) his pictures, as he could encourage.

One day, in the fall of 1907, he called the attention of Mayer to a trade-paper advertisement of a little theater for rent in Haverhill, Massachusetts. It wasn't particularly promising, but Mack suggested it might be worth a look. He and Mayer got on a train and went up to investigate.

Now Haverhill was, without Mayer knowing it (he being green at the time), a most propitious place for the opening of a nickelodeon. It was a shoe-manufacturing city, some thirty miles north of Boston, with a population of some 45,000, mostly industrious mill workers, small shopkeepers, and tradesmen who could be wooed to entertainment that was simple and cheap.

Mayer and Mack found the theater. It was a vacant burlesque house in a fairly poor section of the city, on Essex Street off Washington Place. Built in 1900, with a capacity of six hundred, it had been devoted for a few seasons to cheap "family vaudeville" or burlesque. Now it was dirty, dank, and dismal. Its seats were rickety and its walls were generously splashed along battered baseboards with ugly tobacco-juice stains. It had gone by the currently common but ambiguous name of the Gem. Disgusted citizens had a better name for it; they candidly called it the Germ.

One can vision the hapless little junk man, standing there looking at it in this one-track-trolley-line city, wondering what he could do with it—he who had no experience and was completely unfamiliar with Haverhill. What a contrast between Joe Mack's gold mine and this shabby and fetid dump!

But Mack thought it had possibilities and he took Mayer to see Charlie Chase, a Haverhill real estate man who owned the property. Chase was a canny Yankee. He sized up the applicant and said he could have the theater for a six hundred dollar down payment. That would buy him a lease and cover six months rent in advance.

Mayer had only fifty dollars with him. Chase told him he could put up that to bind the deal on a three-day option while he raised the remaining cash. Mayer knew it would be a struggle, but Mack promised he would help. Miles Brothers would be happy for an outlet in Haverhill. Now was the moment of decision. Should Mayer risk his fifty dollars on an off chance? He did. This was probably the toughest and most critical decision he ever made.

Once made, however, it was heady. He returned to Boston full of steam and started talking enthusiastically among his skeptical in-laws and friends. Maggie was fearful and reluctant, much less certain than her spouse, but she said that if this was what he wanted she would go along with him. Mayer scraped together the money, with the considerable help of Joe Mack, and at 9 P.M. of the last day of his option he got back to Haverhill and paid the money to Charlie Chase. He had himself a theater, or, rather, a nickelodeon.

His first move was positive and appropriate. On the shrewd advice of Joe Mack, he announced that the theater would be renamed the Orpheum and that a new entertainment policy would be introduced. Henceforth it would be dedicated to the exhibition of "high-class films"—"the home of refined amusement devoted to Miles Brothers moving pictures and illustrated songs."

With the help of his wife and a local character, a big rugged fellow called "Bodger" Flynn, Mayer cleaned up the noisome little theater, slapped some fresh paint on the walls, and hired a woman pianist to play for the illustrated songs. He opened the house on Thanksgiving Day, November 28, 1907, with a program of Miles Brothers' pictures. It was, by the most extravagant of calculations, a modest debut.

The event was recorded the next day in the Haverhill *Evening Gazette* with this one-paragraph item on page 18:

The new Orpheum Theater on Essex Street was opened yesterday as a moving picture theater, many changes having been made in the house which has been especially fitted up for the new programme. The painters and decorators have been busily engaged for the past week making the house ready for its Thanksgiving opening and throughout the day a large number of patrons attended, welcoming its change and assuring the new management of a generous support in its new field. The theater is well situated for its purposes with a good stage as well as auditorium so that the change from vaudeville to moving pictures did not entail more than the work on interior decorations [sic]. The programme will be frequently changed as the new reels are received and it is planned to conduct the theater along the same lines as those practiced in the best houses of that kind in the country.

The "best houses of that kind in the country" were, at that instant, being run by such fellows as Adolph Zukor, William Fox, and Marcus Loew in New York, Carl Laemmle and Aaron Jones in Chicago, Tom Talley in Los Angeles—

former furriers and business opportunists who had moved
into the nickelodeon field when its prospects had become apparent. Some of them were later to emerge as great figures in
the vastly expanding motion picture industry.

In its first month the little Orpheum Theater survived and
little more. Attendance was good but not excessive. With
Mayer, it was touch and go. He brought his wife up from
Boston and took rooms in a small boarding house on Temple
Street in a poor section of the city. Maggie helped run the
theater. She sold tickets while her husband scuttled about,
keeping his eye on all the corners and seeing that everything
went properly. "Bodger" Flynn served as doorman, usher,
and bouncer, when the need arose, which was frequent at
first, for decorum was not a notable characteristic of the clien-
tele. "Bodger" was a capable custodian and soon elevated the
tone.

Mayer was not beforehand. Already in Haverhill were two
other nickelodeons, the Cozy Nickel and the New Bijou, the
latter of which was opened only the day before the Orpheum
debut. Competition confronted the new manager.

The notion that nickelodeons were dens of iniquity—
"apothecary shops of the Devil," as one high-school principal
in Chicago loudly charged—was rapidly being circulated by
pious guardians of the public weal who were particularly ardent and active in that day. They proclaimed the little shows
were indecent and that girls were debauched in the dark
theaters. To prevent this notion and the zeal of the uplifters
from prospering in Haverhill was one of the firm steps that
Mayer would have to take.

Thus it was a stroke of sheer genius (or sheer good luck)
that he was able to obtain as the Christmas attraction for his
theater Pathé's *Passion Play*. This was a tableaux picture
which presented "the life of Christ, from the Annunciation to
the Ascension, in twenty-seven beautiful scenes," and was, at
that time, a curiosity that struck great wonder and awe. It
had been filmed by a French company in the vicinity of Ober-

ammergau and had created a mild sensation when it opened earlier that year in New York. Although it was slammed by some preachers as a "disgraceful sacrilege, horribly commercializing the sacred life of Our Lord," it fascinated the public which has ever been prone to commercialized ostentation with a religious tone.

Mayer knew that the film had been successful in the cities where it had been shown; he took a fair chance on its being accepted as a Christmas attraction in Haverhill. To the initial advancement of his fortune and theatrical education, it was.

"Probably no local picture theater has had a larger number of patrons in one day than were at the new Orpheum yesterday afternoon and evening when *Passion Play* was presented in this city for the first time." So the Haverhill *Record and Criterion* reported on December 26.

In later years Mayer often boasted of his success with *Passion Play*. He even took the license of claiming it was the picture with which he opened his theater. It was not—nor was it put on by him "during Lent," as he also liked to recall in making a point of his perspicacity in judging the fervor and tolerance of Christian taste. Such later inaccuracies were minor. The Christmas season is a sacred one, too. Anyhow, what was most important was that *Passion Play* cleaned up for Mayer.

That is to say, it earned him several hundred dollars during its engagement of one week and permitted the tyro theater manager to have the satisfaction of success. The miracle had happened. By one bold move he had salvaged himself.

Significantly, Mayer's next attraction was *Bluebeard, the Man With Many Wives*. Having sanctified the Orpheum, he could piously entice a lowlier taste.

By hard work, diligent attention, and the booking of effective little films Mayer made the Orpheum turn a profit in its first hopeful winter and spring. He was riding the crest of the nickelodeon craze. So well did he do that he was able, come summer, to argue Charlie Chase into "renovating" the little

theater by adding some seats and enlarging the small stage.
Thus he was able, on reopening on September 1, 1908, to
command upper case attention. It was now the New Orpheum.

The Haverhill *Evening Gazette* noted the occasion with
suitable civic pride. The house was "opened for its second
season," it reported, "with a complete program of the latest
in motion pictures and songs illustrated with finely colored
slides. Music was furnished by a ladies orchestra, the concert
program being a feature . . . and Miss Maude Neilson, formerly of the Canobie Lake Opera Company, rendered some
of the latest song successes." (The Canobie Lake Opera Company was a choral group that sang sentimental ballads at a
nearby summer amusement park.)

It is interesting to note that the main picture on this reopening program was Pathé's solemnly sensational two-reel
drama, *The Dreyfus Affair*. It was accompanied by a characteristic mishmash of one-reel comedies—*A Jewel of a Serv-
ant, Just Like a Woman, I Can't Read English,* and *Dan
Casey Joins the Lodge.*

For the next two years Mayer did nicely. The New Orpheum was a success and he was earning a reputation as an
enterprising and reliable citizen. He was gregarious and un-
inhibited, with a knack of making friends. After all, Haverhill was not much different from his familiar Saint John.

Now he was able to move his family to a little frame house
on Merrimac Street in Bradford, a residential area across the
river from Haverhill. This move was a first step up the ladder
of social improvement which Mayer meant to scale. It was, in
his push for liberation, like buying that first baseball glove.

In those two years the hustling theater manager quickly
began to get wise to the eccentricities of show business in a
city of medium size. He soon was able to disassociate himself
from Joe Mack and cut loose as an independent showman
in Haverhill and cities nearby. Through Chase, he became
well acquainted with other property-owning citizens, particu-

larly George Elliott, a merchant of lumber and coal, and Charles Howard Poor, a lawyer. By some persuasive talk, which he was mastering, he convinced them that their city was in need of a new and finer theater than its old Academy of Music, which was committed to straight vaudeville and touring legitimate shows. He soon had them forming a syndicate and putting up money to build the new Colonial Theater, of which he would be the manager.

Even while this was building, he was in on another scheme with real estate speculators in nearby Lawrence to construct a new theater there. That venture was not successful. The Broadway Theater, which was its name, laid an egg, in the later parlance of show business, and Mayer got clear of it fast.

But the 1,600-seat Colonial Theater in Haverhill came out all right. It was opened on December 11, 1911, with a settled policy that had been pioneered by Marcus Loew and others in their growing chains of theaters in New York. It was one of combining motion pictures with four or five acts of vaudeville and offering the programs on a continuous run basis at a 10¢ to 25¢ admission scale.

The grand opening of the Colonial provided Mayer with an opportunity to have his first sip of the strong wine of public admiration and applause. A standard program of speeches and greetings was arranged, with the mayor as the principal speaker. When the latter introduced the beaming manager to a capacity audience as "the man who has done so much to get this fine theater for our city," a "tremendous ovation" occurred. Mayer was so choked with emotion he could only smile and bow. The approval emboldened him, however, to have a portrait of himself done in oils by the theater's scenery painter and to hang it in the lobby where it could be seen by all those appreciative people who hailed him as "the man who has done so much."

Now, with two theaters to manage, the Colonial and the New Orpheum, one might have thought that Mayer had the success he required. In a matter of four years, he had worked up from a dead end in the commerce of junk to the eminence of being the potential theatrical tycoon of Haverhill, Massachusetts. He had long since indicated to his family back in Saint John that he was conspicuously prospering, and brother Rudy was around, looking for some of the pickings. Rudy was initially announced as manager of the Colonial, but that arrangement fell through. Rudy, a little too grabby, was to prove a thorn in Louie's side.

However, brother Jerry was brought down from Canada and installed as manager of the New Orpheum. And Victor Shenberg, Mayer's brother-in-law, was brought from Boston to be operator of the projection equipment at the Colonial. Mayer was strong for the *mishpocha* tradition: he cut in the members of his family. And, also in the tradition, he quarreled with them endlessly.

But this little success at starting theaters only whetted his appetite for more. He was bitten by the bug of show business; he had contracted that infectious disease of *impresarioitis* which wildly inflames the victim's blood. He wanted to move into the big time, to make ever more money. He was convinced he knew the magic that would make him a big man in the theater world.

Being in contact with theatrical people from Boston and New York, the vaudeville performers and road-show managers who came through Haverhill, as well as motion picture people from whom he bought his films, he cast his eyes on horizons beyond.

With the opening of the Colonial, he began hopping down to New York to book vaudeville programs. He usually put up at the Knickerbocker Hotel, which was the hangout of big theater people—the Frohmans, Sam Harris, George M. Cohan—and got a feeling of importance from rubbing elbows with them. Indeed, the legitimate theater had a strong appeal for him. Right now, he was thinking in terms of entertainment that was "live."

One of his New York acquaintances was a man named Ben

Stern, who had been the general manager for Henry B. Harris, a distinguished producer lost in the sinking of the *Titanic*. In January, 1913, Mayer and Stern formed a company "to conduct a general amusement business in New York City, the United States, and Canada." That spring they took a lease on the Walnut Street Theater in Philadelphia, with the idea of operating it as a show place for touring companies. The price scale was to be "popular"—that is to say, one dollar top.

It so happened that the Walnut Street Theater was one of the oldest in the United States—a drafty vault that had been built in 1807 as an arena for circuses and had been later used by such worthies as William Forrest and Edwin Booth. Mayer and Stern did not realize, when they leased the place, that it needed extensive repairing to comply with safety laws. They went through a lot of anxiety and had to spend much money to equip the house.

They had a good fall and winter season with such proven attractions as Edith Thayer in *The Firefly,* Violet Mersereau in *Rebecca of Sunnybrook Farm,* Rose Stahl in *Maggie Pepper,* and Robert Hilliard in *A Fool There Was.* But they ran into trouble with their landlord, and when their one-year lease was out they closed and started suit to recover the six thousand dollars they claimed to have spent on the theater.

That same year Mayer turned his New Orpheum into a legitimate theater and introduced a resident stock company in a run of familiar plays such as *The Rosary, The White Sister,* and *The Lion and the Mouse.* Frank Elliott, "formerly connected with the Keith Stock Company of Woonsocket, R. I.," was the leading man. The leading lady was a stock star from Boston with the alluring name of Miss Valerie Valaire. What the house was, precisely, was a show place for "ten, twent', thirt' "—standard melodrama pitched to the "family trade." Mayer was an ardent exponent of entertainment for the whole family.

His activities in Haverhill showed his vigor. For a time he held a lease on the venerable Academy of Music and attempted to raise its cultural tone by offering the Boston Symphony Orchestra and touring opera companies. He had a resident stage-show troupe at the Colonial, Homan's Musical Revue, in which an eager and active member was a young man named Eddie Dowling. And he also took the Bijou nickelodeon under his wing for a spell.

But change was crowding swiftly upon the new impresario. Mayer had become an American citizen on June 24, 1912, and that year he moved to a new home in a substantial residential section on Hamilton Street. His social as well as his commercial position in the community was on the rise. With pride and a sense of great achievement he was able to visit his parents in Saint John where his father now had a small excelsior factory.

In the fall of 1913 word came that his mother was seriously ill. Mayer grabbed for his Haverhill physician, Dr. W.W. Ferrin, and rushed with him to Saint John. It was found the aging Sarah had cancer. An operation was unsuccessful. On October 14 she died. She was buried in the Hebrew cemetery, close to the home which had been the goal of her wandering life. With her passing, Mayer's last connection with Saint John was cut.

Now Mayer was making his movements in an ever-widening arc. He was soon adroitly to project himself away from Haverhill.

3

Let us now cast a reflective eye on what was happening with motion pictures in those brisk years—those years in which Mayer was beginning to learn show business in Haverhill.

It is notable that the medium grew out of infancy into a state of violent adolescence in about the same time it takes a human being to do so. In 1905, primitive "flickers" were sketchy affairs that crudely conveyed in a few minutes the basic details of simple episodes. The high jinks of low comedians, brief enactments of hold-ups and pursuits, humorous peeks at domestic embarrassments, and short inspections of assorted scenery—these formed the bulk of entertainment flashed on nickelodeon screens. And facilities for distributing and exhibiting these modest pleasures were equally crude.

But within a mere decade, the medium expanded so fantastically that it taxed the belief of sane observers and startled the adversaries of change. In the first place, the form of motion pictures was stretched to increasing lengths, so that it wasn't uncommon for a picture to run a full hour or more. Techniques of story telling were discovered and developed sufficiently that it was possible to offer dramas of considerable plot and range. Such early directors as Edwin S. Porter, J. Searle Dawley, Thomas Ince, and the remarkable David Wark Griffith were making the camera become a clearly potential instrument for the accomplishment of a new art form, and the public was readily adjusting to the image-making tricks that they devised—close-ups, dissolves, quick scene changes, and other fancies of film editing. Griffith's *The Birth of a Nation* which was brought to the ever-marvelous screen in 1915 marked a point of peak achievement, thundering proof of what might be done with film.

And the business of motion pictures was likewise growing in these years, sprawling out of a dime-museum commerce into a form of big-money enterprise. The control of early patent holders and manufacturers of films and machines, who had thought to monopolize the business by forming themselves into a trust, was rapidly challenged and broken by candid pirates and business buccaneers who came tumbling and slashing into the area as soon as its money-making potentials were seen. Some were connivers and con men, but a few were smart entrepreneurs who gathered and shaped the primitive business into the cells from which great corporate giants would grow.

Little Carl Laemmle, clothing merchant and operator of a nickelodeon in Chicago's "Loop," branched out and in 1909 began the independent film making that was to lead to Universal. Adolph Zukor, a former furrier and owner of penny arcades, took to importing films from Europe and formed the Famous Players Film Company in 1912. His expanding, voracious operation was to be formidable in subsequent years, embracing production, distributing, and theater-holding in the name of Paramount.

Jesse Lasky, a vaudeville cornet player, and Samuel Goldfish (later Goldwyn), his brother-in-law who was a successful glove salesman, joined a stage director, Cecil B. De Mille, and launched themselves as independent film producers in 1913.

It was a launching of potent auguries. And an odd little clown named Charlie Chaplin was hired at one hundred and fifty dollars a week to make a series of slapstick films for the small firm of Kessel and Bauman (Mutual) in that same fateful year.

Theaters previously devoted to plays and vaudeville were being brought in for film exhibition in place of the nickelodeons, which quickly became obsolescent with the lengthening and strengthening of films, and, in some of the largest cities, new theaters designed especially for films were built. Exchanges for handling the traffic of films from producers to theaters were gathering scope, and the practices of film selling were undergoing change. From a strictly "ten-cents-a-foot" business, which the transfer from producer to middleman was in the early days, the handling of films by distributors was being arranged through the sale of franchises. A distributor in an area would purchase the rights to peddle a film—or a package of several films—for a specific sum. His income then depended upon what he could get for the film from the theaters, usually on the basis of so much per day or per week.

This was a business that attracted many budding entrepreneurs who were soon to rise to high positions in the spiraling film companies, little fellows who scrambled over others in the shoving and clawing battle to the top. Appropriately and significantly, one of these was Louis Mayer.

By 1913 the Haverhill theater manager had made himself reasonably secure with small-town theater operations. He had clicked with nickelodeons and "combination" shows, had successfully booked bands and minstrels, had offered legitimate road companies. In six years he had got an education in the rudiments of showmanship and, in his somewhat slanted opinion, there wasn't much about theater business he didn't know.

One thing he accurately detected: motion pictures were fast becoming popular entertainment for the masses. They were abundant and cheap and, what was most impressive, they were clearly getting better all the time. Mayer shrewdly saw that opportunity was manifold; the inclination to make something of it was one he could not resist.

Even while busy with theater activities in Haverhill, and before he had dabbled in that venture in Philadelphia, Mayer got his lines out in the business of distributing films on the theory that, as a distributor, he could save money for his theaters; also, if successful, he could make more money for Louis B. Mayer.

As a regular visitor to Boston and a sizeable customer for films, he was closely and cannily acquainted with small distributors there, and he regularly attended the sales conventions that were promoted by producers for theater men. Moving around among the sales boys, a little sharp-nosed man in a derby hat, he picked their brains—or what, with many of them, laughingly passed for brains.

One of his friends was Hiram Abrams, from Portland, Maine, who had started his career as a salesman around New England towns peddling song slides and sheet music to nickelodeons. Now he was in the business of film distributing with Walter Greene, having lately acquired the franchise for handling Zukor's Famous Players releases in New England. Abrams was a go-getter; he was to become president of Paramount, then of United Artists. He had a brain that could profitably be plucked.

Mayer had indicated to him that he was interested in distributing films, although he said he didn't know much about it (which was something of an admission from him). Abrams helpfully suggested a young lady named Fanny Mittenthal as a likely assistant and tutor, if he decided to enter the field. Fanny had worked for Greene at the Plymouth Theater and was now in Laemmle's Boston exchange. Abrams stated that she knew as much about distribution as was to be known.

This was what Mayer wanted, so he got Abrams to arrange a casual introduction to Fanny. It took place on Decoration Day, 1913, at a Boston *Braves* baseball game. The three of them went together, and Mayer talked picture business throughout the game, being more interested in sounding out Fanny than in the fortunes of the *Braves*. This was a token of his fervor, for he was an avid baseball fan. At the end of the game, he offered her twenty-five dollars a week to come to work for him.

Fanny was somewhat irritated. She considered the offer absurd in view of the fact that this little hustler had no office, no pictures to sell, and no experience in the field. Besides, she was already earning thirty-five dollars a week. Much to Mayer's amazement, she politely turned him down.

But he was not discouraged. He continued to snoop around. A few months later, he got back to Fanny and told her he would meet her salary. Furthermore, he was going to rent an office. He was full of enthusiasm and charm, two qualities he had discovered how to use effectively. Fanny was now impressed—not the last woman to fall for his wiles. She agreed to take a chance on his offer and the Louis B. Mayer Film Company was therewith born.

They rented one room on the second floor of the B. F. Keith Vaudeville Booking Office in a building off Tremont Street, in Boston, picked up some second-hand furniture, and had Mayer's name painted on the door.

"What do we do now?" Fanny asked him, noting that they had no films to sell. Mayer told her to write letters to all theater owners in New England informing them that Louis B. Mayer would be offering the best in new, high quality films, the most original and entertaining, and suggesting they write to him.

The response to these letters was encouraging. With this evidence of likely customers, Mayer hastened to New York to buy franchises on some inexpensive films, purchases he financed with his own money. The first he got were some British comedies featuring Stan Lupino, a popular English music-hall clown (and father of Ida Lupino, later a star in American films).

These little pictures rented nicely. Then, one day, a snappy young dude walked in and asked to speak to Mayer. Mayer was out at the moment (he was actually in Haverhill, tending his vineyards in that area), but Fanny conversed with the young man, found out his name was Jesse Lasky and that he had some films to sell. They were films he had produced (and was producing) in California with De Mille and Oscar Apfel directing. Lasky said it had been recommended that he get in touch with Mayer as a new and aggressive distributor looking for franchises.

Fanny latched onto Lasky and told him to come back the next day. Mayer was there (she had summoned him) and a deal for Lasky films was made. They were *The Squaw Man,* with Dustin Farnum (this one was ready to be released); *Call of the North,* with Robert Edeson, and *The Man on the Box,* with Max Figman. With these three five-reel pictures Mayer became a factor in the field.

Years later Samuel Goldwyn, the Samuel Goldfish of the young Lasky firm, insisted that Mayer had got into the business by pulling a fast one at the firm's expense. Mayer had agreed to pay four thousand dollars for the franchise to *The Squaw Man,* Goldwyn said, but he remitted only two thousand dollars and never came through with the remainder. This was a not uncommon practice with distributors in that day, so if Mayer did pull it on the Lasky people he surely had a fast alibi. They all had excuses for defaulting. There were countless dodges to the game, as Lasky and his business manager, Goldfish, were not the first or last producers to learn. No doubt they carefully saw to it that Mayer paid in full for other films before they were sent to him. As Goldwyn himself once said, in explaining his own survival and success in the film industry, "In this business it's dog eat dog, and nobody's going to eat me!"

More important to Mayer's continuity than the three Lasky films was a connection he made in the fall of 1914 with Al Lichtman, a wizard in the game of salesmanship. Lichtman, fresh from a job with Zukor, had fashioned a fancy little scheme for bringing producers and distributors into a mutually helpful group.

His thinking was that small producers were not getting as much as they should for films sold outright to exchange men for franchise costs. At the same time he saw that distributors, always clamoring for more and more films, would be willing to put up some production financing for films they would then get to release on a share-of-the-rental basis, if they could thus assure themselves of a steady supply.

Lichtman, using deft persuasion, got a bunch of distributors in various sections of the country—Rowland and Clarke in Pennsylvania and Ohio; Masbaum in Philadelphia; Grumbacher in Oregon; Engel, Saunders, and others in New York. Mayer grabbed the opportunity to come in as the New England arm of the group. From these distributors, Lichtman got pledges totalling $140,000 with which to start a parallel group of small producers on an output of films. He would advance fifteen thousand dollars for each picture. When a film was sold, the producer would get fifty percent of the revenue (minus the advance), the distributor would get thirty percent, and Lichtman would get the remainder for organizing and operating the pool. The name of the combination was the Alco Film Corporation.

The pictures he acquired were propitious. He got two with young Ethel Barrymore—*The Nightingale* and *Shore Acres,* made by the All-Star Company. He obtained *Michael Strogoff* from Lubin. He contracted with the California Motion Picture Company to do a *Salomy Jane,* with the opera star, Olga Petrova. And from K. & B. he bought *Tillie's Punctured Romance,* with Charlie Chaplin and Marie Dressler. He paid a lot of money for this last one.

The Alco tie was timely and fortunate for small distributor Mayer. It gave him a guarantee of pictures with which to build up a bankroll and prestige. And it soon led to more than that for him. It put him in the way of becoming a figure of some prominence in a national distributors group.

It happened this way: the Alco Company had been operating only a few months when Lichtman made an unwise connection with a fast-talking financier. He put too much trust in this fellow and, the first thing anyone knew, the financier had grabbed Alco's resources and forced it into bankruptcy. This might have been thoroughly disastrous for Mayer and others in the group if the lot of them had not acted swiftly and adroitly to save their collective hides.

Convinced that the idea of Alco was basically practical, they empowered a committee composed of Joe Engel of New York, Richard Rowland of Pittsburgh, George Grumbacher of Portland, Oregon, and Louis Mayer of Boston to find a way of continuing the operation of a producer-distributor group. This committee went into sessions in the Hotel Claridge in New York, and in late January, 1915, came up with a plan for forming a new organization and continuing from where Alco left off.

The new company was called the Metro Pictures Corporation. Rowland was named president. Grumbacher and Clarke were made vice-presidents. The secretary was Mayer. Thus the exchange man from Boston found himself spreading out in the world. With the Metro franchise in New England and a salaried job in the new company, he was gaining strength and experience as a distributor.

Out of the Metro organization a further stroke of good fortune came to him in a personal association of paramount importance to his later life. Involved was a young New York lawyer who had been appointed the Alco receiver. J. Robert Rubin was his name, and his advantage was good connections with Republican politicians in New York. Born in Syracuse and educated at the university there, he was well established with a prominent Wall Street law firm before taking a probative appointment as an assistant district attorney in New York County and later as a deputy police commissioner. Indeed, he was on the way to becoming a political careerist when the job of handling the Alco bankruptcy was casually tossed to him and brought him into contact with the strange breed of movie men.

Rubin was not of their order. He was quiet, reserved, and dignified, a bright young man with distinct professional scruples and social proclivities. But he found himself fascinated by angles in the film industry and was not averse to moving from Alco receiver to the job of counsel for the new Metro group. Thus he was brought into frequent and close association with Mayer, who was soon impressed with his legal competence and personal qualities.

Most of the things that Mayer envied and aspired to, Rubin possessed. He was urbane, sophisticated, and facile and felicitous with words. He had a college education, which Mayer may have outwardly mocked but which he inwardly admired and respected as a token of quality. Furthermore, Rubin was slender and handsome in a definite Nordic way. Mayer keenly cultivated his friendship and used him as his own counsel in New York.

He was soon making much use of him, for now that he had definitely set up shop as a solid distributor in New England and was sitting in with the Metro boys, Mayer was feeling the ambition violently driving him. Already he had started withdrawal from connections in Haverhill by turning the actual management of his theaters over to other men and maintaining only his financial interest and himself in an advisory capacity.

So it was that in 1915, Mayer made the opportune move that was to earn him his first real pile of money and fortify his trust in miracles: he acquired the franchise to release *The Birth of a Nation* in New England for subsequent runs.

No one has yet assembled all the intricate and fabulous details of the wild circumstances under which this picture was brought into being and sold. And that is too bad, for such a record, set against a background of the times, would tell the whole story of the first fine flowering of the over-all potentials, artistic and commercial, of American films.

It would tell how a stubborn visionary struggled and succeeded in breaking through barriers set up by early custom as to the size and dramatic scope of films; of how the Griffith picture hit the public like a tree-toppling storm, overwhelming it with vivid evocation of the great dark crisis that still troubled hearts and minds. And it would show how the system of distributing motion pictures in those days was so naïve that the lion's share of the profits of this great venture finally went to the fellows who hawked it, such as Mayer.

Griffith conceived his picture as an expansion of the novel (and later play), *The Clansman*, by the Reverend Thomas Dixon. This was a florid account of the suffering and strain of people in the South during and after the Civil War. It was well recognized as a fiction that "waved the bloody shirt," and there had been some Negro opposition when it had been offered around the country as a play.

Production was started on the picture in 1914. It was an independent job, with a certain amount of financing furnished by the Mutual company, for which Griffith then worked. But as weeks ran into months without its being finished and costs continued to rise, Mutual directors instructed their president, Harry Aitken, to cancel the company's participation or assume the investment himself.

Aitken did the latter, and he and Griffith and the Reverend Dixon formed the Epoch Producing Company to handle this one exceptional film. More time and money went into it. Aitken had to scratch for funds. It had cost more than $100,-000—an unheard of investment—when it was finally finished at the end of the year. Also unprecedented was its twelve-reel length. This meant a two-hour picture. No film company would dare try to put it through the usual channels of distribution; no theater man would pay the rent they'd have to ask, they said.

Meanwhile the few inside people who got a look at the finished film were either vexed at its mammoth nonconformance or were hugely impressed by it. Word began to spread in the business that Griffith had a dangerous film. "That dirty nigger picture" was the way some referred to it.

Under the circumstances, there was nothing for the Epoch Company to do but make arrangements to exhibit the film itself. Aitken took Clune's Auditorium, a 2,600-seat house, in Los Angeles. And there, on the night of February 8, 1915, *The Birth of a Nation* (then called *The Clansman*) had its world première.

Even before its opening, there were mutterings of trouble to come. Negroes were going to stone the theater, rumor-mongers warned. Police were massed at the première in case any rioting began. The only rioting was that which an enthusiastic audience put on.

From that evening the picture's fame spread swiftly. Prints of it were brought east and plans were made for a New York opening similar to that in Los Angeles. A special screening was given in Washington for President Woodrow Wilson and his Cabinet. The grapevine reported that the President and his guests were amazed and impressed.

The opening in New York was at the Liberty Theater on March 3. Again a fashionable audience was moved to frenzy and cheers by the amazing sweep of the drama and the climactic ride of the Ku Klux Klan. Openings in Boston and Chicago followed immediately. In Boston the opening was at the Tremont Theater, in Chicago it was at the Illinois. These were all under Epoch's immediate auspices.

But now racial opposition to the film was organized. New York's Mayor John Purroy Mitchel was urged to ban it there. The Boston branch of the National Association for the Advancement of Colored People issued a booklet condemning the film. Among the contributors was Dr. Charles W. Eliot, president emeritus of Harvard University. Demonstrations were made on the steps of the State House in Boston and in the lobby of the Tremont Theater.

It was in this climate of agitation and excitement that Mayer got involved with the film.

What happened was that Griffith and Aitken, once they had *The Birth of a Nation* successfully launched and the money from their road-show presentations miraculously rolling in, decided to assign its distribution to franchised salesmen for subsequent runs. They naïvely proceeded on the assumption that their extended road-show presentations would drain the cream.

Mayer was quick to realize that the film would have unlimited appeal, even at advanced box-office prices, in whatever community it might be shown. He was mindful of his earliest experience with the widely circulated *Passion Play*. He rushed in to seek the franchise for the New England area, when he heard Aitken was ready to sell, and was able to close the deal.

Although it did seem a heavy gamble that he agreed to take, at the time, and one that called for some ticklish financing, it turned out to be a hands-down steal. Aitken agreed to let him have the picture for a payment of fifty thousand dollars in advance against the remittance to Epoch of ten percent of the *net* profits received from further bookings of the film!

When you consider that a normal return to the producer of a film today is anywhere from thirty-five to fifty percent of its *gross* receipts in the theaters, and this for any little picture that happens to come down the pike, it is plain that the opportunity so readily given to Mayer (and to others who bought franchises in other areas) was a fortune-showering gift.

Even so, the Boston exchange man was unable to swing the deal by himself. He didn't have fifty thousand dollars, let alone the taste for such a risk. So he did what any enterprising and sensible businessman would do: he went out and drummed up the money from some of his more venturesome Boston friends.

Among those he got as investors were David Stoneman, a lawyer who also made a good business of lending money (at very profitable interest rates); Colman Levin, a successful carpet merchant; Louis Rosenburg, a retail jeweler; A. Morris Greenblatt of the American Sculpta Corporation, and the Ginsburg brothers, paper bag manufacturers.

In his eagerness to raise money, Mayer asked his secretary, Fanny Mittenthal, if she had a thousand dollars she would like to let him put in for her. Fired by his enthusiasm, she scratched up the money and gave it to him. He also invested some of his own money. A company, Master Photoplays, was formed, with officers, of which Mayer was the president. He owned twenty-five percent of it.

A down payment of twenty thousand dollars was made to Epoch on August 2 and the remaining thirty thousand dollars of the advance was paid on August 12, when the contract was signed between Epoch and Master Photoplays. According to the terms of the contract Boston was excluded as release territory until after September 11. Apparently Aitken figured the film would have taken the bulk of what it could get from Boston by then.

No sooner was the contract signed than Mayer started selling furiously. He moved into new and larger offices at 60 Church Street. He took on additional employees, headed by Tom Spry, of the United Booking Office, who was popular with New England theater men. Spry, a tall, nice-looking fellow, thoroughly lived up to his name. He soon became a valuable adjunct and loyal flunky to Mayer, who now consolidated his other distributing functions in the American Feature Film Company.

The experience with *The Birth of a Nation* was another turning point in the career of Mayer. It was evident that he was going to get rich with it. Now he was able to withdraw entirely from his connections in Haverhill and move his home and family down to Boston. He took a sumptuous apartment in Brookline, a fashionable neighborhood, and became a member of the affluent congregation of Temple Ohabai Sholem, a far cry from the environment and association of the little Emerald Street Synagogue.

There is no question but that Mayer and Master Photoplays

handled *The Birth of a Nation* smartly in the New England area. In the time that he had the picture he made a million dollars for his company. That was always his assertion. And a quarter of that profit was all his.

In later years Harry Aitken, who prospered and then declined in the commerce of motion pictures, supported Mayer's boastful claim. He allowed that the Boston exchange man— and many others—became rich on *The Birth*. He also said Mayer did not return him as much money from the territory as was earned, that he never received an accounting and remittance of all that was due.

A recent perusal of the records of Epoch seems to bear him out. The books show that Master remitted close to $15,000 for the first year of its handling the film and $1,500 for the second year. Assuming that Mayer did not make any remittance on the first $500,000 of net profits on the film, since the ten percent due on that amount was discounted against the $50,000 advance, the payments that were sent in for two years would indicate only $665,000 was earned. In the light of Mayer's boast and other evidence, it would appear that Aitken's complaint was justified. But, then, as we've said, exchange men were mostly sharpshooters in those days. No one knows how much of the earnings of *The Birth of a Nation* were diverted from people to whom they were due.

Aitken was not the only person who felt badly used by Mayer. Shortly after the film was in circulation and profits were piling up, the boss had a little talk with his secretary.

"Fanny," he said, "I've got bad news. I've got to give you back the thousand dollars you let me have to put in the company. The board of directors objected when they found out you were in. They said they don't want anybody who isn't a stockholder drawing profits from the company. So here is your thousand dollars."

The young lady, being a lady, barely refrained from spitting in his eye. Why she didn't quit was simple: he was obviously a man on the rise.

4

Success with *The Birth of a Nation* was all it took to embolden Mayer to pursue a still further inclination that had long been enticing him. He wanted to be a film producer. He wanted to get into that realm of fabrication and creation where glamour and excitement were.

As far back as when he was managing theaters in Haverhill, he had talked about making pictures right in his own back yard. Exteriors would be shot in the surrounding country or in the streets of Haverhill; interiors would be photographed on the Colonial's stage in sets built in the carpenter shop. Mayer would undoubtedly have tried it if his local associates had been as keen as he was. But being canny fellows, they weren't ready to go that far.

Now, with his Metro connection and with a small fortune piling up, he was in a favorable position to indulge his productive urge. Naturally, he looked for an entrance through the Metro company.

One of the strongest assets that the youthful company possessed was an arrangement to release the pictures of Francis X.

Bushman and Beverly Bayne. This sedately romantic couple were among the great stars of the day, trailing long streamers of glory in every film they made. Actually, their contract with Metro called for twelve films a year, to be produced by their company, Quality Pictures Corp., of which Bushman was the head.

To approach this great star with a proposition was an audacious thing for anyone to do, especially an uncouth distributor who had never produced a film. But Mayer was nothing if not audacious, and what was more he had a positive conviction that it paid to get the best. When he had his intentions in order, he went to Bushman at his studio in New York and proposed that Bushman join in producing a serial, starring himself and Miss Bayne.

The proposal was not flattering. Serials were weekly sequence films which, though they had a vogue in that period, were considered somewhat beneath a top-rank star. Pearl White was the most famous and typical serial drudge in her *Perils of Pauline*. Bushman sniffed at the suggestion and bluntly turned it down.

But again Mayer was stubborn and persistent. He went to see Bushman several times, expanding his proposition and tearfully pleading with him. Finally, Bushman could not resist him—or his generous offer—and agreed.

Mayer whipped into action. The Serial Producing Company was formed, with Mayer and his investor friends in Boston putting up the funds. Colman Levin, carpet merchant, was the president, but Mayer was the busy beaver who took care of everything.

The serial was called *The Great Secret*. It was made at Bushman's studio in New York, with Christy Cabanne directing. Mayer opened it in Boston, naturally, with an unusual program of promotion. He got Bushman and Miss Bayne to come to town for a round of public appearances on opening day, when he offered the first three or four episodes of the serial in several theaters. Thus anyone wishing to do so could get well into the plot by jumping from one theater to another. The stunt was novel and successful in Boston, but *The Great Secret* generally was not. It was nationally released by Metro and got back little more than its cost, which was mainly the fifteen thousand dollars paid to Bushman and Miss Bayne.

That was in 1916. Mayer found the experience to his taste and set his sights for another opportunity to get into production in a really big way.

Enter, at this point, a minor and oddly grotesque character whose purely by-chance involvement was most helpful to the fortunes of Mayer. This person was a newsboy named Toby, a pathetically hunchbacked dwarf who had a newsstand near the Knickerbocker Hotel in the theatrical district of New York. Mayer usually bought papers from him when he was in the neighborhood and got friendly with the odd chap, who was full of Broadway gossip and bits of news.

But Toby had one big devotion. He was an idolatrous fan of the rapidly ascending film star, Anita Stewart. Miss Steward was a truly lustrous beauty, with fair skin and chestnut hair, and was a particular adornment of the strong producing company, Vitagraph. She had her first break in 1913 in *A Million Bid*, a five-reel drama with which that austere company launched itself in the production of multi-reel films. Her successive roles in *The Goddess*, a serial with Earle Williams, *The Juggernaut*, and *The Girl Philippa* had firmed her position as a star not far below Mary Pickford, Marguerite Clark, and Clara Kimball Young.

From the day that Toby first saw her in *A Million Bid*, Miss Stewart had been his dream girl, and he ardently told her so, in letters and, later, in personal visits which she graciously permitted him. The beautiful actress lived in Brooklyn, where the Vitagraph studios were, and thus was conveniently located for the newsboy to get close to her. Through whatever psychological impulse such curious things occur, he appointed himself her champion and Number 1 buff on Broadway. He obtained stacks of photographs of her and spread them around liberally. Little Toby was what would now be reckoned Miss Stewart's fan-club president.

In conversation with Toby, Mayer no doubt revealed that he was intending to become a producer. He was not the sort to hide such an exciting intention under a cloak of modesty. And Toby was no doubt delighted with the inspired idea, being also a strong admirer of the lively little Boston man. Inevitably, he came to a conclusion: Mayer should produce films with Miss Stewart! What could be more appropriate than that his two idols should be conjoined?

Mayer was not loath to let that prospect flutter before his own eyes. Nothing could suit his fancy better than to be able to snag a star such as Miss Stewart. This was, indeed, his calculation—to get hold of a star already fixed in the motion picture heavens and hitch his little wagon to her.

Stars were the most conspicuous and dependable insurance of success. Customers usually flocked to see their pictures, no matter what they were in. So clearly was this evident that producers usually spent more money advertising their stars than on stories bought for them. Many thousands of dollars were invested in the build-up of a star. These investments were usually protected with contracts, such as the one by which Miss Stewart was tied to Vitagraph.

However, the slight consideration of a star's being committed to someone else would not scare a forthright interloper so avid and relentless as Mayer, any more than it scared off many other sly and determined predators. Star-raiding was as attractive and progressive in those expanding times as was wife-stealing in ancient Troy. When accomplished, it was much more profitable.

For instance, Lewis J. Selznick had just lured Clara Kimball Young away from World with promises of greatness that the vanity of an actress could not resist. World had but recently swiped her from vulnerable Vitagraph, which had a peculiar way of building and then failing to indulge its saucy stars.

Joe Schenck was employing the arts of romance to woo Norma Talmadge from Vitagraph and get her into the Selznick company (and into his own connubial bed). Adolph Zukor's methodical campaign to lure all the worthwhile stars from Triangle and break that sturdy company was just getting underway. And Mary Pickford was the object of wooing of every producer who thought he had a chance. There was too much to be got from a conquest not to make the game extremely popular.

Mayer was suspected of being in it. Robert Cochrane, vice-president of Universal, got wise when Mayer started to ask questions about the salaries and earnings of Universal stars. Mayer's American Feature Film Company was also New England distributor for Universal's "Bluebird" films, and it was on that pretext that he said he would like to know. Cochrane, hep to all the dodges, threw him off by giving him incorrect data.

Then, one day in 1917, Mayer popped into his Boston office in great glee and whooped to his secretary, Fanny, "I'm going to Atlantic City! I'm going to meet Anita Stewart!"

Sure enough, little Toby had talked about Mayer to the star and had got her and her managing mother interested in the expansive ideas of the Boston man. Mayer had shrewdly planted some rosy prospects with the dwarf. An opportunity for a meeting was diplomatically arranged.

When Mayer returned to Boston from the Jersey beach resort, he was bursting with unbounded triumph. "I met her, I met her!" he whooped. "And I danced with her, too! She was a princess! She carried a wand in her hand! You should have seen us! What a picture! Everybody was talking about me!"

Fanny regarded him sourly. "You know what they were saying?" she sniffed.

"What were they saying?" Mayer challenged.

"They were saying, 'Who's the funny little kike with Anita Stewart!' "

The sarcasm cut him where it hurt most. He threw the 'phone book at his secretary's head.

That introduction was all Mayer needed. He followed it up by sending flowers and gifts to the Stewarts at their apartment in Brooklyn and showering them with attentions of all sorts. Pretty soon he was being invited to have dinners with them. In his familiarly adroit and clever way, he devoted a great deal of attention to the matronly Mrs. Stewart. He charmed her with stories of his boyhood and won her confidence with tales of his success. Persuading an actress through her mother became a characteristic technique of his.

Two propitious circumstances were soon recognized by Mayer. The first was that gorgeous Anita was restless at Vitagraph. Although she was earning a salary of $1,000 a week, plus ten percent of the profits of her pictures, with a guaranteed $127,000 a year, she was not content. She objected to the stories they gave her. She claimed the studio did not show her proper statements on which to calculate the profits of her films. She said she was overworked and tired out.

Most important, she was in love.

Anita's leading man in her last three pictures had been Rudolph Cameron, a handsome chap who was ambitious and foresighted. He had thoroughly won Anita's heart. (It was later revealed she was secretly married to him.) His salary was one hundred fifty dollars a week.

Mayer calculated these factors. He saw that Cameron would be susceptible to cultivation in working out a deal. Although he knew Anita had a contract that bound her to Vitagraph until January, 1918, he and his lawyer, Rubin, figured they could get around that.

In May, 1917, shortly after she had begun conversations with Mayer, Anita's doctor discovered she was so nervous and run down that he urgently recommended she go away for a rest. This she did, to a sanitarium in Stamford, Connecticut.

On June 8 she wrote to the people at Vitagraph: "By reason of the continued violation on your part of my contract with you, I have severed my relation with your company."

A heated correspondence followed. Albert E. Smith, president of Vitagraph, preferred to assume that Anita had acted hastily and injudiciously. "I thought some little unpleasantness which had annoyed you in your weakened condition might be forgotten as you grew stronger," he wrote. Presumably the "little unpleasantness" he had in mind was Mayer.

On the basis of Miss Stewart's formal notice, the Boston man later claimed he was advised by her lawyer that he was free to negotiate a contract with her. Then, early in September, it was announced that Anita Stewart, the great star of Vitagraph, was signed to make pictures for Mayer!

The trade paper stories reported she was to receive a salary of ten thousand dollars a week. This was an ordinary garble of an interesting detail. Dennis F. O'Brien, Miss Stewart's lawyer, was a knowing and skillful man. He was a leading theatrical lawyer and wise to opportunists in the field. As a token of Mayer's faith, he demanded a bonus of ten thousand dollars for Miss Stewart. With that amount posted, he felt assured that Mayer was serious.

Actually, Miss Stewart's salary was to be what it was with Vitagraph—that is, one thousand dollars weekly and ten percent of the profits of her films. However, Mayer provided other inducements of a more compelling sort. In the first place, he agreed to set up a producing company bearing the actress' name. Anita Stewart Productions, Inc., was incorporated on September 1. This was designed to provide her with the distinction Mayer insisted was her due, the sort of corporate distinction then enjoyed by Mary Pickford and a few other stars.

However, there was another angle to this corporate device which J. Robert Rubin, Mayer's lawyer, shrewdly recognized. By tying Miss Stewart's name to a corporation in which others would own shares, they would have her so she would not be able to remove it, in case she tried to break her contract with *them*.

Mayer promised to provide Miss Stewart with first-class stories and directors of top rank. And he spoke of moving her productions to California, which was where she was eager to go.

But perhaps the most effective inducement was the agreement to make Rudolph Cameron a somebody in Anita Stewart Productions, Inc. Mayer put him on the board of directors and cut him in for one-eighth of the profits of the films.

This was as bold a job of raiding as was done in those wildcat years.

The ink was barely dry on the contract (and its contents were still unrevealed) when Vitagraph did the expected: Its lawyer, Samuel Seabury, sought an injunction to restrain Miss Stewart from rendering service to Mayer and to prevent him from "enticing, inducing or causing (her) to refuse to work for Vitagraph." An order to the defendants to show cause was handed down in New York Supreme Court on September 6 and an injunction was granted against them on October 23. The lawyers appealed against this injunction, and Vitagraph stood firm; it would make no submissive arrangement and proceeded to file suit against Miss Stewart.

This turn of events quite obviously put a spoke in Mayer's wheel, which appeared to be rolling smoothly up to this critical point. Now it was made to wobble and almost break loose from its hub, so dangerously did it unsettle his complicated affairs.

In the first place, to set up the new company and get financing for making films Mayer was put to the expedient of going again to his Boston friends—"the pawnbrokers," as they were locally known. (Mayer himself and Rubin put up the ten thousand dollars bonus for Miss Stewart.) Colman Levin, David Stoneman, Nathan Gordon, a theater owner, and others became investors in the new enterprise. Those were the days when film financing was a matter of private gambling on a risky scale. The prospect of delay and litigation was not attractive to them.

Furthermore, Mayer's connection with the Metro company was critically unsettled by the revelation that he had made a private deal with the actress. Richard Rowland, the president of Metro, was of a mind that the first vice-president of the company, which Mayer had come to be, should have made such a valuable arrangement on behalf of the company. The fact that Mayer had made it on behalf of Mayer was disquieting.

It was already known that Rowland did not have a warm regard for him. The Boston man was a tireless faultfinder and annoyer in Metro affairs. For one thing, Mayer insisted that Metro should spend more money and make better films. He was a strong believer in "specials" and scorned Rowland's taste for "program" fare. This latest display of his irreverence brought matters to a head. Rowland let Mayer know what he thought of him and the latter returned the compliments. In the fall of 1917, while the status of Miss Stewart was in the scales, Mayer resigned his position with Metro and sold his interest in American Feature Films.

His next move was on the order of a piece of fat jumping out of the pan into the fire. He announced that he had joined Lewis J. Selznick's new Select Film Company as its New England distributor. The prospect of Mayer and Selznick being happy as business associates for very long was about as bright as an arrangement between a bulldog and a panther to share a bone.

Selznick was every bit as tough-grained and aggressive as was Mayer, and, at this point, he had beat his way forward a good bit farther in the motion picture world. Like Mayer, he was the son of Jewish immigrants. As a boy, he had paid small heed to school because he found he could get the kind of learning he wanted much faster in other realms. He was in the jewelry business as a small merchant on New York's lower East Side when he decided the new film business was for him. That was in 1912.

The story of how Selznick broke in is so revealing of the turmoil of the times—and of Selznick—that it bears repeating, even though it may be hard to believe.

At that time, a vicious personal battle for control of the newly formed Universal company was going on between Carl Laemmle and a rugged individual, Pat Powers. The New York office was in the nature of a fortress, of which each was trying to gain command by right of physical possession and mastery over sufficient personnel.

Selznick, calling there one day to sell some jewelry (and case the joint), discovered this crazy situation and decided to act accordingly. He slipped into the office the next morning on the pretext of wishing to see someone, picked out a desk that wasn't occupied, hung up his hat, and sat down. To anyone sufficiently bold to make inquiry, he announced that he was a new employee. No one dared risk disfavor by asking further whether he had been hired by Laemmle or Powers.

Unobtrusively, at first, he merely listened and found out how the business was run—or, at least, how it was supposed to function when a paralyzing battle wasn't on. As soon as he felt he knew sufficient, he promoted himself to the job of general manager, had letterheads printed, and took on the authority. By the time Laemmle won the battle and discovered the subterfuge, Selznick knew a good deal about the business and was known by it in turn.

With Arthur Spiegel of Chicago he proceeded to form World Films, of which he became vice-president and general manager. But so arrogant and persistent was he in trying to dominate World that Spiegel and his associates finally shoved him out. Selznick got back at them; he took along Clara Kimball Young, the statuesque actress whom World had just snitched from Vitagraph.

Selznick formed a producing company with her. He also

set up a company in his name and, on the order of the Metro system, sold franchises to distributors to finance his films. He soon was a sizeable competitor to Adolph Zukor's Famous Players company.

Zukor sensed the challenge and induced Selznick to sell him, secretly, one-half of the Selznick company and change its name to Select. So charmed was Selznick by the intrigue that he failed to realize, until it was too late, that this was a brilliant maneuver to obliterate the Selznick name. The full realization of Zukor's victory dawned slowly and depressingly on him.

It was just at this unpropitious juncture that Mayer became the Boston distributor for Select.

Precisely what intention led him to throw in with Selznick's company, when he was already in a jam, is not convincingly clear. Perhaps he expected to arrange an outlet for the films he hoped to produce. Perhaps he simply wanted a connection while he was waiting for Miss Stewart. In any case, the association was not happy. The arrangement was barely settled when the two began to quarrel. Selznick was demanding and suspicious; Mayer was brash and meddlesome. They stayed together only a few months, then Mayer quit. He and Tom Spry, who had gone with him, pulled out of the company. He and Selznick were bitter toward each other until the day, some years later, that Selznick died.

Mayer, by a quick recovery, bought back into American Feature Films and Metro of New England, assuming control of them. Tom Spry was carried along with him. Mayer was playing a real chameleon game.

It was at this time that there was forming among the nation's theater men the organization that became known as the First National Exhibitors' Circuit. It was inspired by and designed to protect the large independent theater owners from Adolph Zukor's accumulating power. By cornering top producing talent, Zukor was on the way to acquiring a monopoly.

The First National idea was substantially that of Metro, except its members were theater owners. They put up the money instead of distributors. These theater men, one in each key city, had first call on films that were produced. After showing the films in their theaters, they had them for subsequent release.

The First National man in Boston was Nathan Gordon, who had started with penny arcades in the nearby city of Worcester and, over the years, had become one of the top theater owners in New England. Mayer was a close friend of his. In the summer of 1918, they formed the Gordon-Mayer Film Exchange. Once again, Mayer abandoned Metro and went to First National. The purpose this time was apparent. He was making a good connection for release of the films he expected to produce.

During the previous winter the suit to compel Miss Stewart to return to work for Vitagraph had gone to trial in New York and a $250,000 suit for damages had been filed in Boston by the Brooklyn producing company against Mayer and his business associates. In April the New York court ordered that Miss Stewart complete her contractual obligation to Vitagraph. Considering the many weeks she had been idle, the court ordered the extension of that contract to September 3. This was an ominous signal of the probable outcome of the damage suit, so Mayer and Rubin got together with the Vitagraph people and tried to reach a settlement.

They were locked in negotiations when, one day, Miss Stewart and Wilfred North, the director of the picture she had been put to work on by Vitagraph—a thing called *Mind the Paint Girl*—were in an automobile accident. Her injuries were slight, but it was evident that she would not be able to finish the picture before her contract expired. This tempered the Vitagraph people. They agreed to release Miss Stewart to Mayer and throw in two unfinished pictures for seventy-five thousand dollars.

Thus the Anita Stewart wangle was an expensive but encouraging triumph for Mayer. The actress was free to go to work in August. So, you may be sure, was he!

The measure of his determination to make himself distinctive was evidenced by his systematic efforts to insure that his production have quality. Less clever friends in the business tried to tell him that once he had a star he didn't have to worry about a story, a director, or a cast. The star would sell the picture, which was all he wanted to do. Why spend money on "incidentals?" Skimp in those areas.

Mayer didn't go with that thinking. He had seen enough to be convinced that the pictures that pulled big money had other elements of appeal than stars. They told stories of such bold or blissful nature as beguiled the great mass-audience taste, and they were directed and played with such vigor as was popular and impressive in those days. In later years Mayer was commonly regarded as the producer who most firmly relied upon stars, as the man who scorned writers and directors. That was never his theory, from the start.

Even before the Stewart deal was settled, he was seeking suitable stories. One day, his secretary, Fanny, called his attention to a serial story running in *Cosmopolitan* Magazine. She said she thought it would make a good picture. It was called *Virtuous Wives,* and the author was Owen Johnson, a popular fiction writer of the day. Mayer had her tell him the story. It appealed to him. He instructed her to write to the author and inquire about purchasing the screen rights *in her name.*

If he thought this maneuver would permit him to pick up a bargain, he was wrong. Johnson replied that five film companies wanted to buy the story and that it could be had for ten thousand dollars cash. This was far from cheap in that market, but Mayer figured the story must be good, if five other companies were after it. He made a quick check with Miss Stewart and with George Loane Tucker, a top director whom he had tentatively engaged to guide his intended picture. Both liked the story very much, whereupon he had Fanny

buy the screen rights. (Her participation was later overlooked in all the excitement and agitation of producing and
selling the film.)

This, then, was the story on which Mayer's company began,
as soon as the deal was settled and the decks were clear.
Tucker prepared the scenario and a supporting cast was
signed. Conway Tearle, a seasoned matinée idol, was to be
Miss Stewart's leading man. Others were Edwin Arden and a
stalwart stage actor, William Boyd. Prominent among the
ladies was a conspicuously lovely young thing, then the wife
of the famous actor, DeWolf Hopper. In the picture she used
her married name, but she was later to make her way as Hedda
Hopper. That was the beginning of a long acquaintance with
Mayer.

Having settled his quarrel with Vitagraph, Mayer displayed
how impersonal the turmoil was by making arrangements to
shoot his picture at that company's Brooklyn studio. *Virtuous
Wives* was completed in eight weeks, which was rather long
for the shooting of a six-reel film, and Mayer made his deal to
release it—and subsequent Stewart pictures—through First
National.

True to his thorough education in the advantages of powerful showmanship, Mayer made another large investment in advertising his forthcoming film. He bravely and expansively
proclaimed it in trade papers and magazines, directed at distributors and exhibitors, as "a view of high society *with a
moral.*"

It was opened on December 29, 1918, at the Strand Theater
in New York, to a reception marked less by critical approval
than by vigorous audience applause.

"If it is a view of any kind of society," the New York *Times'*
critic wrote, "its only moral is that men and women may
break as many middle-class commandments as they please
without injury to their characters. Some of the people in the
play are unforgivably stupid and others are as vain and vicious as good respectable folks can imagine, but everybody is

miraculously reformed in the last reel and becomes virtuous and intelligent all because a little boy is nearly drowned."

This sort of facile fictional twisting of the behavior of individuals and social groups, based upon dramatic desirability more than upon common sense, was normal in the motion picture culture to which Mayer was firmly allied. His criterion was the response of the mass audience. And the response to *Virtuous Wives* was great. The film went on to earn a sizeable profit and contribute to the making of Mayer.

So impatient for action was he that he and his company were already launched on further production in California before *Virtuous Wives* opened in New York. Arrangements were made by telegraph for Lois Weber, the first woman director of films, to do two pictures with Miss Stewart in a Los Angeles studio. Thither Anita, her mother, Rudolph Cameron, and a small entourage journeyed in November. Mayer followed in a few weeks. Although he did not then realize it, that marked his exodus from the east, his critical move from distribution into production. It was his crossing of the Rubicon.

Thereafter his attachments and his interests in the eastern complex loosened rapidly. Although he maintained an official association with Nathan Gordon and First National, he detached himself from distribution. Indeed, his old friends in Boston were considerably shocked and provoked at the way he apparently dropped them, once he was on his new road.

David Stoneman and Colman Levin, who had furnished his chief financial aid, became disillusioned and resentful because he did not cut them in on future deals. Tom Spry, his loyal lieutenant whom he left behind in the Boston exchange, was promised a job in the west whenever he wanted one. "Just come out and start working," Mayer said. But when Spry wrote a few years later to say he would take a job at five hundred dollars a week, Mayer wrote back and told him he thought it better that he stay right where he was.

Fanny Mittenthal, too, was not remembered when the Rubicon was crossed. She nursed a silent indignation at what had happened on *The Birth of a Nation* and *Virtuous Wives*.

Some years later, when Mayer returned to Boston for one of those gaudy promotional affairs—an engineered civic reception and testimonial dinner—Fanny called upon him at his hotel. In properly expansive style, he grabbed her and gave her a big kiss.

"How are you feeling, Louie?" she asked, using the form of address she always used in the office when others weren't present and she didn't have to call him "Mr. Mayer."

He was about to say he was blooming, then he hedged a bit. "Oh, I'm not so good, Fanny," he whimpered. "I've got this terrible pain here in my hand. The doctor says it is some kind of -itis, but he can't tell me what to do for it."

"I can tell you what to do for it," said Fanny, with solemn solicitude.

"Look who's going to tell me what to do for my -itis!" Mayer mocked, as he did in former days.

"I mean it, Louie," Fanny persisted. "Have you got a fountain pen?"

"Sure, I've got a fountain pen," he answered.

"And a blank check?" she asked.

"Sure, I've got a blank check, but what . . ."

"So take out your fountain pen, Louie, and write me a check for twenty-five thousand dollars," she said. "I guarantee *that* will cure your -itis!"

If a telephone book had been handy Mayer would have flung it at her. . . .

For Toby, the newspaper vendor who started the whole business with Anita Stewart, it is said that Mayer showed appreciation. He helped to pay for the little man's funeral.

## 5

When the erstwhile Boston film peddler arrived in Los Angeles late in 1918 to make pictures with Anita Stewart, it was his first step into that region which was soon to become the center of American film production and would, within a few years, witness his own ascendance to a position of virtual sovereignty.

Although, at that time, as many pictures were being produced around New York as were being made in California, the swing to the west was on. Mayer was but one small producer in the large migration that immediately followed the First World War.

Considering the present metropolis, it is amusing to recollect Los Angeles as it was when Mayer alighted from his Pullman car at the old red brick Moorish-style station of the Santa Fe. It was a sprawling, provincial city on the threshold of its first major boom that was sparked by the oncoming industries of motion pictures and oil. Its tangle of downtown streets gave leg-room to rangy and raw-boned business men, their small-town wives, tourists, citrus farmers, and seedy Mexicans. And the flat areas west and south of the city, stretching from the fringe of surrounding hills to the distant sea, were wide and sparsely settled. It was a real "hick town" in many ways.

Spotted around in the community were the new motion picture studios—open lots with large barnlike buildings on them and crazy clutters of flimsy outdoor sets. Fox had a lot on Western Avenue. Famous Players was in Hollywood, a fast-growing section in the northwest part of the city which was not many years removed from a citrus grove. Over in the San Fernando Valley, beyond dusty Cahuenga Pass, Carl Laemmle's Universal City sprawled amid acres of chicken farms. And miles and miles out toward the ocean, in a new real estate development known as Culver City, Goldwyn had a big lot. The Los Angelinos regarded these mushrooming picture studios as boom-town enterprises, about as settled as traveling circuses.

In fact, the studio with which Mayer made arrangements to rent space for the production of his films had a strong circus flavor about it and was known as the Selig Zoo. It was a place of some thirty acres in East Los Angeles, on Mission Road, belonging to "Colonel" William Selig. It was many miles from Hollywood.

The "Colonel" was one of the earliest motion picture pioneers who had started making films in Chicago and had leaped into a certain amount of fame by shooting a fake news film purported to be of Teddy Roosevelt's big-game hunting trip to Africa.

Roosevelt had refused to take with him a Selig cameraman, so the "Colonel" resolved to get even by making his own "African" film. He hired a Chicago vaudeville actor to impersonate Teddy (who was never referred to by name) and he found a broken down menagerie in Milwaukee that would rent him animals. An aged lion was purchased outright to be shot as a victim of Roosevelt's marksmanship. The scenes were made in a large cage with jungle greenery and with several Negroes acting as gunbearers. The film was called *Big*

*Game Hunting in Africa* and was a huge success. Roosevelt was furious when he heard about it, but later on he forgave the wily "Colonel."

Selig opened his first studio in Los Angeles in 1909. It was in a small building behind a Chinese laundry on Hope Street, not far from the present City Hall. Six years later he acquired some property and established his Selig Zoo as a thoroughly equipped establishment for the making of outdoor and animal films. In mission-style concrete buildings he housed some seven hundred assorted beasts, most of them got from "Big Otto," who had a menagerie in Florida. There were runs for jungle scenes, caves for "illusions," African village sets, and a eucalyptus grove of several acres to be used for sylvan scenes. There were also buildings for indoor shooting. The "Colonel" knew when to come in out of the rain.

Mayer probably selected this studio because he originally intended his first film out there to be a version of *In Old Kentucky,* a popular melodrama which had been a favorite of road companies since 1893 and had been a successful attraction at his theater in Philadelphia. It would require lots of horses, stables, and Kentucky atmosphere. These could be as reasonably provided as African scenery at the Selig Zoo.

In making arrangements for production with Lois Weber, his director, in advance, Mayer had telegraphed her what he expected in a message that indicated the man.

"Thanks for expression of satisfaction with our business relations," he said. "It is mutual. Regarding my idea of leading man, it is the same as my ideas of the play and cast, namely the best. My unchanging policy will be great star, great director, great play, great cast. You are authorized to get these without stint or limit. Spare nothing, neither expense, time, nor effort. Results only are what I am after. Simply send me the bills and I will O.K. them. Best wishes."

That was Mayer. Miss Weber undoubtedly figured she was working for a multimillionaire.

Actually, his resources were modest. He was not so lavish when he got on the scene. And Miss Weber did not direct *In Old Kentucky* without stint or limit, as she had been led to expect. She did two quick potboilers with Miss Stewart. They were *Midnight Romance* and *Mary Regan,* the latter based on a mildly popular play. The fact that they were both finished and in release by April is an indication of how rapidly they were made.

To direct *In Old Kentucky,* which followed, Mayer obtained the distinguished Marshall Neilan, who had directed no less than Mary Pickford and Blanche Sweet. Neilan was a fine and flashy fellow, a peer in that fabulous breed of silent film directors who marched around in puttees, wore their caps backwards, and communicated their subtle instructions through megaphones. His invariable nickname was Mickey. In the manner of most early directors, he scorned "money men."

Since Mayer knew very little about production he spent endless hours on the sets, listening to and watching the director and all the activity that went on. Neilan, being a champion, had his own personal crew of assistants, cameramen, and stagehands, and he acted the full lord of his domain. It annoyed him to have the little producer on the set, first looking and then asking questions. "Why do you do that? It's not in the scenario." Neilan would attempt explanations and arguments would ensue.

After several days of this, Neilan blew up. He called for all work to cease at one of Mayer's interruptions, sat down beside him wearily, and said, "Well, my little student, what lesson shall I give you today? These interruptions are costing you plenty, but it's your money, not mine." Then he studied his watch and glanced benignly at the crew sitting on their hands. Mayer may have been burned by this sarcasm, but he was not discouraged from doing all he could to learn the techniques of film making and the operation of a studio.

Shortly after his arrival in Los Angeles and his commencement of operations at the Selig Zoo, he had made a momentous maneuver. He hired a secretary. She was a handsome young woman named Florence Browning, a tall, somewhat statuesque blond, conspicuously different in appearance from small Fanny Mittenthal.

Mayer first saw Miss Browning in the office of his Los Angeles lawyers, Edwin and Joseph Loeb, where she was employed as a clerk. He was struck by her. "That's the sort of person I want working for me!" he told Ed Loeb. "I want high-class people!" He offered Miss Browning a job, and on Loeb's recommendation she went to work for him.

To her, a native Californian, he was a new sort of person, indeed—a tough little man with sharp, hard features, in somewhat dandyish clothes, who rode around in a Ford and boasted confidently that he was going to become the best producer in that part of the world. He seemed to her to have no inhibitions, no sense of embarrassment at his unrestrained self-approbation. She should have known he was the coming "Hollywood."

Mayer's office at the Selig Zoo was a little enclosed space off in one corner of a large loftlike room where the cameramen kept their paraphernalia and the cowboys and animal trainer kept their gear. It was a miserably meager establishment, even in those inelegant times—a slum by later Hollywood standards—but it was presently adequate for Mayer.

Despite Mickey Neilan's repulses, he was ceaselessly acquainting himself with every technique of picture making. He spent most of his days out on the sets or on the lot, questioning the electricians, the carpenters, the wardrobe people, the property men, as well as studying the directors, the actors, and the camera crews.

He was eternally vigorous and impetuous, and when he came into his office in the afternoon to take care of his mail and other duties, he would bluster and fume elaborately. "Tell him to go to hell!" he would snort at Miss Browning, in dictating a reply to someone making a presumptuous suggestion or demanding payment of a bill. Or, "Give this sun-nava bitch a nasty answer." Miss Browning would dutifully decide what he wanted said with less profanity and write the letters for him.

Now and then, she would put into the letters words he didn't know or understand. When he hit one of these in read-ing the letters he would call her into the office and de-mand, "What kind of damn word is this?" She would tell him the simple meaning. He would look at her critically and snort. But she noticed he usually used the words later in con-versation. Correctly, too. He learned fast.

Sometimes, when he was dictating, he would get madder and madder as he went along until the intended letter stretched to ridiculous length. Florence would patiently take it and tell him she would type out a draft. Naturally, she would cut it and put it into an orderly, comprehensible form. Often a three-page original would end up three paragraphs. Mayer virtually never questioned, or even noticed, what had been done.

On most occasions, however, he made an effort to show friendliness and charm. He was intent on getting the best out of people and did everything he could to captivate them. He had no diffidence about approaching those he wanted and selling himself to them. He was one of the most effective "romancers" that Hollywood ever had.

Florence would go to a bank where Mayer owed money and kept a slim account. Her friends there would ask her, in bewilderment, "What sort of fellow is he? Is he crazy? He owes us money and he still calls us and demands that we come out to see *him!* If he wants to see us, let him come *here!*"

And yet, in those days of his wing-spreading as a producer, Mayer also had secret attacks of sudden paralyzing depression and emotional instability. Many times, when he had an ap-pointment to see someone he regarded as "big," Florence would go into his office before the person arrived and find him sitting in frozen terror, tears pouring from his eyes. She would fetch him a glass of water and tell him gently and patiently, "Here, now, drink this; it will make you feel better." He would grasp the glass in both hands and drink it, as a child would, with the apparent confidence that it really did have some magical power. Then he would sniffle a little and wistfully wipe his eyes. A few minutes later, when Florence took the visitor into the office, Mayer would be sitting there and would jump up to greet the arrival with the cheer and self-assurance of a man thoroughly collected and in supreme command.

About this time he was also prone to "seizures," or his well-known "fainting spells." Caught in a difficult situation from which he obviously needed an out, he would suddenly groan and fall face forward on his desk or reel and slump to the floor. People who weren't familiar with these seizures would be aghast and rush screaming for aid. Florence Browning would calmly go to him, help him onto a couch or into a chair, splash a little water in his face, whereupon he would "come to" with painful gasps and sighs. This would reassure the visitor, who would then discreetly go away.

Most of the people in the office soon became familiar with these spells, which were a standard maneuver in the Mayer histrionic repertoire. So obvious were they that their occurrences turned into private office jokes. Once, in the midst of one of them, Bess Meredyth, a popular scenarist, appeared at the office door with a towel wrapped around her head, nurse-fashion, solicitously bearing a basin and a bottle of ink. "How is the patient?" she whispered to Florence Browning, as the latter came out after ministering the usual dousing.

That sort of thing could happen before anyone held Mayer in great awe.

He himself had a kind of sense of humor and could joke about his circumstances, too, although it certainly did not amuse him when others made light of him. There was the time when a small fire started in the studio. This happened to coincide with a low point in the fortunes of his company.

Mayer watched the conflagration blandly, as others leaped
for the telephone. "Don't call the firemen," he said casually.
"Let the damn thing burn."

Mayer remained on the West Coast until the summer of
1919, during which time Marshall Neilan completed the two
pictures with Miss Stewart that he had contracted to do. They
were *In Old Kentucky* and a wistful romance called *Her King-
dom of Dreams* written by Agnes Louise Prevost.

*In Old Kentucky,* incidentally, was a drama about a girl
of the bluegrass country who fell in love with a horsy young
blade, saved his prize mare from a fire in his stable and then,
in the disguising togs of a jockey, rode the mare to victory in
a major race. It was the sort of wholesome, sentimental
drama that Mayer and millions of customers loved. An indication of its popular reception was the fact that, when it
opened in Los Angeles, a touring company of the play that
was there at the same time lost out so badly that it was forced
to close.

When Mayer first told Miss Stewart they would do it she
nervously cautioned him that she had an allergy to horses and
he assured her she wouldn't have to go near one. However,
when the time came for the big scenes the horses were on
the sets and Miss Stewart was compelled to act with them.
This was an indication to her that Mayer was a stubborn
producer and that he sometimes made promises which, under certain circumstances, he found it inconvenient to keep.
She was going to have further troubles with him as their association continued.

Furthermore, if she and Rudy Cameron had any pretty
ideas that Mayer was conscientiously intending to devote all
his attention to them, they were mistaken. His wish to oper-
ate a stable of stars had been tacitly indicated when he gave
out a story to the Boston press that he was going to produce
films with Mary Pickford as well as with Anita Stewart.
This was in early 1918, before the Vitagraph trouble was
cleared, and had no more foundation than the fact that Miss

Pickford had signed to make films for First National. Mayer was wishfully thinking and picking up a little side publicity.

But now, in June, 1919, just before he returned to New York, he accurately announced that he had garnered Mildred Harris Chaplin as his next stellar protégée.

Miss Harris—or Mrs. Charlie Chaplin, as she happened at the moment to be—was not an actress of any notable talent or popularity. She had knocked about in movies since she was a little girl and had played in several Universal pictures, in supporting roles, when Chaplin met her at a very gay house party of Hollywood blades and babes and provided her chief claim to distinction. He gallantly made her his wife.

The marriage was not one framed in heaven; it soon became holy hell. However, the newspaper writers made it appear a lovers' dream. Chaplin was then coming into his great fame and popularity, and the public was avid for details of his first marriage, which this one was. Writers attempted to provide those details as best they could.

This naturally gave pretty Mildred an aura of romance, which Mayer recognized as good for business. Although it was privately agreed by the newlyweds when they were married that Mildred would give up her screen career, this arrangement was not pleasing to her after a few months of less than bliss. By the spring of 1919, Mayer was dangling a contract in her face, with the inducement that he would set up the Mildred Harris Productions Company, just as he had done for Miss Stewart.

As it happened, Miss Harris was one of the Universal people whom Robert Cochrane had deliberately oversold to Mayer when the latter was casting about for prospects a year or so before; a bloated notion of her proven attractions may have further excited his zeal. By June he had made a deal with her, even though she was pregnant at the time. When he returned east that summer, he was in business with two female stars.

Mayer had now decided to move to California permanently, leaving his eastern representation to Robert Rubin and a small clerical staff in New York. Through Selig he made arrangements to have a new studio built for him in the eucalyptus grove that adjoined the Selig Zoo, at 3800 Mission Road. Work was well started on it when he returned with his family and moved into a rented house on North Kenmore, between Sunset and Hollywood Boulevards.

The new studio was ready in January, a small but attractive facility in keeping with the ambition of Mayer. The main building was styled to resemble the château of Chenonceaux; there were four stages, and dressing bungalows for Miss Stewart and Miss Harris were set prettily among the trees. Miss Stewart's was decorated in crimson and yellow, Miss Harris' in lavender and light gray.

With the expanded studio Mayer's activities increased. He had heralded the signing of Miss Harris with a big advertising campaign, again boasting the incomparable beauty, talent, and popularity of his new star, and proclaiming that her first picture would be *The Inferior Sex*. This was a tale of domestic discord, with Miss Harris cast to play a wife who missed by a hairsbreadth falling into infidelity.

Shooting had been completed and it was in the editing stage when an accident in the cutting-room caused ruin to some of the negative. Thus Mayer was compelled to hasten completion of her second picture, already in the works, and release it first. This was *Polly of the Storm Country,* a generously mawkish yarn about a "squatter" girl, abused by "hilltoppers," who ended by marrying one of them. Some of the exteriors were shot in a fishing village on the California coast.

Mayer had this romance written for him by Grace Miller White, whose previous *Tess of the Storm Country* had been a popular vehicle for Mary Pickford and whose *The Secret of the Storm Country* had served Norma Talmadge equally well. Therefore, he felt the "storm country" would do for Miss Harris and for him.

By the time *Polly of the Storm Country* was ready for release, Mayer and his publicity people somewhat amended their regard for her skill. In suggesting to theater managers how to sell the film, they said:

"Mildred Harris Chaplin is still new enough as a star to be exploited as the famous comedian's wife. She will attract more attention in that way than by referring to her ability. . . . The moral of the story is a good one. Send invitations to the clergy and win their support, as the picture emphasizes the power of brotherly love."

The irony of this pious advice was that "the famous comedian's wife" was even then engaged in a public battle of mudslinging with her spouse. She was righteously protesting that Chaplin had been cruel and inhuman to her; he was replying, via the newspapers, with a few lurid charges of his own. Whatever the effect upon the clergy, this was good publicity —something that Mayer was not averse to. He added a little on his own.

On an evening in April, 1920, he was with a party in the fashionable dining room of the old Alexandria Hotel in Los Angeles. The party included Mrs. Mayer; Anita Stewart; her husband, Rudy Cameron; and J. Robert Rubin and his wife, who were on their first visit to California to see Mayer's new studio.

Everything was going along nicely, when Chaplin and some friends came in and sat at a nearby table. Looks and then words were exchanged. Chaplin was noisily protesting against what he thought was meddling by Mayer in arrangements for a financial settlement he was trying to make with his estranged wife.

Mayer got up and went to the lobby. Chaplin and other gentlemen followed him. There Mayer said something to the comedian that he did not wish the ladies to hear.

"Take off your glasses!" Chaplin challenged. Mayer removed his pince-nez with his left hand and with his right, swinging out at the same moment, clipped Chaplin neatly on the jaw. The comedian tumbled backwards into a potted palm, from which he was rescued by Jack Pickford, as the other gentlemen intervened. Chaplin was led away bleeding and Mayer, flushed with victory, said to his friends who offered polite approval, "I only did what any man would have done."

This was not the last incident of fist swinging in which Mayer was to be involved. He was one of the frequent scrappers in the boom days of Hollywood.

During his one-year contract with her, Mayer produced five films with Mildred Harris (who was compelled to drop the helpful name of Chaplin after her divorce). In addition to *Polly of the Storm Country* and *The Inferior Sex*, they were *The Woman in His House, Old Dad* and *Habit.* They were not very successful films, after the flurry of public interest created for the first two, and the contract was not renewed. Mayer incidentally indicated he was unsympathetic to divorce.

By this time, Anita Stewart's contract was also running out, and her experiences with the producer were not such as to encourage her to renew. She found him a tough taskmaster. In the three years she worked for him, he got fifteen pictures out of her, not counting two she completed as part of the settlement with Vitagraph.

Miss Stewart and Rudy Cameron had frequent quarrels with Mayer. She wasn't satisfied with her stories, and Cameron had other complaints. The constant work and tension upset her, she suffered badly from "nerves," lost weight and looked ill in her later pictures. When her contract expired, she was so exhausted that she took an extended rest. Sometime later, in reminiscing, she said a bit wistfully, "I have often wondered since if it would not have been better if I had remained in dear old Brooklyn with Vitagraph."

Considering Mayer's early insistence upon the value of stars and his repeated reliance upon this theory in his later career, it is interesting that he continued without conspicuous stars for a spell, after the completion of his contracts with Miss Harris and Miss Stewart. Now he depended on directors to deliver his "quality" films. His two particular meal tickets were Fred Niblo and John Stahl.

Niblo was a former Ince director who had gone with United Artists when it was formed in 1919 and had there made a couple of mild successes with his wife, Enid Bennett, as star. Mayer got him to do the last two Stewart films, *The Woman He Married* and *Rose o' the Sea,* and to remain in association with the Mayer company.

Stahl was an interesting acquisition. He was first brought to Mayer by the then successful agent and later producer, Edward Small. He had been a prominent stage director with the Jewish theater in New York and had done a couple of pictures for companies in the east, but they were not sufficiently impressive to give him any kind of prestige.

When Stahl arrived in Hollywood, Small took him to William Fox. "There are no Jewish directors in this business; why don't you give a job to one?" Small asked. Fox was not moved by that suggestion, so Small took his man to Mayer and put the same question to him. Mayer thought the question fair, but he was more interested by the fact the he could get Stahl on very good terms. He put him on the Mildred Harris picture, *The Woman in His House,* which was not particularly impressive. But Stahl was, and stayed.

All of Mayer's pictures, up to this point, had been distributed through First National. But an opportunity to expand his output and distribution now presented itself. Metro, his erstwhile connection, had been sold to Marcus Loew, the theater chain operator. Richard Rowland, Mayer's nemesis, was out. Robert Rubin, who was one of Loew's counsel, had helped to arrange the deal. Now, with Metro needing more pictures—and better ones—to release, it was natural for Rubin to suggest that an arrangement be made with Mayer. Loew took the suggestion and made a contract with Mayer to produce four pictures a year for Metro, in addition to his output for First National.

The little Mission Road producer was moving rapidly ahead. Another miracle was in the making. He could feel it in his bones.

# 6

Let it be duly noted that Mayer's concern for morality on the screen was particularly exercised and evident in what he later called his "Mission Road days." Most of the Anita Stewart and Mildred Harris films followed the general formula of the poor but decent girl conducting herself with honest purpose, always against temptations and harsh assaults, with a full reward for her virtue bestowed in the happy end.

He was downright passionate about virtue. Some producers and directors were following a trend toward fleshy, salacious pictures, such as *Male and Female* of Cecil B. De Mille or the *Sheik* films of Rudolph Valentino or *The Queen of Sheba* of Fox. But Mayer stuck to dramas of honor, fidelity, and virtue-sorely-tried, for which there were terminal compensations. He doted on self-sacrifice.

It was in this interesting period, 1919 through 1921, when the social and moral climate of the nation was changing radically as a consequence of the First World War, that the motion picture medium came under severe attack as a deteriorating influence and contributor to the corruption of public morals. The succession of sexy pictures (which were naïve by standards of today) and the occurrence of several incidents that suggested riotous living in Hollywood had started a wave of agitation among the clergy and women's clubs for censorship of the movies and the closing of theaters —on Sundays, anyhow.

To counter this ominous agitation, leaders of the industry agreed to employ as the champion of the movies a man of impeccable prestige. For this position they chose Will H. Hays. His first qualification to be the "czar of the movies," as he later came to be known, was that he had helped, as a Republican leader from Indiana, to accomplish the presidential nomination of Warren G. Harding in a smoke-filled room. For this respectable service he was later appointed Postmaster General in Harding's cabinet, a post from which he was able to dispense much Federal patronage. This, of course, qualified him as a man of impeccable prestige. Another strong recommendation was that he had high standing in the Presbyterian church.

Hays was made president of the newly formed Motion Picture Producers and Distributors of America in January, 1922. One of his first orders of business was the disposal of the "Arbuckle case."

In the previous fall, comedian Fatty Arbuckle had been sensationally involved in a wild party in San Francisco which resulted in the injury and death of a minor movie actress by the fortuitous name of Virginia Rappe. The case was luridly reported, and it was felt that something should be done to show that motion picture people did not condone this sort of thing.

Adolph Zukor, whose Famous Players company released the Arbuckle films, was persuaded by Hays to shelve all those it had in release or in the works. Zukor went through with it righteously, at a big financial loss. Needless to say, Arbuckle was officially ostracized. (The poor man was later absolved of guilt in the death of the actress, but by then his career was ruined.)

Although Mayer was not a big enough producer to partici-
pate in the hiring of Hays, he followed the extraordinary
proceedings with inherent sympathy. He was much in favor
of the idea of the film industry protecting itself, and he issued
his own public statement after the ban of the Arbuckle films.

"I haven't any particular love for Adolph Zukor," he said,
"but, in this instance, he certainly backed Hays up man-
fully, despite the fact that it cost his company about $2,000,-
000." Then he added, with a slight suggestion of smugness
and piety, "So far, I have to be thankful that no picture of
mine has ever come under the ban of any censorship. I have
always striven to keep them clean."

Mayer's solemn impulse to virtue, as well as his general
disposition, was revealed to writer Frances Marion, a top
scenarist, when she first met the budding titan in 1922. He
had asked her to come to his studio to discuss the adaptation
of a play he had purchased for production. It was *The Famous Mrs. Fair,* by James Forbes.

Then there was no tiresome waiting to see the not yet so
famous Mr. Mayer. He bounded out of his office to greet
Miss Marion the moment she arrived, led her in, sat her
down, and for fifteen minutes talked enthusiastically of his
interests and intents in producing films.

"I will make only pictures that I won't be ashamed to have
my children see," he said, and he pointed with pride and affection to a large silver-framed photograph of his wife and two
teen-age daughters, Edith and Irene, that faced him across
the desk.

"I'm determined that my little Edie and my little Irene
will never be embarrassed. And they won't, if all my pictures
are moral and clean."

Meeting him for the first time, Miss Marion was touched
and impressed. She was one of the valuable people to suc-

cumb to his ardent salesmanship. Years later, when she knew him much better, she reflected wryly on that meeting. "Thus did we start out with Mr. Mayer's own brand of castile soap to keep the slate clean for little Edie and little Irene," she said.

It hardly need be added that Miss Marion did prepare the scenario for *The Famous Mrs. Fair,* which was directed by Fred Niblo and was one of Mayer's more successful pictures, released by Metro in 1923. It was the drama of a woman who had to choose between fame and her family. Knowing Mayer's predisposition, it is not hard to guess which she chose.

But his artistic ardor for conformance was particularly manifest in the films John Stahl directed for him, such as *The Child Thou Gavest Me* and *One Clear Call,* the latter a tearful drama in which a hopelessly tubercular husband committed suicide to relieve the strain on his family. Most memorable of Stahl's films, however, and the one which was recalled by some of Mayer's veteran associates in his later years was a stern middle-class morality drama called *Dangerous Age,* made from an original scenario by Frances Irene Reel.

As the New York *Times* tersely described it (January 29, 1923), it had to do with "wayward middle-age, the lingering taste for romance in a man of forty whose wife gives him sulphur and molasses in the spring and spends a moonlight evening darning his underwear. He goes to New York on a business trip and meets a young girl there. He satisfies his appetite for romantic moonshine with her—even to the point of writing his wife he wants his freedom so he can marry the girl. But the girl herself has no such serious design, the wife wakes up to her husband's needs, and the husband comes to the conclusion that 'a man at 40 is not so damned young as he thinks he is!' "

In the role of the husband was Lewis Stone, who was again to play a character whom Mayer found fascinating years later in a famous series of films.

Such fondness and pride did the producer have for *Dan-*

Louis Mayer as a youth, hobnobbing with a ship-wrecking crew aboard a hulk in Saint John, New Brunswick. Note the dash of class in his vest, watch chain, and charm.

The Haverhill, Massachusetts, nickelodeon magnate, in derby hat, chesterfield, and pince-nez, attends an early convention of film exhibitors in 1911. The gentleman in white motoring cap is Albert E. Smith, president of Vitagraph, the producing company from which Mayer later "stole" Anita Stewart. At left, behind Mayer, is Nate Gordon, who became his partner in a Boston film exchange.

Here is where Mayer started in show business—the new Orpheum theater in Haverhill. This photo was made on the occasion of Mayer's triumphal visit to the city in 1925, but the place looks much as it did when he first acquired it in 1907, even to the pool hall above.

*United Press International*

Nance O'Neil in *The Fires of St. John,* a big hit at the Colonial in 1912.

Eddie Dowling, a favorite in Homan's Musical Review, which played the Colonial (with weekly variations) for twenty-two weeks.

*Joe Laurie, Jr., Collection, N.Y. Public Library*

A life-sized oil painting of Mayer, made from this photo by a clever scenery painter, hung in the lobby of the Colonial theater in Haverhill when Mayer opened it.

Lorne Elwyn, leading man in the Orpheum theater's stock company in 1912.

*Museum of Modern Art Film Library*

A desperate situation in the 1917 serial film, *The Great Secret,* the first production financed by Mayer. The handcuffed gentleman in the boiled shirt is Francis X. Bushman, outstanding star of the day.

Beautiful Anita Stewart protects Mrs. DeWolf (Hedda) Hopper, in this scene from *Virtuous Wives.* This was the film with which Mayer successfully launched his producing career.

*Museum of Modern Art Film Library*

A Mayer company (*The Fighting Shepherdess*) on location in the early Hollywood days. The star, seated in the wagon with the bulldog, is Anita Stewart. Standing, in puttees, is her husband, Rudolph Cameron. Cameraman Tony Gaudio steadies his instrument; Director Edward José leans on wagon wheel.

*Museum of Modern Art Film Library*

*Museum of Modern Art Film Library*

Mildred Harris Chaplin, looking a bit plump for a star, poses in this chummy photo on signing to make films for Mayer (1919).

Moving up in the world Mayer consults with Fred Niblo and theater magnate, Marcus Loew, on the set of Mayer's Metro production, *The Famous Mrs. Fair.*

*Museum of Modern Art Film Library*

The key to the future. Mayer, flanked by his associates, Harry Rapf and the youthful Irving Thalberg, at ceremonies which marked his taking over as the head of the merged Metro, Goldwyn, and Mayer studios in April, 1924.

This is the way the Culver City lot looked at the time of the merger. Stage 1 has been "decorated" as an outdoor set.

Mayer and his family on location for filming of scenes for *Ben-Hur* at Livorno, Italy, in 1925. Left to right, Irene, Mrs. Mayer, Dr. Jones, Fred Niblo, Carey Wilson, Mayer, Edith, and Bess Meredyth.

A typical luncheon for a celebrity in the Marion Davies "bungalow" on the Metro-Goldwyn-Mayer lot. Seated at the head of the table are G.B. Shaw, Miss Davies, Mayer, Clark Gable, and George Hearst, son of W.R.

*Culver Service*

*gerous Age* that he had Stahl repeat the formula in two or three subsequent films.

It was now, in this Mission Road period, that there casually occurred for Mayer a stroke of fortune—or fate, as some might call it—which was a major event in his career. That was his introduction to Irving Thalberg, a frail young man who was then in the employ of Universal as a sort of head of studio.

This hesitation about his position is due to an odd circumstance: Thalberg himself was not quite certain what position he held. As a protégé of Carl Laemmle, the pintsized founder and undisputed head of unusual Universal, he had been brought to the West Coast studio in a secretarial capacity only a couple of years before and had been left there as a glorified watchman for his employer when the latter departed for a trip to Europe.

Such was Laemmle's custom. He generously gave people jobs, especially his relatives, and then neglected to tell them precisely what the jobs were. He had taken young Thalberg into his office when the Brooklyn youth had got to him through a slight friendship with the Laemmle family at a Long Island summer resort. And he had hauled the young man to California on the pretext of needing him to take care of some correspondence on the trip out. Then Laemmle planted him at the studio.

Fortunately, Thalberg was able to look out for his own interests as well as those of his boss. Although he was only nineteen when he arrived on the Coast, he was vastly ambitious and resourceful. Most important, he was fascinated with films. He rapidly got to know the business, which was fairly new and crude, and soon was making suggestions on productions and then taking a hand in them.

When Laemmle came back to visit some months later, he found Thalberg well entrenched and, for all his youth and boyish nature, exercising some small authority. This pleased the little Napoleon (which Laemmle liked to think he was).

He empowered the young man to take over more authority
in the running of the studio. With this new status Thalberg
preëmpted the production of many films and soon ran afoul
of Erich von Stroheim, a headstrong writer-director-actor
whom Laemmle had employed.

Thalberg's battles with Von Stroheim when the latter was
making *Foolish Wives* were such as to justify legends still
awesome in Hollywood. He grimly stood up to the tough
Teuton whose extravagances were absurd. He also carried on
a contest for position with a couple of other uncertain
"heads" of the studio. In these difficult maneuvers he learned
to be patient and strong. That was the character of Thalberg
when he was starting life in Hollywood.

Mayer first came upon him in 1922. Their introduction
and subsequent encounters occurred in the home of Edwin
Loeb, who was the lawyer for both Mayer and Laemmle and
an early friend of Thalberg. Loeb had met young Thalberg
when he was just out from New York, still a little lonely and
homesick, and had quickly invited him to his home. There
he found the young man to be bright and sensitive, shy in
social contacts, and as green as a kid off a farm. Loeb was
struck by a homely little detail: the chap wore long woolen
underwear even in the California climate. Back home, he had
been a "mama's boy." His mother, Henrietta, was a powerful
force in his life, as everyone who knew Thalberg soon
learned.

Although the young man was extraordinary in devotion
and application to his job, he found time to pay attention to
Laemmle's dark-haired daughter, Rosabelle. A clumsy romance developed. It was not much beyond puppy love, but it
puzzled and upset Papa Laemmle, who wasn't sure that he
entirely approved. Eddie Loeb had discovered one time, when
he had his doctor see Thalberg at his house, that the lad's
heart was weak from an illness that had kept him in bed for
several months as a boy. Whether he told this to Laemmle

and whether Laemmle was worried isn't certain. But the papa was further puzzled when the romance perceptibly cooled.

All of this was coincident with Thalberg's struggles to cut his way through the disorder and intrigue at Universal. Loeb was able to see that the pressures were getting too much for him, that the young man was nearing collapse. Finally, he spoke to Laemmle and warned him he had better do something quick to make things easier for Thalberg, if he wished to keep him in his employ. Laemmle's answer surprised him.

"For God's sake, Eddie," he said, "do me a favor, will you? Take that young man off my hands."

Loeb was unable to figure whether Laemmle was more concerned about the health and welfare of Thalberg or about the feelings of Rosabelle. Anyhow, he took the suggestion and, a few days later, spoke to Joe Schenck, who was then making films for First National.

"Why don't you hire this boy?" he asked.

"Listen Eddie," Schenck told him, in preface to what was probably the worst piece of judgment of his career, "I'll pick the people to make pictures. You stick to the law."

Loeb then dropped the suggestion into the ear of Mayer, who was more receptive. He had come to like Thalberg and was impressed with the young man's knowledge of picture making and his serious concern for quality. Mayer had a keen eye for talent and he recognized it in "this boy." Furthermore, he considered Thalberg's attachment to his mother a most auspicious sign. Perhaps he began to have the feeling that this might be the "son" the Almighty had never seen fit to give him but that he might miraculously find.

Mayer's enthusiasm for Thalberg, once he had discussed the possibility of making an association with him, is evidenced by the generosity of the proferred deal. He offered to set up a separate producing company, subsidiary to his own, which Thalberg would run, and give him twenty percent of the profits of the films this company made. But when this arrange-

ment was found inharmonious with Mayer's contract with
First National, Thalberg was hired on a straight employee
basis at six hundred dollars a week. His switch-over from
Universal occurred on February 15, 1923. His job this time
was specific: he was the vice-president and production assistant to Mayer.

It would be a surrender to fancy to encourage the happy
thought that it was all sunshine and profits with Mayer's company during these embryonic days. It was not, not even when
Thalberg presumably added the magic of his incipient intuition and skill. Mayer was far from being one of the top producers of Hollywood. He was a small, enterprising operator
doing the best he could to supply First National and Metro
with the pictures they had contracted for. There were many
others like him, clawing to get minor stars and unattached
directors to make their pictures and help them to get ahead.
On some films they picked up profits, on others they definitely did not. The business was always a gamble for them, as
it was for Mayer.

The precarious nature of operations is evident in the
deal Mayer had with First National. He received fifty percent
of the gross receipts from the distribution of his pictures
*after* First National had taken out the amount of money it
gave him for each picture on delivery of the negative. Although First National guaranteed him $125,000 for each nega-
tive, his costs often exceeded this figure so that Mayer was
always gambling for his cut. In those days, if the average
picture grossed $250,000 for the distribution company, it was
doing well.

During one period of slight embarrassment he sublet space
in his studio to B.P. Schulberg, another independent, who
was no larger than he and likewise made up in aggressiveness
for what he lacked in size. Mayer was east, looking after matters in the New York office, which he continued to maintain,
when Schulberg put a sign, "B.P. SCHULBERG PRODUCTIONS,

INC.," on the studio. Mayer's secretary, Florence Browning, wired him what had occurred, fearful that he would be outraged. Mayer made no reply. When he got back he shrugged off the incident. "We need the rent money," he said. "What do we care if he shows off a little?" Mayer could sympathize.

Actually, the Mayer and Schulberg families were good friends in these days. The Mayers with their two teen-age daughters and the Schulbergs with a daughter and two sons, one of whom, Budd (then Buddy), was to write knowingly of Hollywood, would often get together for Sunday dinners at the Mayer home on North Kenmore and feast royally on the special dishes that Mrs. Mayer so capably prepared. They were socially sympathetic, both families recently out from the east, remote and still a little lonesome in this strange community, where the papas were both striking boldly for glittering motion-picture gold. Neither could foresee the future, but each had his limited dreams which came out in guarded conversation on these Sunday afternoons.

With the addition of Thalberg to his production staff, Mayer stepped up his output of pictures. A new director, Reginald Barker, had been brought in to do mainly outdoor epics, which were always in demand—such mighty and muscular dramas as *Hearts Aflame,* a fiery saga of logging, and *Eternal Struggle,* a discovery of the eternal triangle with the Northwest Mounted Police.

In the latter he had Renée Adorée in the role of a vivacious French-Canadian barroom girl who fell in love with a handsome Mounted Policeman, even though she was promised to marry his stern superior. Implicated in a murder, she naturally ran away and the Mountie was dispatched to retrieve her, preferably alive. This took a bit of doing, what with a perilous canoe trip on the way, but of course it was eventually accomplished and all ended happily. The Mountie was played by Pat O'Malley, who had worked for Mayer in Haverhill, and his stern superior was Earle Williams. Also in the cast were Barbara La Marr and Wallace Beery, a popular "heavy" well favored by Mayer. An outdoor drama of this nature excited his lusty showmanship.

Barker's next picture after this one—a society drama called *Pleasure Mad*—is notable in the Mayer output because it gave first prominence to a young actress who was to be a powerful factor in the Mayer-Thalberg hegemony. This was a Canadian girl, Norma Shearer, who was pursuing an indifferent career as a minor actress in New York when she was put under contract to Mayer's studio in the spring of 1923.

Her emergence was a matter of pure good fortune. Robert Rubin had called Edward Small, a talent agent, and urgently requested a nice, refined-looking girl—any girl—who could be sent to California right away to do a job for Mayer. Small said he had this young Canadian actress whom Mayer could have for one hundred fifty dollars a week, provided he paid her expenses and her mother's to the Coast. Rubin, relying on Small's judgment, accepted. That's how Miss Shearer got her job.

The picture for which she was intended was *The Wanters,* to be directed by John Stahl, but he didn't like her appearance when he got a good look at her in a gaudy gown she had selected for her screen test. He dropped her to a mere "bit" role.

Even so, Mayer and Thalberg decided to give her another chance and turned her over to Barker for the ingénue lead in *Pleasure Mad.* This was the role of a society girl who had to make a choice between her father and her mother when they were getting a divorce. Clearly, it was another of those morality tales that Mayer loved. Unfortunately, Miss Shearer and Barker did not get along at all. She couldn't seem to take direction from him, and he badgered and browbeat her. Finally, he went to Mayer and told him he could not use the girl. This could have been the finish of her career at that studio.

However, Mayer was less despairing and proceeded in a

way that was characteristic of his perception in handling talent. He called the actress to his office, let her tell him her side of the case, the while listening patiently and politely to throw her a little off guard. Then suddenly he leaped from his chair and sprung at her.

"The trouble is you're yellow!" he cried. "Here you are given a great chance, the chance of your life, and what do you do? You throw it away because maybe you don't like the director or something! I'm through with you!"

The actress stood quietly for a moment, too stunned to say a word. She hadn't expected this sort of violence from the presumably sympathetic Mr. Mayer. Then she put on what he later termed "the most magnificent act" he ever saw. She drew herself up in indignation, dramatically paced the floor, thumped his desk with her fist, and flashed defiance.

"I am NOT yellow!" she cried. "I'll fight it out! I'll show you I can do it! Give me another chance!"

Here was a show of spirit such as Mayer instinctively admired. It revealed the reaction he wanted in a cheering histrionic display. He turned Miss Shearer over to Thalberg, who gave her the gratifying news that the shooting already done on the picture was photographically poor and they would start over again. When they did, she pulled herself together and was a lamb. *Pleasure Mad* was not a great picture but it saved Norma Shearer for bigger things.

As much as the motion picture business was expanding generally, it was doing so in a crazy, reckless fashion that made it liable to periodic slumps. Producers, ever optimistic, would tend to overspend and overproduce in periods of booming attendance; they would overinvest and overstock, so that a slow-up or setback in the public's responses would leave them in a financial jam. One of these—a bad one—came in the fall of 1923.

A modest decline in movie-going found producers and distributing companies with large inventories of pictures, made more or less expensively. This classic economic disorder meant a crisis in the industry. Adolph Zukor ordered a shutdown of production at his Famous Players studio. First National issued instructions that all its producers should "retrench."

Marcus Loew, president of the company that owned the Loew theater chain and operated Metro, called for "rigid economies" and analyzed the dilemma from the invariable point of view of the theater man. He blamed Hollywood producers for "extravagance, inefficiency, lack of brains and" —something that was going to be conspicuous in their isolated area—"jealousy."

"The exhibitors can afford to pay for big pictures and high costs and all that," he said, "but they *can't* pay for extravagance and waste and inefficiency.

"I can tell you this now," he added, with the prudence of a sober businessman who thinks of jittery stockholders, "because the house is being cleaned."

To observe the progress of his house cleaning, Loew made a trip to the West Coast a few weeks before Christmas, 1923. He was accompanied by Robert Rubin, one of his lawyers, as well as counselor for Mayer. They paid an important visit of inspection to Mayer's studio. There Loew was hospitably welcomed and given a sizeable helping of Mayer charm. He was taken to watch the shooting and meet the directors and casts of two rather important pictures being prepared for Metro release. One was *Thy Name Is Woman,* Fred Niblo directing, with Ramon Novarro and Barbara La Marr as stars; the other was a Reginald Barker picture, *Women Who Give.* Mayer introduced Loew to Thalberg and made sure to impress him with the intelligence, economy, and efficiency with which he ran his studio.

This was a particularly potent move, for Loew was anything but impressed with the quality of the operation of his own Metro studio. Under the management of Joe Engel, it was rapidly going downhill, providing inadequate pictures at illogical costs. Loew and his board of directors were so displeased and discouraged, by and large, that they were seriously given to wondering whether they should abandon the studio.

Then came that chance occurrence which did for the future of American films something comparable to that done for science when an apple hit Isaac Newton on the head.

Loew had returned from the West Coast with a bad cold. After Christmas he went to Palm Beach to rest and recuperate. There he ran into and got to talking, more or less casually, with the president of another film company who was even less happy than he. This was Frank Joseph Godsol, head of the Goldwyn Company, which he had been sent to manage after the unseating of its founder, Samuel Goldwyn, two years previously.

Godsol acknowledged that his company was in a precarious way, stuck with heavy investments which it was finding hard to recoup. Its principal assets were a half-interest in the Capitol Theater in New York and the well-stocked studio in Culver City that had belonged to Triangle and Thomas Ince. Without being devious about it, he let it be understood that he'd be glad to make an arrangement whereby Loew would take the whole business off his hands.

Loew wasn't in sound health, but a little light came on in his brain. Rather than abandon his Metro studio, why not build it up? Why not merge with the Goldwyn Company, use its facilities, and develop a smart producing operation which would be able to provide his theaters with a full and economical supply of films? His health did not permit him to deal with Godsol personally, but he called Robert Rubin and Nicholas Schenck from New York—Schenck was his top lieutenant, in charge of theaters—and turned the job over to them.

After long and involved conversations, the negotiators arrived at a plan whereby the Loew company would take over the Goldwyn Company through a simple exchange of stock. Loew's Metro producing company and the Goldwyn Company would be merged into the Metro-Goldwyn Corporation. Preferred stock in this corporation would be exchanged for the shares of the Goldwyn Company, at the rate of one share for one. The common stock would be given to Loew's, Inc., for its Metro company. It remained for directors and shareholders of the Goldwyn Company to accept the plan.

However, a still urgent matter had to be met by the men of Loew's. That was the selection of someone to head up the prospectively merged studios. Joe Engel of Metro was excluded. Indeed, he was actually discharged from his position with that company before the merger was assured. Abraham Lehr, the head of the Goldwyn studio, was regarded unfavorably. He was a nice fellow but not an executive; this was a job that called for a man who was able and strong.

Needless to say, Robert Rubin had just the man in mind. When the moment was right, he 'phoned Mayer and advised him to hasten to New York. Mayer came, prepared to do some dealing. Although the job looked desirable, it was not the sort he would jump for without favorable *quid pro quo's.*

Rubin arranged a meeting for Mayer with Loew and Schenck. The reason for the meeting was tacitly understood. Conversations were started and continued for several days, with Mayer and Loew guardedly sparring and Rubin deftly moving between. Loew was impressed with Mayer's performance but knew he would be gambling on him. Mayer was in the strong position of having a successful studio, well staffed with young Thalberg and good directors, if not an impressive group of stars. He had, even that month, added a new supervisor, Harry Rapf. What Mayer had to offer was a propitious combination of productive skills.

Eventually an arrangement was worked out. Mayer would blend his studio and his people into the Metro-Goldwyn merger, if and when it occurred. He would become the first vice-president and general manager of the new producing company at a salary of $1,500 a week. Thalberg would be second vice-president and supervisor of production at $650 a week, and Rubin would be the secretary at $600 a week. He would be the eastern representative, with offices in New York.

There were other significant understandings.

Each motion picture produced by the new company would say on the main title, at Mayer's option, either "Louis B. Mayer presents" or "Produced by Louis B. Mayer" or "Produced by the Metro-Goldwyn-Mayer Corp." And "in all advertising and paid publicity the name of Louis B. Mayer shall be prominently mentioned as the producer of said motion picture photoplays." Mayer undoubtedly remembered how Lewis Selznick's name had been lost when he formed the Select Company with Adolph Zukor. He would not have that happen to him.

All contracts with stars, directors, and writers would be made in the name of Louis B. Mayer, but no contract could be made until approved by Loew, Schenck, or Rubin. Loew reserved "the right to propose" stories, actors, and directors.

The whole kit and caboodle of Mayer's property, including cameras, equipment, and furniture, both at the Mission Road studio and in the company's offices in New York, were to be purchased outright by Metro-Goldwyn. (The figure eventually paid was $76,500, which shows the small value of the company in everything but skills.)

Included in the transfer were the contracts of Mayer's personnel. They included Fred Niblo for five pictures, Reginald Barker for three, John Stahl for two, and Hobart Henley for three; Elinor Glyn for two stories; Harry Rapf to supervise three productions; and the contractual obligations for various periods of Huntley Gordon, Robert Frazier, Norma Shearer, Hedda Hopper, and Renée Adorée.

A clause was also included which specified that if, after two years, less than fifteen pictures were turned out in any one year, the contract could be terminated. This protected Loew's against the possibility that Mayer would not come through.

Most important was a small clause which specified that twenty percent of the profits of the Metro-Goldwyn company would be paid to the members of the "Mayer group." Profits were to be reckoned after payment of an annual dividend of two dollars a share on the common stock. Members of the "Mayer group," as it was cryptically termed, were Mayer, Thalberg, and Rubin, who among themselves would privately arrange to whack up whatever bonuses might accrue.

This deal for twenty percent of the profits was not revealed to stockholders for several years, and was arrived at after an attempt by Mayer and Rubin to arrange a bonus in stock had failed. "I would rather make you shareholders in the pictures than stockholders in the company," Loew said, thus choosing a form of inducement that was to cost Loew's, Inc., millions over the years. For the share-of-the-profits arrangement, which seemed fairly safe and conservative at the time, became a gold mine for the producers when the company swept to prosperity.

A contract between Mayer and Metro was reached and signed on April 10, 1924. A few days later, the fateful merger was formally ratified.

# 7

When word of the merger of the Metro and Goldwyn companies got around, there was no great surprise or breathless wonder in the motion picture industry. Adolph Zukor, William Fox, and Carl Laemmle, reigning powers of the day and heads of major companies, did not shudder with anxiety. In general, the new amalgamation was seen as a desperation move, designed as a last attempt to rescue two tottering studios. And Mayer, far from being regarded as an executive with miraculous powers, was figured as a shrewd opportunist with more to gain than lose. Mergers had been so common and so often futile in the growing industry that the chances of this one succeeding were quoted at even, no more.

However, that sort of skepticism had no place in the thinking of Mayer. He was fired with optimism. For him, the miracle had happened; in a matter of less than six years he had become head of an extensive studio. A fine plant and plenty of talent, experienced artists, were his to command. If he couldn't make them make good pictures, he figured it couldn't be done.

The plant to be used was the handsome Goldwyn studio on Washington Boulevard in the outlying flats of Culver City. It had been started by Thomas Ince as the home of Triangle, the first big combine of top directors and top stars. Ince, D.W. Griffith, and Mack Sennett were its prime supports. When it fell apart, the studio was vacated. The Goldwyn Company had taken it in 1918.

Now it was a forty-acre layout lying behind a high white wall and a three-story office building, fronted by an austere colonnade. It had six large glass-enclosed stages (to take advantage of natural light), storage buildings, shops, laboratories, bungalows, and dressing rooms. All were set serenely and neatly among well-kept lawns and drives. It was a long way removed from civilization, but it was the community's most ample studio—quite a spectacular contrast to the distant Selig Zoo.

The people inherited from Metro (whose old lot was abandoned and sold) were of no particular distinction. Most notable among them were directors Rex Ingram and Victor Schertzinger—and, as it soon turned out, Ingram was annoyed by the arrangement and refused to work with Mayer. He made his own separate deal to produce pictures independently in Europe for Marcus Loew.

But the roster of Goldwyn people was impressive. It was strong in directors—Robert Leonard, Charles Brabin, Victor Seastrom, Rupert Hughes, Frank Borzage, Erich von Stroheim, and Marshall Neilan, Mayer's old friend. Among its stars were Mae Murray, Eleanor Boardman, John Gilbert, Lon Chaney, and William Haines. Since Mayer would have his own group to work with, he felt the auguries were fine.

His initial attack was characteristic. Without waiting for the date on which the merger would be officially effective, May 17, he began getting plans formulated as soon as he returned from New York. He and Thalberg started sifting story properties, calling conferences, and lining up arrangements for productions in a feverish way. Within two weeks of ratification, he called for a formal ceremony to "dedicate" the Culver City studio.

Mayer liked to do things grandly, with pomp and display. That was the way of the showman, and he was certainly one. A large wooden platform was erected on the expanse of pretty green lawn that extended between the office building and the first of the glass stages. It was draped with red, white, and blue bunting in Fourth of July style, and an American flag was given prominence. This was an historic day.

Somebody made arrangements to import a Navy band, and a group of military and civic dignitaries were present, most of them important. These included Admiral Samuel Robinson, commander-in-chief of the Pacific fleet, and his staff; Major George Ruhlen, Jr., of Fort MacArthur; Mayor C.V. Loop of Culver City; and Judge Summerfield. Film stars were on the platform to balance the visiting "brass": Mae Murray, John Gilbert, Lon Chaney, Ramon Novarro, Antonio Moreno, Lillian Gish. Joe Schenck was there as a tacit stand-in for his brother, Nick, and Marcus Loew. Fred Niblo was master of ceremonies, and Will Rogers, a former Goldwyn star, was one of the distinguished visitors asked to say a few words.

Called to come to the platform from among the five hundred or so studio employees gathered on the lawn—the time chosen for the dedication was the lunch hour on Saturday, April 26, 1924—Rogers ambled up, grinning broadly, and apologized for being late. He said it was because he had to turn around and go back home when he was halfway to the studio, "on account of he discovered" he had left his chewing gum in his other suit. That's what he got for not wearing his every-day clothes, he said.

However, he continued, he was sure glad he got there in time to hear Mayor Loop, on account of it was the same speech the Mayor had made not many months previously at the opening of a new race track that had already gone broke. The implication got a laugh from everybody, including both the mayor and Mayer.

More serious activities included the reading of telegrams from President Coolidge and the Secretary of Commerce, Herbert Hoover, a Californian whom Mayer had recently met at a civic luncheon and by whom he was solemnly impressed.

Abe Lehr, who was marked for dismissal, then handed over to Mayer a floral piece in the shape of a giant key as a token of transfer of control of the studio. Mayer accepted it firmly, with tears in the corners of his eyes.

"I hope," he said, "that it is given me to live up to this great trust. It has been my argument and practice that each picture should teach a lesson, should have a reason for existence. With seventeen of the great directors in the industry calling this great institution their home, I feel that this aim will be carried out. . . .

"This is a great moment for me. I accept this solemn trust, and pledge the best I have to give."

He meant it, as sincerely and profoundly as if he were taking the oath to serve as President of the United States.

He did not grab all the glory. Proudly, he introduced Thalberg and Harry Rapf, who he said would serve as his "associates" and help him get a flow of pictures from the studio— many of which were already on the way to production, he proclaimed.

The one ominous incident of the occasion came when Marshall Neilan disturbed the attention of the gathering by making a considerable show of walking out and taking several people with him, right in the middle of Mayer's speech. He was then in the final stages of shooting a production of *Tess of the D'Urbervilles,* and his pulling his crew and the people of his company away from the gathering brought disturbing snickers and guffaws.

Neilan later explained he did it because the ceremony was "taking too goddamn long" and he couldn't afford to waste his time and the time of his people "listening to all that gab." He wished to remind everybody that he himself was responsible for the costs on his film, and every minute they wasted was adding to costs. But the inescapable suspicion was that he did it deliberately to show his contempt for Mayer, whom he and other lordly directors, such as Ingram, frankly considered a parvenu. Neilan had got his fill of Mayer when he was making the Anita Stewart films.

Such candid disdain of the producer, manifested by Neilan's attitude and by the flat refusal of Ingram to be subordinate to Mayer, reflected a fundamental conflict that openly existed at the time between largely autonomous directors and what they scathingly called "the money-men." Leading directors considered themselves the elite—supreme and secure from restriction in conceiving and creating films. Although they acknowledged dependence for necessary funds on the fellows who put up the money, usually the distributors, they inherently assumed that they would make all artistic decisions. The "money-men" were mere promoters who were capitalizing on art.

This concept of the director as the paramount creative control in the manufacture of motion pictures stemmed from early days when directors, such as Ince and Griffith, were trailblazers for the medium. They and their brash contemporaries —E.S. Porter, Cecil B. De Mille, J. Searle Dawley, George Loane Tucker, Ingram, John S. Robertson—made pretty much what they wanted. They chose their own stories, their casts, approved the designs, picked their locations, and spent as much money as they wished—or, at least, as much as they could wangle from their yammering entrepreneurs. The latter did not intrude as critics, so long as they were eager for the films.

It was only as costs began to rocket in the period after the First World War—that period of splurge and competition that culminated in the crisis of 1923—that businessmen putting up the money saw that brakes would have to be applied, that some means of controlling top directors and compelling the regularity of their pictures would have to be devised. Order within the giddy area of film creation was the great longing of the industry.

Tacitly, this was the initial and primary purpose of Mayer —to bring about order and efficiency in the Metro-Goldwyn studio. He had to organize production, get the pictures that were then in the works to the quickest possible completion, and *then* get new ones underway and consolidate operations so that there would be a minimum of duplication and waste. The rigid demand of Loew's, Inc., was for a regular flow of new films possessing distinctive attraction and produced at not too great expense.

That Mayer undertook to do this with only two supervisors to help—with Thalberg for the more important projects and Rapf for secondary films—is a notable indication of his audacity. He was biting off a portion that it would seem ten men could scarcely chew. But it also indicated how much the industry did rely upon directors in those days and, again, how simple, by later standards, was the production of silent films.

Pictures already in production or almost ready to be released were *The Arab,* made by Ingram; *Bread,* from a novel by Charles Norris, and *Revelation,* with Monte Blue and Viola Dana—all from the Metro studio. Independently made for Metro and almost ready to be released were Buster Keaton's *The Navigator* and *Little Robinson Crusoe,* with Jackie Coogan, the child star.

Mayer brought over *Broken Barriers,* with Norma Shearer, *The Red Lily,* a Fred Niblo special, and *The Great Divide,* with Alice Terry and Conway Tearle. And the Goldwyn studio offered *Circe,* with Mae Murray, Neilan's *Tess of the D'Urbervilles,* and a particularly thorny item, Erich von Stroheim's *Greed.*

This uncommonly ambitious production, based on Frank Norris' novel, *McTeague,* was one of the most talked-about projects in Hollywood. Von Stroheim had got the go-ahead on it from Frank Godsol and Abe Lehr as one of their last reckless gambles for the Goldwyn Company, and they had given him pretty much the carte blanche that he loftily maintained was the director's due. He took full advantage of it. Spurning the "cardboard sets" of the studios, he went to San Francisco and Death Valley to shoot his grimly realistic tale. Time was unimportant to him; he took endless weeks on the film and literally tortured his actors in tearing from them a searing drama of greed for gold. What was more—and most bewildering—he had no restraint about the length of his film. When he presented his final cut to the Goldwyn people, it ran for forty reels, nearly six hours!

Told that it would have to be shortened, Von Stroheim angrily refused, held out a few weeks, and then acceded to cutting it to twenty-four reels. Beyond that amount of excision he simply would not go. He said he would not be restricted by the stupid conventions of Hollywood. Lehr despairingly gave it to June Mathis, one of his leading scenarists, to cut. She trimmed about a third more from it. And that's where it was when Mayer took control.

*Greed* was not the greatest of the problems to which Mayer and Thalberg fell heir, but their unhesitating handling of it gave a major indication of how they were going to run things. They did not intend to let any director have his way with them—especially Von Stroheim, with whom the youthful Thalberg had had plenty of trouble back in his Universal days. They called in another cutter, pulled two more reels from the film, and told Von Stroheim he could like it or lump it, but that was how it would be. He didn't like it, but he grudgingly submitted to the terms of his contract, which had some time to run, and started looking for another story to make for the new company. This amounted to service of notice by Mayer and Thalberg that directors had better stay in line.

Meanwhile, another top director, Victor Seastrom, had

been put to work on what turned out to be the first production launched in the merged studio. This was an adaptation
of a Broadway play, *He Who Gets Slapped,* a drama of a
clown in the circus whose love for a beautiful bareback rider
was doomed. He died defending her honor—in line with
Mayer's taste for self-sacrifice. Lon Chaney, the distinguished
character actor, was secured to play the clown. Norma Shearer
played the bareback rider, and John Gilbert was assigned to
play a handsome circus performer who loved the girl. Everything went nicely on the picture. Seastrom was allowed to have
his head. Thalberg, his supervisor, only occasionally looked in
on the sets.

When *He Who Gets Slapped* was finished shooting (and
that was in a matter of a few weeks), Mayer called Seastrom
to his office and warmly congratulated him. The picture was
great, he told him, and done precisely as the company desired.
It was good to have a director who could do things properly.
Indeed, it was so gratifying that he would like to show his appreciation by tearing up Seastrom's old contract and writing
a new one.

He noted the old contract called for Seastrom to receive ten
thousand dollars per picture plus a percentage of the net
profits of each. This, Mayer told the director, was hopelessly
unfavorable to him. Net profits were impossible for him to
check, Mayer said. The only way he could do it would be to
hire a lawyer and put him on a full-time job. So why not just
drop that business of the percentage of the profits and make a
new deal whereby Seastrom would be paid thirty thousand
dollars for canceling his old contract and then twenty thousand dollars each for his next three films?

This sounded fine to Seastrom. After all, he had not seen a
single penny of percentage bonus from the Goldwyn Company. And he had no way of knowing that the distribution
system of Loew's would be much more efficient in gathering
profits than that of his erstwhile employer. He gratefully ac-

cepted Mayer's offer and thereafter regarded him not only as his benefactor but as his true and respected friend.

Not so happy were some other associations. Neilan gave Mayer a hard time with his virtually independent production of *Tess of the D'Urbervilles*. Not unreasonably, Neilan had adapted Thomas Hardy's classic so that the heroine, Tess, played by Blanche Sweet, went to the gallows at the end. Mayer didn't like this finish. He claimed that audiences would be depressed by seeing the poor, tormented woman pay for her misfortunes (and for murdering her husband) in such a way. He insisted that Neilan shoot an alternate scene in which a messenger arrived at the last moment to say that Tess had been reprieved. Neilan fought against this insistence. He called Mayer every kind of boor. But Mayer compelled the alteration. He was now in command.

This indicated to Neilan the new direction of the wind. His contract called for two more pictures. The first of these he arranged to shoot abroad. It was called *The Sporting Venus*. Again his star was Miss Sweet. His leading man was a new young British actor, Ronald Colman, whom he picked up when he went to Scotland to shoot the film. After that Neilan did one at the studio, *Mike*, then unregretfully departed and returned to First National, where he could still make films independently.

There was naturally much confusion in the studio during the first few weeks. The influx of new people from the merged companies created traffic jams. Technical staffs were disordered and there was wrangling over space. An example of the consequential chaos was reported in the trade paper, *Variety*:

"Last week, Hobart Henley was working on a set and used a large amount of electrical equipment and a large crew. Robert Leonard was working on a Mae Murray picture (*Circe*). He passed Henley's set, looked in, saw no director or cast, only the electrical crew. He told the crew to take the equipment and themselves to his stage and begin work for him. Of course, complaints were made."

They were, indeed! And there were plenty of others. But Mayer, Thalberg, and Rapf worked day and night to straighten out the difficulties and get everyone in proper place. Apparently, they were sufficiently successful to satisfy Marcus Loew, for in June he issued a statement that had an enthusiastic ring:

"Mr. Mayer, as everyone knows, has no equal as a producer. His past record speaks for itself, and during the short time that he has been in charge at the Culver City studios, he has accomplished wonders. There are twenty-two companies now at work. We are way ahead of our schedule. By the first of September, there will be prints of twenty-five productions in our exchanges. That is going some!"

But there was one mighty cloud on the horizon, one project in the works that disturbingly dwarfed all the others. That was the lagging production of *Ben-Hur*.

This huge enterprise, then shooting on locations in Italy, was supposed to be outside the interest and responsibility of Mayer. It had been acquired as a separate and special project of the Goldwyn Company, and it was clearly understood that the "'Mayer group" would not share in any profits it might earn. Indeed, from the way things were going, it was doubtful whether there would be any profits at all. It was rapidly becoming the most expensive motion picture ever made.

The spectacular project had been launched by the Goldwyn Company as one of its last extravagant efforts to salvage waning prestige. Screen rights to the famous stage drama, which was based on the equally famous book by General Lew Wallace, *Ben-Hur: A Tale of the Christ,* had been acquired from a syndicate that owned them in a truly fantastic deal which specified that this syndicate would receive *one-half* of every dollar the picture earned. June Mathis was the Goldwyn employee who had done most to push the project along, and she was the one accepted by the scrupulous syndicate to prepare the scenario. Charles Brabin was selected as director, George Walsh was picked to play Ben-Hur, and the company had been sent abroad to shoot the picture in mammoth sets constructed in Rome and in various scenic places in Italy. It had been in the works for almost three months when the merger occurred, by which time it was fairly obvious that it was going to be a headache, king-size.

Press stories sent back from the Eternal City were couched in superlatives, but private reports indicated that Miss Mathis and Brabin were in a jam. The immensity of the historical drama and the problems of staging its numerous spectacle scenes had made for delays and misadventures. Walsh was frequently sick. Brabin seemed stumped by the awesome prospect of directing the World's Greatest Film. Marcus Loew was soon sending instructions to his management team on the Coast to select a set of key replacements and have them ready to go to Italy.

This had to be done in strictest secret, for the contract on the screen rights specified that Miss Mathis was to be in control of the picture and the director must be approved by Abe Erlanger, the theatrical producer who headed the syndicate. Mayer and Thalberg assembled their people with the stealth of conspirators, barely letting them know what they were in for before shipping them on to New York.

They picked Fred Niblo as director, young Ramon Novarro to play Ben-Hur, and Bess Meredyth, an experienced screen writer, to revise the scenario. It was notable that all three were veterans of Mayer's Mission Road studio. They were sent to Europe with Marcus Loew in July.

Mayer didn't make that journey. He went only as far as New York and there consigned the community interests of the "Mayer group" to Robert Rubin, who did go abroad with the group. There was too much demanding attention in Culver City that summer for Mayer or Thalberg to go to Europe to tackle a problem as knotty as *Ben-Hur*.

With diplomatic talking Loew did the delicate job of getting the dedicated Miss Mathis to relinquish her authority. With difficulty he got Niblo and Novarro ensconced. Then he left Rome, leaving Bess Meredyth and Carey Wilson, another writer whom Thalberg had picked, to size up the situation and revise the scenario. They did both and returned to New York with Loew in August, thence proceeding directly to the Coast.

Mayer and Thalberg heard their estimations and their reading of the scenario. They telephoned Loew and naturally told him the latter was the best they'd ever heard. They also told him they thought the production should be pulled out of Rome and completed at the Culver City studio. Loew replied, "If our company cannot maintain the distinction of producing this great film in Italy, then we had better shut up shop."

It was partly to prevent that off-chance hazard which Mayer saw as a possibility if his people didn't do a job on *Ben-Hur,* that he accepted the suggestion of Loew that he take himself over to Italy and see that there were no more delays on the film. The grapevine had it that Niblo was having trouble getting things underway. Mayer also liked the idea of a trip to Europe with all expenses paid. He hadn't been back across the Atlantic since he had arrived in America as an immigrant boy.

With his wife, his two daughters, now young ladies, his family physician (whom he wished to have close by) and the personable Carey Wilson, he left for Europe in September. First they went to Paris. Mayer insisted on seeing all the sights and was as pleased with the standard attractions as any tourist first visiting the City of Light. He sent his daughters to do the town with Wilson, whom he sternly cautioned to be most careful where they went. He wanted them to see Paris thoroughly, he told them, because he didn't know when they'd have a chance to do so again.

Then they went down to Italy, arriving just in time to see the shooting of the scenes of the great sea battle between Roman and pirate galleys off the coast near Anzio. An accidental fire in one of the galleys caused a near catastrophe, giving Mayer a graphic demonstration of the kind of troubles with which the company was beset. Nevertheless, he was far from sympathetic when he got to Rome and saw the little that Niblo had accomplished in the almost two months that he had been there. What's more, the footage shown him did not appeal to Mayer. He blistered the hide of the director, and Niblo, indignant, said he'd resign.

"You're not resigning," Mayer told him. "As of this moment you're fired!"

It took considerably pacifying on the part of several associates to cool him down. Mayer suspected that Niblo was succumbing to a sense of power. He was not going to let this director pull an Ingram on him.

Another old friend who got the sharp edge of his tongue in Rome that trip was the statuesque Francis X. Bushman, who was playing Messala, the antagonist of Ben-Hur. Mayer accused Bushman, a theater veteran, of deliberately stealing scenes from the less experienced Ramon Novarro, whom Mayer was nurturing as a romantic star. Bushman was hurt and bewildered. He could not honestly deny the minor charge, but he was dismayed at the fury with which he was set upon by the man whom he had helped make his first film.

Mayer stayed in Rome a week longer, then he and his family departed for Berlin, leaving behind Carey Wilson with tacit instructions to keep a close eye on the chastened Niblo and do all he could to make things move. Mayer was more convinced than ever that *Ben-Hur* should be finished at the Culver City studio.

One of the many things the producer hoped to accomplish on this trip was to pick up some new talent in European capitals. Foreign directors and actors had proved profitable additions in Hollywood—this, of course, being at a time *before* actors had to speak in films—and Mayer was hopeful that he might find a few.

In Berlin, he was shown some pictures, as he was in Paris and Rome. Among them was one made by Mauritz Stiller, a Swedish director, whom Victor Seastrom had urged him to meet. It was full of snow and reindeer. Mayer said he would like to see what Stiller could do with people; he wasn't interested in hiring reindeer this trip.

Stiller had someone call the next day and say he would like to show Mayer his latest film, *Gösta Berling's Saga,* from a novel by Selma Lagerlöf. They met at a screening room. There Mayer discovered that Stiller was a tall, lantern-jawed man who could not speak English. They sat down to watch the picture with an interpreter.

Early along, a little actress, Mona Martenson, came on and Mayer made some comment about her. Stiller merely grunted a reply. Then, a few scenes later, the heroine appeared. She was a lovely, slender, spiritual-looking blonde. Mayer asked who she was. The interpreter transmitted the question to Stiller, who roared, "Look at the picture! Look at the direction!" He boomed in Swedish. Mayer was amazed at his violent response.

After seeing the picture, he detected that Stiller was afraid he was interested only in the actress and might wish to hire her away. When he explained that he liked the whole thing, including Lars Hanson, the male lead, Stiller said the girl's name was Greta Garbo and he'd be happy to bring her to meet Mayer.

They met the next day for dinner at the Adlon Hotel. When Mayer arrived, he noticed that Stiller had set the actress so she could be most favorably viewed. Even so, he was a bit disappointed to discover that she was on the plump side and had rather heavy ankles. But her face and her eyes were divine! He immediately set about negotiating with Stiller for him to come to Culver City and bring Miss Garbo with him. They reached an understanding before dinner was finished.

As Mayer was about to leave the table he said to the interpreter, "Tell her that, in America, men don't like fat women." The actress accepted this information with a solemn nod.

That evening he cabled Rubin and Thalberg to inform them of what he had done and to request their okay. They sent it and the contract was signed. Stiller and Miss Garbo were to come to Culver City the following year. Mayer also signed Lars Hanson and Mona Martenson.

No wonder he was frank in saying, when he arrived back in New York with his family on December 10, that he was greatly impressed with the quality of European films. "The continental producers are learning to do things remarkably well," he said. "We can learn things from them."

Little did he know how much he had!

Thus, with a coup of talent-scouting that was to prove one of the smartest ever made, Mayer achieved an historic climax for that already momentous year. The merger had been accomplished, new pictures were flowing favorably, and everything seemed happy at the Metro-Goldwyn studio.

But already there were underground rumblings. While Mayer was still abroad, rumors began circulating that he intended to resign. Loew, on a visit to the studio, frankly took note of them and told an informal gathering of studio employees that they were false.

"I view the association of Mr. Mayer, Mr. Thalberg, and Mr. Rapf with the greatest satisfaction," he stated. "It is, as a matter of fact, the happiest association I have ever had in my life. And there will be no change involving any of them."

The statement was absolutely honest. Loew was immensely pleased. But there were certain unmentioned factors that were making for disharmony. From some areas of friction rose a certain amount of tell-tale smoke. Those certain areas of friction were soon to be more clearly exposed.

The old saying that love of money is the root of all evil may not have universal endorsement in this motivation-researched age, but it bluntly defines the popular passion that long beset members of the "Mayer group." This urge for money—and that other human impulse that money feeds, vanity—were demons that chewed at their vitals and unsettled their harmony, with their employers and with each other, almost from the day they were joined.

Money was not an extraordinary passion with people in the business of making films. Money was the be-all of their labors, most avidly pursued, more desperately and intensely strived for than artistic satisfaction and acclaim. To get close to the nozzles from which the great wealth of motion pictures gushed in those days, when wells were daily opening and business still had the tentativeness of boom, was the impulse of hundreds of people, most of whom were picture makers by chance, getting their first bright look at riches. The infection touched Mayer and his friends.

The germ of the "Mayer group's" infection was the profits-participation plan, arranged when they contracted to give their services to the Metro-Goldwyn studio. This was the plan that called for members of the group to receive, in addition to their salaries, twenty percent of the net profits of pictures they produced, profits to be calculated after annual dividend payments of two dollars a share on the common stock of the company had been deducted.

On the face of it, this arrangement appeared simple and harmless enough—no more than a smart inducement to make profitable films. But within it were such provisions and technical niceties, not to mention the latent peril of strife over the private division of spoils, that this plan became the infection that diseased the relations of the group. As a judge later put it, more poetically, "With it, the seeds of friction were sown."

The first and most cogent core of trouble was the provision that a charge of thirty percent should be levied against total rentals received from the theaters by the distributing organization to offset costs of its services. This meant that Loew's, Inc., which handled the films of the studio, would take three hundred dollars out of every one thousand dollars of rentals that came in, passing along the remainder to the producing company. Out of this remainder total production costs had to be paid and the dividend fund subtracted before profits were calculated.

Mayer and his group had no objection to the charge of thirty percent for the costs of distribution. This had by now become the standard charge for that service within the industry. In previous years it had been higher. After all, Mayer retained ninety percent of the dollars he collected from the rentals of *The Birth of a Nation* in New England.

But what he did object to—and that most strenuously—was the preferential lower-rate rental of pictures to Loew theaters. He found, or strongly suspected, that the films the studio produced were being turned over first to Loew theaters and quietly rented to them on terms well below the rentals that such pictures would ordinarily fetch in the trade. This meant less return to the distributor than should, by right, come in, and thus less return to the studio and, finally, less profits on the films.

Obviously the prime value of the studio to Loew's, Inc., was to provide its theater chain with new pictures, the best that could be produced, and give its houses the advantage of playing these pictures first. This was the main consideration that moved Marcus Loew and Nicholas Schenck, his theater-managing lieutenant, to arrange for the larger studio. Mayer understood that. The arrangement to keep the films in the family, as it were—or, at least, to give the "family" first pickings —was entirely within his ken. But to slip the theaters an advantage which would result in a reduction in the producer's profits of the films—that was a "family" privilege that he certainly did not bargain for.

Arguments over this issue began as soon as Mayer suspected what was going on. Knowing distribution and all the dodges that might not show up on the books, he was quicker to be perceptive, or intuitive, than another might have been. He spoke to Loew about it. He also spoke to Schenck.

Significantly, this practice was one that would give the theaters a break on their operations. With studio pictures costing them less, they could show a more favorable balance. This would redound to the credit of Schenck, who was, at that time, completely in charge of the company's theaters. Such a personal beneficence, naturally, did not appeal to Mayer. He saw no reason whatsoever for making Schenck's balance sheets look good.

This was a point of contention that had already been discreetly raised before Mayer went to Europe to have a look at the production of *Ben-Hur.* Indeed, it was over this issue that he had words with the men in New York and thus contributed to early rumors that he and his associates were thinking of leaving the studio. It was while he was in Europe that these rumors spread alarmingly, to the extent that it was necessary for a denial by Loew.

However, that denial did not dispel the vigilance of Mayer, who had his people in New York, headed by Rubin, keep as close an eye as they could on the Loew books. Nor did the dispatch of Eddie Mannix, a "Schenck man," to Culver City while Mayer was abroad to be a watchdog on the studio operations tend to pacify the head on his return. It is true that Mannix, a rugged Irishman who had first gone to work for Schenck as a youthful and enthusiastic "bouncer" at the latter's sideline-run Palisades Amusement Park, soon became a wide-eyed admirer and loyal friend of Mayer. But the initial cause for his presence rankled. The lines were early drawn between Schenck and Mayer.

With the favorable flow of pictures in the first year of operation of the studio and with every prospect of a continuance as they moved on in 1925, Mayer clamored more loudly about the matter of rentals to the Loew theaters and the jeopardy in which this placed the income of the "Mayer group" from the profit-sharing plan. The sum total of the group's bonus in 1924 was only $15,000. This was piddling. And indications were that the Loew's, Inc., earnings would be doubled during 1925. Obviously, this surge of prosperity was due in the main to the films coming from Culver City. Mayer hollered on behalf of his group.

Finally, in October, an understanding was reached. The contract with Mayer was amended to the considerable advantage of him and his group. First, all three members got raises. Mayer's salary was upped from $1,500 to $2,500 a week. Thalberg was raised from $650 to $2,000 (a sturdy boost, bespeaking the young man's growing importance) and Rubin from $600 to $1,000. More substantially, they were guaranteed that the group's annual bonus would be a minimum of $500,-000. The contract, which originally was written for three years, was extended to five. In return the "Mayer group" pledged to turn out no less than forty-four pictures a year.

Thus the first internecine struggle growing out of the profit-sharing plan was won by Mayer. But this was only the beginning. There were to be more bitter quarrels within the group.

As in family disputes, however, squabbles on the level of family heads did not noticeably affect the daily routines of getting things done—at the start. While Mayer was arguing rentals and distribution receipts with New York he was also performing the many functions of an industrious and able studio head. And the studio was running full blast, under the supervisory surveillance of Thalberg and Rapf.

Today it is amazing and a little depressing to reflect upon the youthful enthusiasm and ferment of group activity that prevailed in the Culver City studio during that heyday of silent films. Everybody was busy, everybody had ideas, and few persons were bothering to try to cut other persons' throats. Pictures were being manufactured, not all of them historic, it is true, but pictures that had qualities acceptable to mass audiences. And some of them were historic. Some have been enshrined in the archives of motion pictures and in the hearts of millions who still recall the beautiful pleasure of seeing them all those years ago.

*Ben-Hur* was brought back from Italy in the winter of 1925 and put through the torments of completion on the Culver City lot. A huge, full-scale slat-and-plaster replica of the ancient coliseum at Antioch was built on a five-acre barren off Venice Boulevard, and there some three thousand extras, eight chariots each drawn by four-horse spans, most of the principals in the drama, and hundreds of spectators gathered one day for the filming of the crucial chariot-race sequence in *Ben-Hur*. It was, in the memories of old-timers, one of the great events in the history of Hollywood.

The completed *Ben-Hur,* an epic picture, was one of the greatest of all silent films.

The studio was pounding out others. Von Stroheim the Troublesome was embarked on *The Merry Widow* in the fall of 1924. It was his own rather grotesque conception of the light operatic story of Franz Lehar, in which a youthful and beautiful widow pursues a dashing prince who was her girlhood love. The glamorous Mae Murray and John Gilbert were cast in the romantic roles, and the big scene was supposed to be their dancing in a great ballroom to the famous "Merry Widow Waltz." (The music was to be provided as an accompaniment by theater orchestras.)

There was trouble on this one. Again Von Stroheim assumed what he stubbornly (and no doubt sincerely) considered a director's prerogatives. He took his time shooting the picture. He injected some realistic scenes that suggested sexual deviations among the supposedly romantic Viennese. And, more disturbing to Thalberg—and *most* disturbing to Mayer —he failed to pay due attention to the favorable presentation of his star.

Miss Murray rushed to the front office one day, screaming that she had been insulted by the director, who had also called her names. Mayer and Thalberg listened, then summoned Von Stroheim to account. He flatly refused to favor Miss Murray and protested, in turn, that she had called him "a dirty Hun."

Mayer was not moved by this objection. He had small use for Von Stroheim, anyhow—had considered him a crude and loutish fellow ever since Von Stroheim had remarked, in Mayer's (and some other people's) presence, that "all women are whores." Mayer was outraged at this opinion. He demanded that Von Stroheim state it again so he could be sure he had heard him correctly. Then he punched the startled Teuton in the nose. "You can't talk that way about women in *my* presence," Mayer stormed indignantly as a couple of hefty bystanders hustled Von Stroheim out the door.

To settle the quarrel with Miss Murray, Mayer instructed Von Stroheim to apologize. He refused, and to assert his independence would not return to the set. This was all right with Mayer and Thalberg. Von Stroheim's contract called for him to receive a percentage of the profits of his pictures, but this he would forfeit if he did not finish his film. Mayer im-

mediately assigned the direction of *The Merry Widow* to
Monta Bell, a rather pedestrian director recently brought to
the studio.

The next day, when Bell tried to take over, the stagehands
refused to work. They were sympathetic to Von Stroheim,
who was always liked by his crews. Mayer was quickly summoned. Here was a crisis, indeed. The studio workers were
attempting to boycott the assignment of a director by the
studio head. Such insurgent endeavor would have to be
scotched at once.

He hastened to the set with Eddie Mannix, jumped up on
a stool, and began to read the riot act to stagehands. His language was emphatic and blunt. Mayer had a coarse vocabu-
lary and, when angered, would put it to use. One of the stagehands closer to him moved forward menacingly. Mannix,
standing stalwartly beside Mayer, saw the move and dropped
the fellow with one sharp blow. There was a moment of
frightening tension. Mayer and Mannix stood their ground.
Other stagehands subsided and took the warning. They had
been shown that Mayer was in command.

The tiff with Von Stroheim was later settled when Miss
Murray apologized to him and he apologized to her, where-
with they went ahead and finished the picture, which ran extremely long. Thalberg told Von Stroheim to cut it. He said
this could not be done. Again they were at an impasse which
had to be settled by Mayer. They finally agreed that Von
Stroheim would be relieved of his obligation to cut the film,
if he would give up his percentage and burn his contract,
which he surprisingly did. Thus Mayer saved the company a
lot of money (and perhaps a lot of headaches, too), for *The
Merry Widow,* carefully edited by Thalberg and Margaret
Booth, was one of the studio's most profitable films.

Still another extraordinary picture accomplished in the
same momentous year was King Vidor's surpassing drama of
the First World War, *The Big Parade*. This one was started
modestly in February, 1925, when Thalberg brought the play-

wright, Laurence Stallings, out from New York to prepare a scenario for Vidor, who had expressed a wish to do a war film. A script was prepared with another writer, Harry Behn; and John Gilbert, the busiest actor in Culver City, was cast to play the lead. It was the role of a wealthy, carefree clubman who became a doughboy, went to France, and discovered the horror of warfare in the Battle of Belleau Wood.

It was started as a "Jack Gilbert special," meaning a low-budget program film, but Thalberg soon perceived that Vidor had a picture underway with a dramatic potential far beyond the scope of money allotted him. He asked Mayer to increase the budget so they could build up the scenes of war. Mayer freely complied, after waging a battle with people in New York. The additional expense made all the difference. Vidor was able to create a tremendously graphic picture which went on to become a phenomenal money-maker, a historic silent film. It still stands as the classic silent drama of the First World War.

The tandem operation of Mayer and Thalberg on *The Big Parade*—their harmonious working together to get potential results, Thalberg doing the creative scouting and Mayer materially and morally supporting him—was the perfect example of their method of collaboration in those days. Thalberg was creative; this was understood. He had the imagination and judgment to control creative elements. Mayer was the business organizer, the executive provider of support and, what was vastly important, the diplomatic liaison with New York. He was also a showman, an inveterate optimist, and a loving admirer of Thalberg, whom he now liked to think of as "a son."

And what a clever calculator and convincing counselor he was. His skill was shown in the way he talked Seastrom and Von Stroheim out of their percentage-of-the-profits deals. He did the same with Vidor on *The Big Parade*. Vidor's contract, carried over from the Goldwyn Company, called for him to receive twenty percent of the profits of his pictures. It was the

same sort of contract as was held by the other men. But when
it appeared that the picture was going to be a big success,
Mayer got hold of Vidor's lawyer (the director was immersed
in another film) and talked him into abandoning the percentage arrangement in lieu of a settlement. The settlement
was based on the assumption that the picture would earn
$1,500,000. Mayer impressed the lawyer by obligingly point-
ing out that only a handful of pictures had ever earned that
much. *The Big Parade* earned more than $10,000,000 and
Vidor had to comfort himself with the satisfaction thereafter
of being one of the favorites of Thalberg and Mayer.

It was he who drew the prize assignment of directing Lillian Gish, the great dramatic star of D.W. Griffith, when she
came to the studio to do *La Bohème* in 1925. And it was he
whom Thalberg stoutly backed up when he wanted to make
a picture called *The Crowd,* a sober drama of white-collar
workers, which was one of the last distinguished silent films.

Yes, they made films those years in Culver City. Lon
Chaney, the finest performer of weird characters that ever
worked for the screen, was doing such fascinating pictures as
*The Monster, The Unholy Three, The Road to Mandalay,
The Black Bird,* and *Tell It to the Marines.* William Haines,
Ramon Novarro, and Norma Shearer were being starred in
at least three films each a year. Then there was the young
Greta Garbo, whom Mayer had signed when he was abroad.

When this tall, taciturn Swedish actress arrived at the studio in the summer of 1925, she appeared a most unlikely
prospect to match such svelte and exotic stars as Pola Negri
and Nita Naldi. She appeared gawky, her English was poor
(though that was not then a serious problem), and she was
depressingly shy. Thalberg took one look at her and then discreetly refrained from passing an honest opinion on the judgment of Mayer.

Her first film, called *The Torrent,* was a tear-jerking tale
of a Spanish peasant girl who couldn't marry the man of her
dreams and became a great, lonely opera star. The actress was

pretty good in it, though she was not directed by her friend, Mauritz Stiller, whom Mayer brought over with her. She was directed by Monta Bell.

She went from that into *The Temptress*, a drama of a Latin *femme fatale*. Stiller was allowed to start this one, but he proved too finicky and slow, one of those "difficult" directors that were now being got out of the studio. Fred Niblo was assigned to take over. The picture was no ball of fire. But before it was released, Miss Garbo had met Jack Gilbert and fallen in love.

At least, that is what the press agents and gossip columnists proclaimed and what the ebullient Gilbert was happily led to believe. While playing together in her next picture, *Flesh and the Devil,* under the direction of Clarence Brown, he and Greta made beautiful music which was joyously piped to the world. By the time the picture was ready the Garbo-Gilbert romance was a thoroughly publicized trailer for this voluptuous and plushy boudoir film. Mayer didn't like the picture, but he certainly liked the money it brought in.

Indeed, he was full of satisfaction over the remarkable development of his hand-picked star, when all of a sudden Miss Garbo somewhat let the air out of his delight. After finishing *Flesh and the Devil* and being assigned to another film, she solemnly informed Mayer and Thalberg that she wanted a raise in pay. Her contract—the one made in Germany—was now getting her six hundred dollars a week. She felt this inadequate for a star of her importance. She thought five thousand dollars a week would do.

Mayer almost exploded. He told her that was absurd. Such a salary was out of the question! And such ingratitude! Here he had brought her to this country, given her a chance to star in American films, spent money to give her a build-up—and this was the appreciation she showed! Miss Garbo was unmoved by his anguish. She coolly walked out and went home. And there she remained, for seven months, until Mayer and the company gave in. She was encouraged in her recalcitrance by Stiller and by Harry Edington, a clever business manager whom Gilbert had fondly brought to her.

This little set-to with his treasure was *one* contract fight that Mayer lost. But, of course, Greta Garbo continued as a top asset of the studio.

Technically in this category was another actress not yet mentioned here, but one whose delicate presence had a status and distinction all its own. This was Marion Davies, a pretty and personable blonde who happened to be a very close companion of the powerful newspaper publisher, William Randolph Hearst.

Hearst had been smitten by the lady and had undertaken to make her a movie queen when she was merely an undistinguished show girl playing in the musical *Watch Your Step* in New York. This was in 1918. Hearst had already been interested in motion pictures as a mass communication device; for several years he had owned a newsreel, and he had produced a few serial films which were not dissimilar in spirit to the type of journalism he espoused. Now, with a new creative interest, he acquired a studio in New York and launched a program of feature-film productions to promote Miss Davies as a star.

Large sums were spent on her pictures, which Hearst insisted should be stories of sweet young maidens and gauzy romantic heroines. Miss Davies wanted to play tough babies, hard-boiled blondes and comic types, but her patron visualized her in innocent and noble roles. Out of a dozen pictures made between 1918 and 1924, only one was of any consequence. That was *When Knighthood Was in Flower*.

Hearst's outfit was called Cosmopolitan and it was releasing through the Goldwyn Company at the time of the merger. For a few months, he hesitated whether to set up his lady with the new company. He decided to do so, however, when a generous arrangement was devised whereby Metro-Goldwyn would finance his pictures, which were to be made at the Cul-

ver City studio, give him a share of the profits and Miss Davies
a handsome salary. In return, it was tacitly agreed that Metro-
Goldwyn and its people were to receive most favorable attention in the Hearst press.

The importance of this association to the company and to
Mayer was not so much in the prospect of having Miss Davies
as a star as in the promise of prestige and kudos that the
Hearst proximity would provide. And these were soon forthcoming. A fourteen-room "bungalow" that had something of
the elegant simplicity of the "dairy" of Marie Antoinette was
built for Miss Davies on the front side of the Culver City lot,
and she moved into it with the splendor of an arriving queen.
The "Davies bungalow" soon became the center of the social
affairs of the studio, as well as the technical location of the
actress' "dressing-room." All important sightseers and visiting
celebrities eventually landed there and were usually treated
to fancy luncheons after touring the studio. Hearst was often
present for these receptions, as, of course, was Mayer. The
social stimulation thus provided was of vast satisfaction to
him.

And Hollywood was, indeed, a magnet for tourists in those
years of the middle and late nineteen twenties, when the "era
of wonderful nonsense" was going strong. No community in
the country offered such an elaborate display of human and
architectural eccentricities and glamour running rampant on
the hoof. Rococo buildings and oil wells, Aimee Semple Mc-
Pherson holding forth with steamy evangelism in her Angelus
Temple, movie stars in high-powered foreign cars racing in
flashy ostentation along palm-fringed boulevards—where in
the world could the tourist see such an exciting demonstration of the folderol of the modern age?

Those were the years when Hollywood was truly the Great
Phenomenon, the newly established capital of the fables that
were girdling the world. Kings and politicians, queens and
courtesans passed through the colonnaded portals of the Cul-

ver City studio. This was the Versailles of the movies that visiting nabobs had to see on their grand tours of the famous
West Coast city. And its reigning Louis was Mayer.

It takes a sympathetic person with wisdom and tolerance to
understand the powerful psychic pressures of ambition and
vanity, to appreciate (and pity) the pneumatic effect upon
the man of finding himself hobnobbing with "the most important people," especially Hearst. It wasn't so long since he
had crumpled and cowered in his office at the Selig Zoo,
whimpering with frozen terror at the prospect of facing someone "big." Now he was regularly greeting and playing the
proud, possessive host to people whom the embryo producer
would have met with clumsy dread.

There was something almost apostolic about the feeling of
Mayer for Hearst, which began and rapidly developed with
the association of Cosmopolitan and the studio. Here was
Hearst, solid inheritor of a pioneer experience and wealth,
who had, by his own further efforts, become mighty and mas-
terful on the American scene. He was autocratic, fired with a
fierce, defensive zeal for the abstraction known as The People
that he reached through his vast newspaper chain. These were
manifestations that Mayer uncritically approved. Was not
Hearst a great patriot and successful? What else did a man
strive to be?

And here was Mayer, born in the slums, a nondescript immigrant child, inheritor of nothing except stamina and a ma-
nia to get ahead. Maybe he wasn't raised on Nob Hill and in
a mansion in Washington, maybe he hadn't gone to Harvard
and run for governor of New York. He had worked himself
up to a position of power and considerable control over a medium that was serving the world with notions of a sort that
turned in his own head. He was somebody in his own jungle.
A lion could look at a king.

That these two established an attachment that lasted over
the years, through a couple of painful disagreements and numerous minor differences, is a token of the basic affinity of

their minds and temperaments, caught up in the beautiful deception of their own happy illusions about themselves. Each was essentially a showman who played to the plain credulities and soft emotions of the masses of people without conscious awareness of their guile. It may be truly calculated that neither Mayer nor Hearst ever thought they were gulling anybody with their products. They succeeded in deluding themselves first.

Hearst was always stage struck. He loved the theatrical. This was one of the aspects he particularly liked about Mayer. He liked his lively disposition, his histrionics, his spunk. And he liked him because he "knew show business" and could do things to "help Marion." This was perhaps the most fervent and consuming desire of Hearst's life—to create a glowing Galatea out of his bland and benign little blonde.

Mayer, on the other hand, liked Hearst for reasons more formidable. He liked him because he was lordly and carried the weight of the world. Hearst's physical size impressed him. Hearst was an aristocrat. His concept of Hearst was compacted in a spontaneous eulogy he pronounced at a company sales convention a few years after the merger had occurred.

The salesmen of the company had gathered in Los Angeles, and Mayer was the principal speaker to boost pictures of the coming year. After giving a warm recital, as he was thoroughly able to do, he made so bold as to ask whether anyone would like to put a question to him.

"Yes," said Bob Lynch of Philadelphia, "I would like to ask why do we handle the pictures of Marion Davies?"

This was a question, indeed, and its delicacy was obvious. Everyone in the room knew that the pictures with Miss Davies were difficult to sell. Of the films she had made since her arrival at the studio—*Lights of Old Broadway, Zander the Great, Beverly of Graustark* and *The Red Mill*—only the first had been a money-maker. The remainder had been extravagances. It was hard to persuade exhibitors to take them at the necessary high terms.

Mayer fixed his questioner with a stern eye. For a moment he didn't speak. Then he patiently asked him to remember the success of *Lights of Old Broadway*. He cited the personal charm of Miss Davies and the fact that she was the friend of Mr. Hearst, whose newspapers were in a position to be a great help to the company.

The mention of Hearst's name seemed to give him a sudden afflatus of zeal, and with that he began an oration on the greatness of Hearst. He glowingly recollected how Hearst's father, as a young man, had crossed the country with the forty-niners, had acquired the Comstock Lode, built up a fortune in California, and become a United States Senator. Then he traced the career of William Randolph from his riotous boyhood to his position as the most powerful publisher in the United States.

"This," he said to his audience, "is what I want to impress upon you gentlemen. This is the spirit that has made America great. We live in a land of opportunity! God bless America!"

He boomed the last words with passion, as tears glistened in his eyes. The salesmen were stunned by his fervor, then burst into applause. Mayer solemnly acknowledged their approval and addressed himself to Lynch.

"Does that answer your question?"

"Yessir," the salesman replied.

A pronounced affection for publicity was noticeable in Mayer in these years, and it was generously fed by frequent attention in the Hearst press. Prophetically, the first photograph transmitted by telegraph wire from San Francisco to New York in April, 1925, was of Mayer presenting a make-up box to Miss Davies upon her arrival at the Culver City studio. Thereafter, he was a regular participant in the Hearst brand of news.

That fall the New York *American* ran a contest to discover a new child star. Mayer went to New York "to see personally the progress" and to proclaim that "nationality is no bar to a child." His frequent blasts at "salacious pictures" were warmly approved by the Hearst press. The powerful patron of Miss Davies agreed completely on the desirability of a high moral quality in films.

"Today the only people who would take a chance with a frankly salacious picture are the little fly-by-night producers," Mayer proclaimed to a reporter for the *American* in 1926. "They want to do something startling and sensational. The big producer doesn't have to do that.

"Of course, we shall have sex," he continued. "As long as we have men and women in the world, we will have sex. And I approve of it. We'll have sex in moving pictures, and I want it there. But it will be normal, real, beautiful sex—the sex that is common to the people in the audience, to me and to you. A man and a woman are in love with one another. That's sex and it is beautiful, in the movies and in life."

Mayer's thesis was regularly dittoed in ringing editorials signed by Hearst.

The two were also in agreement about politics, in which Mayer was now becoming peculiarly interested. His leaning in this direction had begun soon after he arrived in California and took up horseback riding as a pleasure consistent with his urge for physical action and his position as a rising gentleman. He did his riding on Sunday mornings, renting his horse from a stable near Griffith Park—the Griffith Park Riding Academy—which was a favorite spot for gentlemen riders in Los Angeles. It later became headquarters of the Breakfast Club, a spirited bunch of community boosters of whom he was one of the most spirited.

Here he came into contact with substantial citizens whose interests were such as to make them concerned about local politics. Mayer was by disposition an ardent Republican, and Republicans were strongly entrenched in Los Angeles. He felt that an active association would benefit him and the community.

His entry, however, was modest. It came through Ida Koverman, a San Franciscan who had been a secretary to Herbert

Hoover when he was a California engineer. She had been active in Los Angeles in the campaign to elect Calvin Coolidge to the presidency in 1924. Mayer was brought to her as a willing worker by a man named Rasty Wright, who had been instructed to get a motion picture projector for showing some campaign pictures. He turned up with Mayer.

A more eager and robust enlistment in Republican ranks has seldom occurred. Mayer campaigned, as much as his being abroad allowed him, in the fall of 1924. Later he hired Miss Koverman to be his secretary. Florence Browning was dispatched to New York to be the custodian of affairs of the "Mayer group" in the office of Loew's. Through Miss Koverman's close friendship with Hoover and others, Mayer was rapidly advanced in party councils. Naturally, it didn't hurt that he also had the close friendship of William Randolph Hearst.

It was partly the active involvement of Mayer in other affairs that caused the first individual protest of Irving Thalberg against what he considered inadequate recompense for what he did. Certainly it was his attention and that of the group of bright men he was gathering around him—Bernard Hyman, Albert Lewin, and Paul Bern—that was setting creative patterns for the studio product. Mayer was an earnest observer and highly important to the operation, but he was imperceptibly allowing creative functions to slip from his hands.

Thalberg made his initial protest in 1926, less than a year after his and the salaries of Mayer and Rubin had been raised. He insisted on getting more money. Mayer could not deny him his due. This matter and others concerning recompense of the "Mayer group" were again taken up with New York. Again there was haggling and bickering. Most of it was done by Mayer and Rubin with Nicholas Schenck and certain members of the board of directors, because Marcus Loew was ill. Eventually, they came up with a formula. Thalberg was to receive a raise in salary to $4,000 a week and a guarantee that his annual income from salary and bonus would not fall below $400,000 a year. This meant that, in a matter of two and a half years, his income had been jumped from a minimum of $32,500 a year to a minimum of $400,000.

To maintain a proper balance, the twenty-percent-of-the-profits spoils received in a lump sum by the "Mayer group" was divided so that Mayer received fifty-three percent, Rubin twenty-seven percent, and Thalberg twenty percent. Thus, although Thalberg's salary was greater than that of Mayer, it was still a mathematical likelihood that Mayer would receive a larger total compensation than he.

There were other changes at that time. The contract was modified so that the twenty-percent-of-the-profits was figured on the profits of Loew's, Inc., rather than on the profits of the producing company. This eliminated the continuing suspicion of Mayer that the theaters were getting preferential treatment. Mayer had previously asked the right to approve contracts to the theaters. Now the profits of all branches of the company went into one pile. And it was a pile, indeed.

Finally, in January, 1926, the name of the company was officially made Metro-Goldwyn-Mayer. Vanities were being appeased.

After this arrangement Thalberg wrote to Schenck and said he would be perfectly happy until the end of his contract, which was now extended to 1932. That was a fond thought, unrealistic in the light of the rate of change.

For the very next year brought changes that complicated the already tangling relations of people in this tight and temperamental group.

In the first place, a financial scandal that broke in California in June, 1927, dragged in, among its host of suspects, the name of Mayer. This was the famous scandal of the Julian Petroleum Company, a giant oil firm that had been kited in the era of tremendous boom. Mayer was among those indicted for usury—for making loans at exorbitant rates of interest to those who were trying to support watered stock pools. Although he was in good company of California financial names, it was not a flattering situation for the head of the Metro-Goldwyn-Mayer studio. The case was only started with the announcement of the Julian bust. It was to drag on for three years and build up one of the most odorous scandals in California history. While Mayer's involvement was minor, it was an embarrassment and annoyance.

Then came the economic crisis of 1927 in industry, and in September two more events which precipitated changes. Mayer's good friend, Marcus Loew, died, to be succeeded in the presidency of Loew's, Inc., by his not-so-good friend, Nicholas Schenck. A few days later Irving Thalberg and Norma Shearer were wed, with Mayer standing as best man and his daughters serving as bridesmaids.

And, the following month, in October, a motion picture opened in New York, a Warner Brothers picture called *The Jazz Singer,* which was to start a revolution on the screen.

In the summer of that year, 1927, Mayer turned forty-two.

The coming of sound to motion pictures and the pressures
that this inevitably put upon the whole creative process and
thus upon studio personnel did not occur in a brief time,
though that now seems the general impression. It was not a
case of "This week, *The Jazz Singer;* next week, All-Talking Films!" The radical and profound transition was spread
over two or three years. Compulsion more than planning im-
pelled it, against resistance within the industry.

Sound as an adjunct for the "flickers" was actually an old
idea. Thomas Edison had intended in the beginning to combine pictures that moved with his phonograph. Dozens of in-
ventors had tried to do it, with something less than success,
mainly because their mechanisms all lacked an efficient am-
plifying device. It was not until the early 1920's that this essential appliance was devised by Western Electric researchers,
using the audion or radio vacuum tube.

The Western Electric people, working for the Bell System
(telephone), tried hard to interest film producers in their device for adding sound. None of the large producing companies

was remotely interested. Why should they endeavor to tamper with the satisfactory medium of silent films? Music, which was all they ever reckoned would be added by sound anyhow —that, and perhaps some realistic noises—was being provided by pit orchestras. The addition of mechanical music would be only an expense.

But, in 1925, Warner Brothers, one of the smaller producing companies, joined with Western Electric to experiment with sound films. Quietly they went about producing a group of musical shorts, starring famous concert performers, and a synchronized musical accompaniment for the feature film, *Don Juan*. These novelties were first offered to the public at the Warner Theater in New York on August 5, 1926, and were received with enthusiasm. The new system was called Vitaphone.

But for all the excitement and approval of sophisticates in New York, the system was not regarded as anything more than a novelty by the remainder of the industry. A second series of shorts and another feature equipped with a synchronized musical score were brought out by Warners in October. These two programs were shown in a dozen theaters around the country. Vitaphone was predicted to be a dud.

Hopes for expanding the system were further discouraged by the slump that hit the motion picture business in the spring and summer of 1927. Theater men saw no percentage in going to the expense of installing costly equipment while attendance was falling off. They dourly accepted the premise that this was a cyclical drop and all they could do was seek the shelter of stiff economies.

While they tended to blame their misfortune on the new wonder of broadcast radio, which swept into great popular favor in the mid-1920's and became a fixture in millions of American homes, they regarded this new medium as merely a competitor for their customer's time. They failed to grasp that it was rapidly rendering the silent film commercially obsolete. They did not conceive the crisis in its broader terms

—namely, that a basic evolution in mass mechanical entertainment was occurring with the exposure of the public to image-forming sound.

The first inkling of this phenomenon came in October, when the Warner's historic *The Jazz Singer* was presented in New York. This latest of the synchronized sound pictures was different from those that had gone before only in that its leading character, played by Al Jolson, sang two songs and spoke a few lines of dialogue. Toward the end of the picture, he faced the audience, and for the first time spoke in audible words instead of in printed subtitles. He said, "You ain't heard nothin' yet, folks!" Then he began singing "Mammy," a particularly sentimental song.

The effect was galvanizing. Suddenly the character was brought alive and made capable of giving vocal expression to the already tearful sentiments of the plot. The illusion was so affecting that the audience cried and cheered.

That première marked the beginning of an inevitable change to sound, even though the misgivings of industry leaders were substantially the same as before. For the public's response to *The Jazz Singer* was tremendous, wherever it was shown. People flocked to see it in incredible swarms. While well-recommended silent pictures were doing only passably well, the Warners' "part dialogue" feature was an invariable sensational hit.

This was enough to give the tip-off to the nation's top theater men that there was something magical and potent about pictures with music *and* spoken words. They began clamoring for sound equipment and for more films with the built-in success. Studios in Hollywood were driven to begin providing them.

The consequence was an upheaval in the producing community the likes of which had never been experienced in previous phases of growth and slump. Writers, directors, and producers who had been accustomed to making silent films were compelled to meet the mighty question of what to do with sound. How much talk should there be in pictures? Should the screen become a replica of the stage? And what was to be done about actors and actresses who didn't know how to talk?

This latter consideration caused hysteria. Many of the most successful players were powerless to speak dialogue. Their careers were suddenly threatened. They desperately rushed for coaches and speech schools. Studios which had them under contract pondered the prospects of doom.

And then there was the immediate difficulty of solving the mechanical riddles of sound, installing the new equipment and discovering what to do with it. The problem was complicated by the fact that Vitaphone was challenged by other sound systems as soon as its success was foretold. Studio technical departments were put to frenzied work to devise ways of building or combining sound systems that would give optimum results. But they couldn't get around the basic patents of Western Electric on the audion, which was unique and indispensable in the effective projection of sound. As Cecil B. De Mille crisply put it, when the inevitability of the transition loomed, "Well, boys, it looks as though we're all going to work for the telephone company."

In this period of crisis people at Metro-Goldwyn-Mayer were no less confused and frightened than any others in Hollywood. They were running a large operation with an extensive group of stars. How they would manage to guide the studio was anybody's guess. Their facing up to the problem was also somewhat delayed by the fact that Nicholas Schenck, the new president of Loew's, Inc., stubbornly held out against sound. He did not accede to the inevitable until *The Jazz Singer* had proved a great hit, and then he reluctantly approved necessary expenditures for equipping the studio and theaters.

But in this respect he was no different, no more doubtful and rigid, than was Mayer. The latter had no belief whatever in the practicality or desirability of films with sound. He had seen several previous endeavors to promote the idea when he was a theater man. In his estimation sound films were, at best, a novelty.

True, he had given his permission in 1925 for a young engineer, Douglas Shearer, the brother of Norma, to work up a stunt for publicizing a new picture in Los Angeles by simultaneously showing a trailer in several local theaters, with synchronized dialogue broadcast to it from a radio station. But the stunt proved a laughable foul-up when the synchronization went off, and Mayer was not amused or encouraged by this evidence of the awkwardness of sound. He would not listen to Shearer's petition to be permitted to continue with experiments, and it was only when *The Jazz Singer* was booming that he got Shearer back to the studio and gave him the nod to proceed.

Even with evidence of the public's avid interest in films with sound, Mayer was not convinced of their intelligence or that they were "here to stay." He frankly delegated to Thalberg the job of planning the production of sound films, while he kept himself free to act as observer and advise Eddie Mannix in directing physical adjustments in the studio.

Thalberg went at the assignment with his usual eagerness and energy. Although he, too, was chary of the new thing (he had said in June, 1927, that he did not believe the talking motion picture would ever replace the silent drama), he was interested and optimistic. To those of his associates who despaired of being able to master the new medium, he cheerfully said, "We know as much about sound as anybody does."

The first of the studio's pictures to be partially equipped with sound was a scenic romance with Raquel Torres and Monte Blue called *White Shadows in the South Seas*. A musical score and a few sound effects were added to it after it had been shot as a silent film. It was presented in New York in July, 1928, and several others, similarly equipped with music or "part dialogue," were sent out before the end of the year. In that time the studio had started on a first experimental musical comedy which was called *Broadway Melody,* and its first all-talking drama, *The Trial of Mary Dugan,* in which Norma Shearer was starred.

Under the pressure and uncertainty that prevailed in the motion picture business during this critical year of 1928, it is hard to believe that an executive with the responsibilities of Mayer could have had the audacity or energy to get himself further involved in politics. But doing the unreasonable or audacious was a tendency with Mayer. He chose that time to make his first big flourish as a Republican on a national scale.

Having employed Ida Koverman to be his secretary and having completely dedicated himself to Herbert Hoover as a presidential candidate, he began the usual fence-building even before the intrusion of sound and was one of the "original Hoover Republicans" prior to the "presidential year."

As a Republican State committeeman he was, therefore, committed to attend the Republican National Convention in Kansas City in June, 1928. Already he had made the acquaintance of Mabel Walker Willebrandt, a strong California Republican and chairman of the important committee of accreditation that year. She and Mayer were regarded as key people who might swing the essential support of William Randolph Hearst to Hoover, if and when the opportunity arose. The great newspaper publisher virtually controlled state delegations from California, Texas, and Illinois.

Mayer had already done some groundwork, with Ida Koverman, in bringing Hearst and Hoover together. In meetings at his home he had got Hoover to assure Hearst of his interest in a program of public works and national reforms to save the nation from the crisis of economic stagnation that Hearst foresaw.

Even so, when they went to the convention Hearst had not committed himself to support of Hoover. His preferred candidate was Andrew Mellon, Secretary of the Treasury in the Coolidge administration.

What Mayer did at that convention in the hot summer of 1928, when sound was rumbling in the movies, was not of historic consequence. There was some talk that he might be selected to make the Hoover nominating speech, but his California friends were a little uncertain what he might do if he got on his feet. He was a vigorous talker but not a particularly logical one, and he had a tendency to ramble and neglect to notice when it was timely to come to an end. Further, he was a "new" Californian and, more discouraging, he was a Jew. The honor of delivering the nominating speech fell to a "native son," Hon. John L. McNab.

Mayer kept himself conspicuous in the councils of his friends and, accompanied by Miss Koverman, stayed close to Hearst. When the latter finally saw that Mellon did not have a chance and threw his delegates to Hoover, Mayer was a triumphant man.

That fall he put in time and effort campaigning for Hoover among people in the motion picture business. His advocacy had ironic point, because it was known that Nicholas Schenck had contributed twenty-five thousand dollars to the campaign of Hoover's rival, Al Smith. Thus it was a great satisfaction to Mayer when Hoover won. He tended naïvely to imagine that he had much to do with it.

His satisfaction was expensive, however. His absorption in politics, while the studio was in the middle of the problem of switching to sound, did not sit well with Irving Thalberg. Already the latter felt that he was carrying the brunt of creative responsibilities of the studio. Even though Mayer had been the keystone to the arch of the "Mayer group," Robert Rubin had been its architect and now Thalberg felt himself its chief support. He mentioned his discontent to Rubin and the latter inclined to agree with him. Together they quietly calculated what they should and could do.

Thus an uncomfortable climate of suspicion, anxiety, and doubt began to develop within the "Mayer group" during the latter part of 1928. Suddenly Mayer was confronted with the stark and disquieting dread that his two much admired and envied partners were cutting themselves away from him, that they were up to something desperate, plotting behind his back.

Had it been anyone else, this suspicion would not have distracted him. He was a rough and rugged contender against persons who might wish to steal his power. He would have gone in slugging and depended on the best man to win. In past tests of strength and cunning he knew that the victor was usually Mayer.

But this time he had no taste for battle. He felt strangely paralyzed, for openly to fight with his partners would only weaken and maybe destroy himself. He knew as well as anyone how dependent he was on them, on the creative potency of Thalberg and on Rubin's artfulness. His frustration in this weird dilemma was pathetically revealed in a small encounter he had one winter evening with a young studio employee.

In those first months of working with sound films the complexity and scarcity of projection equipment was such that there was only one theater in the surrounding area where new pictures with accompanying sound could be tried out. That was in San Bernadino, some fifty miles from the studio. Getting there on the night of a tryout became a sort of group ritual, presided over by Thalberg and joined by most of the key personnel.

A car of the Pacific Electric interurban railway would be brought alongside the studio in the afternoon and stocked with assorted delicatessen, soft drinks, and playing cards. At 6 P.M. Thalberg and his cohorts, all the people who formed his inner group and the department heads and writers and technicians responsible for the quality of the film, would get aboard the streetcar and off they would go to "San Berdoo," playing bridge (which Thalberg loved) and generally having a cheerful, relaxed, and chummy time. It was in such congenial relations with his associates and the artisans of the studio that the essentially attractive personality of Thalberg expanded and glowed.

One evening, the car had departed and the studio was emptying for the night when a new employee, Fred Wilcox, was passing the executive office building on his way home. Outside was Mayer's automobile, waiting, with chauffeur at the wheel. As Wilcox approached, Mayer came from the building and strode head down toward his car. The two men nearly collided, and as Wilcox jumped aside Mayer looked up and recognized him. The two had briefly met. The young man was the brother of Pansy Wilcox, a former show girl, who the year before had married Nicholas Schenck.

Mayer paused uncertainly for a moment, then grabbed the young man by the arm and dragged him into the automobile. "Come along, Wilcox," he said, "I'll drive you home."

There was no use declining the offer, even though the young man was shy and rendered exceedingly uncomfortable by the incongruous situation of being driven home by the studio boss. Mayer asked where he lived, instructed the chauffeur, then sat back and said nothing more. Nor did Wilcox. For several minutes they rode in silence, both looking straight ahead.

Suddenly, Mayer started weeping, fitfully at first, then in an unrestrained torrent. Wilcox looked at him abashed, not knowing what had happened or how he should behave. Mayer kept right on crying, regardless of the embarrassment of his guest, who finally blurted in great confusion, "Mr. Mayer, what's the matter? Is there anything I can do?"

Bawling like a youngster, Mayer caught his hand and sobbed, "They all went off and left me! *They didn't ask me to go along!*"

Wilcox felt like a dummy. What could a fellow say?

A couple of months passed, months of waiting, wondering and worrying what was afoot. Mayer was cautious and guarded in talking to Thalberg, trying to find out. If his partners were really against him, if they were plotting something with Schenck, there was not much that he could do about it but accept the blow when it fell.

Then something incredible happened, something so amaz-

ing and grotesque that it utterly preëmpted the attention and
the anxiety of Mayer—and, for that matter, the anxiety of his
partners, who were as starkly exposed as he.

Among the more predatory creatures who had prowled successfully in the ever-widening jungle of the motion picture
industry was a man we have previously noted, the former
cloth sponger, William Fox, whose name was as appropriate
as any could possibly be. From a small nickelodeon operator
in Brooklyn, he had scuffled and fought his way to a position
of greater prominence in the business than that of Mayer.

Fox had first assembled a few theaters, in the manner of
Marcus Loew; then he had gone into film production to free
himself of dependence on anyone. Through the 1920's, he
prospered with his competent Fox Films.

When the prospect of sound was looming, Fox providently
got control of some patents to a parallel mechanism labeled
Movietone. He and his able associates brought this process
along simultaneously with the inauguration of the revolution-
ary Vitaphone. Fox's Movietone features came hot on *The
Jazz Singer's* heels.

Now Fox had been an ardent fighter for "independence"
in the days when "the trust" was attempting to maintain complete possession of the infant industry, and he had got an education in the workings of monopoly. He had seen that the
only way to tie up the business, if one had that in mind, was to
command not only mechanical devices for the manufacture
and projection of films but also the major theaters. And Fox,
being greedy, obviously had that in mind. He owned a pat-
ented method for the manufacture and projection of films
which he hoped, through legal maneuvers, to make the exclusive mechanism for sound. Now he wanted to get control
of as many theaters as was financially possible.

Already owning a few houses in cities across the land he
started a campaign of theater acquisition in 1927 by grabbing
the new and spectacular Roxy in New York. In rapid succession thereafter he cleverly got control of the Westco chain in

California, the Saxe circuit in Wisconsin, the Poli circuit in New England, and started forming the strong Metropolitan circuit in New York. It was well recognized in the business just what he was trying to do.

Even so, a flurry of rumors in the late fall of 1928 to the effect that Fox was attempting to gain control of Loew's, Inc., were treated with incredulity. It was utterly absurd to imagine he had a chance to move in on the large, successful properties of Loew's.

But people who laughed at those rumors failed to credit the wiliness of Fox or the passion for gain of other people who owned large blocks of shares in Loew's. For, indeed, Fox was more than attempting to move in on the powerful company; he was studiously bent on acquiring sufficient stock in it to give him control.

The details of a secret maneuver by which Fox persuaded Nicholas Schenck to assemble and sell him enough shares of Loew's stock to give him this control need not now be recounted. But they make a story, indeed—how the president of Loew's, Inc., actually canvassed a select group of stockholders, including the widow and sons of Marcus Loew, to get enough stock together to sell out to a competitor—all, it must be noted, at a profit of several million dollars to Schenck.

What is pertinent and important is that the motion picture world was struck all but dumb with amazement when this negotiation was revealed by Fox and Schenck in a public announcement on March 3, 1929. And even more startled and dumbfounded were the three men who comprised the "Mayer group." They were probably the most amazed men in the whole amazed motion picture world.

Literally, Mayer, Thalberg, and Rubin were kept completely in the dark about the planning for this momentous sellout of the company for which they had done so much. Mayer had been given an inkling that Fox would like to buy, when he was approached by one of the latter's lieutenants sometime in 1928 and asked if he would be willing to help swing a deal. (This was before the arrangement for the in-road was set up with Schenck.) Mayer told the man to go to blazes, or saltier words to that effect. Furthermore Mayer did not own stock in the company, so Fox's offer to pay a sizeable bonus on all blocks bought did not fascinate him. He heard no more about it, after that tentative advance.

Of course Rubin had heard rumors floating around in the trade, but he couldn't bring himself to believe them, especially when they were publicly denied by Schenck. "Were it not for the fact that such reports are apt to do harm," Schenck had said, "this rumor would be the most ridiculously amusing gossip I've heard in years." Once Rubin asked Saul Rogers, a Fox attorney, if his boss was angling to get Loew's. "You ought to know," Rogers told him, then tactfully asked to be excused. Rogers was amazed to learn later that the "Mayer group" had not been made privy to the sellout by Schenck.

Actually neither Mayer, Thalberg, nor Rubin had any sizeable holdings of Loew's stock, so there was no point in Schenck going to them and inviting them in on the deal. Although they had been top executives of the company for almost five years, and had made a lot of money from it, they had neglected to accumulate its stock. Perhaps Schenck considered that omission sufficient reason to leave them uninformed. Perhaps he also knew there was disunion among the three executives and so believed them unable to do or demand anything.

However, when they did learn of the sellout the three men were rendered aghast. That Schenck could have sold control of the company to Fox was beyond belief.

The tip-off to what was happening came with a telephone call from Eddie Hatrick, Hearst's man for his motion picture interests, to Florence Browning at her office in New York.

"Florence," Hatrick fairly shouted, "they're over at the bank right now, signing papers to sell the company to Fox!"

Miss Browning was flabbergasted. Rubin was on the Coast and Mayer was on a train bound from California to Washington to attend President Hoover's inaugural. She called Rubin first. He took the news grimly and said he was returning to New York right away. Then she relayed calls to catch Mayer and finally got through to him in New Orleans.

When he heard the news of the sellout he reacted as though hit on the head. Then, after a pause, he said, "Well, Schenck is president of the company. He can do what he wants with it!"

It was with that knowledge gnawing at his innards that he arrived in flag-decked Washington.

After the inauguration, Mayer came on to New York. Rubin and Thalberg had preceded him. No one knew what was going to happen. There was not only the sellout to Fox but also the pregnant possibility of disunion within the "Mayer group." As Florence Browning put it, "Everything could have fallen apart right then."

When Mayer walked into the New York office Rubin was there to greet him and put out his hand. They faced each other squarely, clasping hands, without words. Mayer later confided to Florence Browning, "When Bob held out his hand, it was like the clouds had broken and the sun was shining again."

Such was the dubious dissipation of that first ominous strain within the "Mayer group."

What happened thereafter on the Fox deal, which in 1929 appeared to forecast the most potent amalgamation yet made in the motion picture industry, is a matter of complicated record, some of it still obscure, and some of the intimate personal details are lost forever in the dust of men now dead. But the ultimate consequence was that Fox, getting more and more involved in his efforts to pyramid his holdings and his delicate financial deals, was forced into the hands of a receiver which placed the Loew's stock in trust and eventually threw it on the open market. There was never an amalgamation of Fox's companies with Loew's.

However, for a few weeks after that announcement in 1929, there was nervousness and consternation in the ranks of

Metro-Goldwyn-Mayer. Schenck was angrily assailed and assaulted by the three members of the "Mayer group" who charged he had selfishly traded on the excellent studio and on the increasingly rich company they had helped to build. Loew's had expanded from a gross income of some $19,500,000 in 1923 to $116,200,000 in 1929—almost six fold! The fact that Schenck and his associate, David Bernstein, the treasurer of Loew's, had got more than $9,000,000 profit for themselves and their conspirators from the Fox deal was the realization that most infuriated them.

There are now several interesting versions of precisely what occurred in the heated personal relations of Schenck, Mayer, Thalberg, and Fox. As the last named told the story to his biographer, Upton Sinclair, published under the title of *Upton Sinclair Presents William Fox,* Mayer, Thalberg, and Rubin had several conferences with him, protesting their outrage at what happened. Fox defended the action of Schenck and told the three men they had shown no faith in their company by failing to buy any of its stock. As a consequence of his position Fox said, "I incurred their animosity."

As Mayer himself later told it, he was called in Washington while he was there for the inauguration by A.C. Blumenthal, the Fox lieutenant who had previously spoken to him, and was informed, in cheery fashion, "L.B., your new boss wants to talk with you." Fox then came on the phone and said, "L.B. this is Bill Fox, and I just want to let you know I'm proud to be associated with you." They made a date to meet in the apartment of Winfield Sheean in New York a few days after the inauguration. Sheean was Fox's top executive.

When Mayer went to the apartment Fox was full of friendliness, "Call me Bill," he told Mayer. The latter said he preferred to call him Mr. Fox. They went into a discussion of the state of the studio. Among other things Fox indicated he was unhappy about a new contract that had recently been signed with John Gilbert.

This contract, which was drawn in December, 1928, bound

Gilbert for four pictures at $250,000 each. It was one of the largest figures ever paid a star and turned out to be a disastrous deal for the studio. Sound was on the threshold, and Gilbert soon proved inadequate to it. He fell down in his first talking film and did not thereafter recover his great silent popularity. Fox was right; the Gilbert contract was one with which to be displeased. (Fox didn't add, however, that he had a personal antipathy to the star; he had fired him before he went to the Goldwyn Company because Gilbert had a slight bulbousness at the end of his nose!)

Mayer replied that he had nothing to do with the Gilbert contract, that it had been arranged and signed by Schenck. Mayer himself had no use for Gilbert. It seems that shortly after they had made *The Big Parade,* Gilbert was telling Mayer his life story and casually remarked he believed his mother was a whore. "What's that you say?" Mayer hollered. "I say my mother was a whore," Gilbert replied. This horrified Mayer so profoundly that he leaped on Gilbert in violent wrath and was pounding the astonished actor when associates pulled them apart. Ever after, the innocent Gilbert was held in scorn by Mayer.

When Fox heard that Mayer disliked Gilbert, he was gratified. "I'll tell you how to get rid of him." he said, confidingly. "Give him a couple of bad parts. That'll make him mad."

Mayer, according to his story, candidly replied, "See here, Mr. Fox, I don't want to break contracts—and I don't like anybody who does."

Fox was still trying to be friendly. "Come on, call me Bill," he insisted. Then he turned and winked at Sheean, "We know how to break contracts, don't we, Winnie?"

This didn't move Mayer, who stood his ground. "I won't be a party to putting my foot out in the dark and making the man stumble," he said.

It was on that delicate point of honor that the two men discovered themselves in hopeless disagreement.

In a subsequent conversation Mayer, still angry, mentioned to Fox that he (Fox) might find himself in trouble with the antitrust division of the Department of Justice as a consequence of getting control of Loew's. The amalgamation of the two large companies might be regarded as a monopoly, he said.

Fox answered (according to this story), "We've taken care of that. My friend Greenfield (Albert M. Greenfield, a Philadelphia banker who had lent the money to buy Loew's shares) has President Hoover in his back pocket."

This was touching close to Mayer, who was, of course, a friend and strong supporter of the new president.

"I don't know anybody who has President Hoover in his pocket," he said.

A few days later, on March 12, Mayer was back in Washington with his wife and daughters to enjoy what for him, at that particular moment, was a triumph sweetened with revenge. He and his family were there to have dinner and spend the night at the White House. They were the first informal guests entertained by the Hoovers after moving into their new home. The occasion seemed so newsworthy to William Randolph Hearst that he saw that it got a full column report in the New York *American*. The visit to the White House was preceded by a small reception at the Hotel Carlton for the Mayers, arranged by Ida Koverman and her friend, Mabel Walker Willebrandt. (That reception was fraught with embarrassment, incidentally. Trunks containing the new dresses of the Mayer girls did not arrive and they had to appear before the Republican politicians wearing their grubby traveling clothes!)

While in Washington, on that happy occasion, which was further adorned by the fact that Mayer was being bruited as the likely new ambassador to Turkey (it stopped at that), he naturally mentioned to Hoover what had happened to his company and made some comment about the Fox purchase opening the way to a possible monopoly. Hoover advised him to speak to people at the Department of Justice, which Mayer did. He spoke to the new Attorney General, William Mitchell, giving him, as he said, "information for file on the consolidation." There he let the matter stand.

Now it should be realized that Fox had already made inquiries, before completing the Loew's buy, as to whether it would be permitted. He had been told, according to his story, that it would. However, the new Attorney General was not the man Fox expected him to be. Within a few months Fox was being investigated and told to divest himself. He hastily endeavored to mend his fences and make sure his purchase would not be assailed.

From a leading Republican politician, Fox, to his amazement, learned that the man who might be helpful to him was none other than Louie Mayer. So again, in June, Fox arranged a conference with the resentful studio head. This time, by Fox's own admission, it was his intention to make Mayer his friend.

After a bit of further wrangling over the injustice done to Mayer and his associates, Fox offered to draw a new contract of generous scope with the "Mayer group," and on the side said he would give a $2,000,000 bonus to Mayer himself if a consolidation of the Fox and Loew companies could be achieved *without* any further annoyance or objection from the government. This proposal put a new complexion on the desirability of the deal.

"Apparently Louis B. Mayer was able to do in the Attorney General's office what Herbert Hoover wasn't able to do, for nothing more was heard about the order to William Fox to divest himself of the Loew shares." So Upton Sinclair reported in the Fox biography.

However, this is not quite accurate, in the light of what later occurred, and also according to the private recollection of John Lord O'Brian. Mr. O'Brian was the Assistant Attorney General appointed that June to head up the antitrust division of the Justice Department. There he found one of the top-priority issues to be that of the Fox-Loew deal.

His associates who had worked on the case informed him that Mayer had already expressed strong opposition to the purchase. Thus O'Brian was surprised indeed when Mayer came to see him a short time after and said he was not now opposed to the deal by Fox. This change of heart disturbed him, for O'Brian knew that Mayer was Hoover's friend. He also was convinced that the law had been violated. This was subsequently proved when O'Brian and the Justice Department were able to bring the case to trial.

For all this, Mayer solemnly insisted—and continued to insist in later years—that he made no overtures to anyone at any time on behalf of Fox. Indeed he maintained devoutly that his only desire was to see that the wily would-be monopolist did not get away with the deal.

And he didn't. In July of that year, before any consolidation could be commenced, Fox was badly injured in an automobile accident while en route to play golf on Long Island with, ironically, Nicholas Schenck. He was totally immobilized for a few months. Then the stock market crash of 1929 occurred and Fox's financial pyramids began to crumble and fall. Two weeks later the Justice Department filed its delayed suit against him for operating a trust, and in December he was compelled by court order to relinquish control of his companies to a board of trustees headed by his largest creditors.

Thus, Mayer's only final satisfaction from the fabulous Fox deal was to see the man who would have gobbled up his company started on a long road to ruin.

What was done privately within the circle of the top Loew's executives is another story—and a not edifying one. The three members of the "Mayer group" felt that they should be recompensed in some way for what had happened. They couldn't see Schenck and his friends getting away with all that booty.

The question was simply how much and under what circumstances the members should be paid.

Mayer and Rubin each claimed they never took a cent from Schenck, although Mayer said that he was offered $100,000 as settlement. However, both Mayer and Rubin insisted consistently that Thalberg did accept $250,000 as a conciliatory settlement from Schenck and went back to Hollywood placated.

"His only weakness was love of money," Mayer observed.

Thalberg was not the only individual prone to that alleged frailty.

Although the incipient rupture of the "Mayer group" was thus forestalled by the weird circumstances of the Fox deal, Thalberg was still not appeased. He continued to insist that he was not getting his just deserts for the work he did. In December, 1929, Mayer consented to give him ten percent more of the group's bonuses. This brought Thalberg's share of the division up to thirty percent and reduced Mayer's to forty-three.

Slowly the frail and sensitive "genius" was eating away at Mayer's magnificent lode.

It was just a matter of time before the two mutually dependent men would clash.

Within his own family circle, during these complicated times of difficult studio expansion and personal rivalry, Mayer grandly played the stern parent. He fancied himself a patriarch, because that was what his inclinations and traditional upbringing prescribed that the head of the family should be.

His own father, now in his eighties, was a resident in his home, in the elegant ocean-front villa that Mayer had bought in Santa Monica in 1925. Thoroughly warped and wizened, old Jacob Mayer was but a wraith, a rheumy and wretched relic to remind his son of the painful past—of the childhood misery in Russia, the boyhood labors and yearnings in Saint John, the self-sacrifices of the mother who had died in the harness of her toil. The old man was oddly incongruous in the expensive and elaborate house which was part of the façade of the grandee that Mayer was acquiring in the community. He still had the look of an aged peddler in this fine mansion of a millionaire. He coughed and hawked and had crude manners. His throat was so badly clogged he could scarcely talk.

Yet Mayer maintained his father in the bosom of his own

family and dutifully gave him the illusion of being honored as a grandparent should be. He *schmoosed* with him, and pretended to seek his counsel, even though he perceived that the old man had not the slightest understanding of the world of films. Every so often, the ex-peddler would get into a chauffeur-driven Ford and go to the studio, where he would put on the elaborate airs of a big boss. His foolish and vain behavior would greatly embarrass his son.

Maggie Mayer, now a settled matron, saw to it that her father-in-law's meals were cooked and served in accordance with orthodox dietary laws, and she was always conscientious about getting him to the synagogue. Mayer submitted to the authority of his parent to that degree.

But toward his wife and daughters he acted the master in every way, insisting that these females in the family conform to his notions of propriety. When they first moved to California, the daughters were sent to the Hollywood School for Girls, an ordinary private day school, undistinguished academically. However, it was socially more suitable for the daughters of a man determined to make himself distinguished than were the Los Angeles public schools. Among their more memorable schoolmates were Margaret and Agnes De Mille and Harlene Carpenter, a stringy lass who later developed, under the name of Jean Harlow, into a sexy movie star. There were also two lone, embarrassed boys attending the school at the time—a toothy lad, Douglas Fairbanks, Jr., and a gangling one named Joel McCrea.

Mayer's notions of female propriety included rigid ideas on the not uncommon practice of having dates with boys. He was violently opposed to his teen-age daughters going out at night and forbade such behavior until the girls were virtually grown. Then he diligently screened their venturous escorts and insisted they have the girls home by midnight. His stern and repeated precept was that a woman's place was in the home, and he saw to it that his wife taught their daughters how to cook and sew.

This nigh pathological insistence on the observance of strict formalities was, in part, a carry-over from his own background, in part an accretion from his exposure to middle-class New England gentility. It was, in a sense, a reflection of his own mixed-up morality. He was moved by a passion for conformance, and also by caution and fear. He felt the worst thing that could happen to him, socially, would be to have his daughters become connected with the fast life of Hollywood.

The anxiety was valid because Hollywood, in those days, was a gaudy and carefree community. The elite of the motion picture colony, into which Mayer's family naturally fell, were given to extravagant doings. Big costume parties were the rage. They usually ended in drunken brawls, auto races along the night-shrouded boulevards, and encounters with press and police. Mayer understandably quailed at the thought of any of his family being involved.

Edith, the older of the two girls, was artistically inclined. She was elected president of the dramatic club at school and dreamed of becoming a singer, an actress, or a dancer, as do most girls. Her father let her take singing lessons and study acting, painting, and ballet. He literally idolized Edith, a pretty and fragile girl. His pet name for her was "yingele," an affectionate diminutive. But he sternly resisted any vain hopes that she might attempt a professional career.

Irene was more the intellectual. She had a stubborn hope that she might be permitted to go to college, after the Hollywood School for Girls. But her father hooted at this notion.

"A daughter of *mine* go to college?" he scoffed. "Become an *intellectual?*" He flung the word with a sneer. His contempt for that category of people—"intellectuals"—was frequently proclaimed.

Instead he encouraged Irene in the wholesome outdoor pursuits of horseback riding, swimming, and tennis. She was his frequent companion on the horseback rides he took on Sunday mornings at the Griffith Park Riding Academy. There were those who strongly suspected that Mayer secretly wished Irene were a boy and consequently tended to treat her with a sort of masculine camaraderie. She was brunette and prone to be chubby, very much as was he; in a way, she probably did provide him with some of the companionship he might have got from a son.

Inevitably the grown daughters began to think seriously of beaux. Husbands were naturally to be expected for two young ladies as eligible as they. Mayer was loathe to accept this expectation, other than theoretically. He acknowledged matrimony as a proper prospect for young ladies, but he had a hard time acknowledging any individual as an adequate suitor for his girls.

Some people thought Irving Thalberg would make an ideal husband for one of them. He was bright, energetic, wealthy, and on a suitable social plane. And there's no doubt this obvious prospect was contemplated by Mrs. Mayer and the girls. But Mayer ridiculed the speculation, whenever it was mentioned, usually in the intimacy of the home. "Stay away from Irving," he ordered. "He's sick; he has a weak heart."

Mayer, of course, knew the awesome secret of Thalberg's illness as a boy and the terrible dread of his idolizing family that he had a "rheumatic heart." Such an intimate and fascinating detail of physiology would not have escaped an associate as sensitive to illness as was Mayer. It was talked about in the Mayer family, time and time again, as a solemn reminder to the daughters that they should never think of marrying a man who might die young.

However, it is reasonable to suspect that the anxious father, deep in his heart, let his growing resentment of Thalberg affect his regard for him as a possible son-in-law. The thought that one of his priceless daughters, one of his jewels, might transmit her love to his increasingly vexatious partner could have filled him with jealousy. He was ever inclined to be disparaging toward anything he sensed he could not possess.

The marriage of Thalberg with Norma Shearer in 1927 removed that peril to his home.

But, sooner or later, it was inevitable that serious suitors would come along. And they did. For Irene it was David Selznick; for Edith, William Goetz. The two young ladies became acquainted with the two young gentlemen at about the same time, and their hectic and difficult courtships roughly paralleled.

Dave Selznick was the youngest, most impetuous, and physically most attractive son of Mayer's old nemesis, Lewis J. Selznick, so there was good cause for him to be disturbed. Young Selznick, in his middle twenties, was actually working at Metro-Goldwyn-Mayer when he met Irene at a New Year's Eve party and became attracted to her. (On that particular evening she was allowed to stay out until 1 A.M.) He was working then as an assistant to the dutiful Harry Rapf, having been employed over the violent objection of Mayer.

How this phenomenon happened is pertinent to the story here told.

Selznick had come to Hollywood in 1927 and had applied for a job to Rapf, who had previously worked for his brother, Myron, in a minor way. Rapf was inclined to hire young Selznick, but when he put it up to Mayer the latter popped with indignation. "I'll have no son of a Selznick working here!" he said.

Rapf regretfully reported this to the young man, who was not to be squelched so easily. He happened to note in a newspaper that Nicholas Schenck was in town.

Now Selznick was happily mindful of an incident that had occurred a few years back, involving his father, old Pat Powers, and the austere Schenck. The elder Selznick and the ever-enterprising Powers had gone to the office of Schenck with a proposition involving screen rights to *Ben-Hur*. The proposition smacked of a swindle, of that you may be sure, and Schenck was in the position of trying to parry the attempt.

It so happened that Papa Selznick, who always studiously tutored his sons in the ways of high-level dealing, had young David along with him. The youth was sitting quietly in a corner, listening to the wrangling of the men. Suddenly the elder Selznick turned to his son and said, "All right, so I'll leave it up to Davey. Shall we go through with it or drop it?"

"Drop it," the young man answered, probably because he was getting bored.

"That's your decision?" asked the somewhat baffled father.

"That's my decision," David replied.

"So be it," said the elder Selznick, to the great relief of Schenck.

As the men were leaving the office Schenck stopped the younger Selznick and said, "That was a wise decision, Davey; let me know if I can ever do anything for you."

Now Selznick had occasion to ask a favor of Schenck. He purposely encountered the new president of Loew's, Inc. (Schenck had just succeeded to that job), coming out of the barber shop of the Ambassador Hotel.

"Well, Davey, what are you doing in this town?" Schenck greeted him cordially.

Selznick said he was trying to get a job at Metro-Goldwyn-Mayer.

"So what can I do for you?" Schenck offered.

Selznick told the story of how he was opposed by Mayer.

"Call me this afternoon," Schenck answered.

Selznick called and was told he had the job.

Here was another reason for Mayer to resent the young man. He was not one to be indifferent to a person going over his head. Mayer's feelings were quickly manifest when Irene began going out with Selznick, who had a lot of his father's push.

"Keep away from that *schnook*," he warned her. "He'll be a bum, just like his old man!"

This crude and unkindly reference was to the fact that the elder Selznick had come to a harsh and untimely end as a

film baron in 1923. Partly through his own high-handed dealing, partly through the assaults of his enemies, among whom
Adolph Zukor was conspicuous, he was forced into bankruptcy
and had not been able to recover in the rapidly consolidating
world of films. No tears were shed by his erstwhile fall-guy,
Mayer.

But Irene refused her father's warning. She was carried
away by energetic and exciting young Selznick, who was rapidly rising in the community. Less than a year after landing
his job at Metro-Goldwyn-Mayer, he was out for disputing
Thalberg on a matter of policy. Right away he went over to
Paramount and got himself a job. Apparently Zukor bore no
grudges against the Selznick tribe. And within a few months
he was climbing blithely up other people's backs. He was a
fascinating fellow, especially to Irene Mayer.

Meanwhile sister Edith had met and fallen in love with
"Billy" Goetz, a modest and well-mannered assistant supervisor at Fox. Mayer had nothing against him; he rather liked
him, in fact—thought him a nice young fellow, much better
than "that Selznick bum." But when Edith and Goetz informed him they wanted to be married quietly, he was angered and upset.

"Why should my daughter go off and get married in some
backhouse?" he demanded. "I'm not going to have people say
I couldn't give my daughter a big wedding. The Biltmore is
where it'll be!"

Edith pleaded with her father. She and Billy didn't want
that sort of thing; they just wanted to be married quietly,
with the family and a few friends present, she said.

Mayer derided the notion. He wouldn't pay for her trous-
seau, he said. A man in his position had to show the community that he could marry his daughter in proper style.

"What do you want, a cottage with green vines growing
up it?" he jeered. He dismissed such nonsense with a gesture.
"Dreamer! Dreamer!" he cried.

His attitude was so stubborn and intemperate that Edith

was reduced to tears. She rushed from the house with her fiancé and didn't see her father for several days.

In the meantime he cooled off and regretted the scene he had made. He attempted to extend peace offerings through his distracted wife. This was a standard maneuver, to enlist the services of a third party for conveying messages or patching up quarrels. Seldom, *very* seldom, would he make direct overtures to anyone whom he had offended. He got others to convey what amounted to his apologies.

This time the mother moved gently between her husband and daughter. She soothed and comforted Edith, trying to make her understand the stubborn pride and impetuousness of her father, which, heaven knows, the whole family had observed. In a few days she had Edith softened.

Then one morning, Mayer went to his daughter's room, knocked on the door, timidly entered, and abjectly fell on his knees. He literally crawled to his daughter, grabbed her hands, held them to his face, and started sobbing and weeping until her hands were soaked with his tears. He said she could have anything she wanted, that he couldn't bear being separated from her. Edith melted and also began crying. She told her father she would do as he desired.

Mayer was delighted and exuberant. He told her, "You say you love this boy? Then how you get married shouldn't matter. You should have only eyes for him!"

Edith followed that counsel with iron determination when she and Goetz were married on March 19, 1930, in an elaborate ceremony at the Biltmore Hotel. It was a highly regarded social function. All the top people of Hollywood were there. Edith was lavishly outfitted in a gown by Adrian, swanky dress designer at the Metro-Goldwyn-Mayer studio. But she looked at no one—not her mother, not her father, not at any of the guests—only at her future husband, as she walked down the aisle.

With Edith's wedding as encouragement Irene and Selznick decided to be wed, even though Mayer continued to

oppose this with uncompromising disdain. He was so nasty to
Selznick that once the young man rushed out of the house,
telling Irene, "I'll be damned if I'll stay here and let him talk
to *me* that way!"

The issue of planning a big wedding with paternal approval was ruled out by the timely death of Mayer's father on
April 19, 1930, at the age of eighty-three. This humble family bereavement made it appropriate to have a quiet wedding
in the Mayer home, some ten days after the old man's death.
The irony of the son of Lewis J. Selznick marrying the daughter of Louis B. Mayer and of the Selznicks actually being present as guests in the Mayer home did not escape the notice of
pundits in Hollywood. Some of the more romantic were
minded of Montagues and Capulets. The toniness of the allusion would not have pleased the father of the bride.

So within a space of less than two months, in the spring of
1930, the Mayer home was reduced by the aged father and
the two daughters whom Mayer was so loathe to let go. The
emotional change all this brought upon him over the next
few years was profound.

Remember, he was still a comparatively young man—forty-
five, officially—at a point of considerable efflorescence in a
lush community. For the first time in years he had no pressure
of family responsibility. His parents were dead, his brothers
and sisters were more or less out from under his wing. Brother
Rudy was the only one who gave him trouble. He was a sport
and a thorn in Louis' side.

Sister Yetta was remote with her own family. Ida Mae
lived in Hollywood and basked in the growing glory of Louis.
Brother Jerry, obliging and good-natured, had a job at the
studio, acting as purchasing agent and doing pretty much as
he was told.

Now Mayer's daughters had married and moved into homes
of their own. And, to cap it all, he was suffering a slow estrangement from his first adopted "son."

His relations with Thalberg, whom he truly had grown to love in the early years of their association, continued to deteriorate after 1928 under the pressures of frequent disagreements and deep resentments. The coming of sound and the changes this brought in films only added to bickerings over money and the jealousies that were already existent.

The addition of dialogue to pictures necessarily forced and nurtured smarter plots, more subtle emotional complications, and more care in articulating them. The stage, with its wealth of "modern" dramas, became a more important feeder to the screen. The call was for more taste in picking stories, more diligence with working dramatists.

At this there was no one better than Thalberg. He had a superior gift for choosing interesting material and developing it with the proper men. From the theater he drew such dramas as *The Last of Mrs. Cheney, The Divorcée, The Guardsman, Anna Christie,* and *Strange Interlude.* And he brought such witty writers to the studio as Frederick Lonsdale, Scott Fitzgerald, and Moss Hart.

It was generally felt by the artists, the top creative people on the lot, that Thalberg was the animating spirit and the "genius" of Metro-Goldwyn-Mayer. And his coterie of close associates—Bernie Hyman, Al Lewin, Paul Bern, King Vidor, and several others—did the internal boasting for him that he was inherently too modest or too discreet to do.

This praise might have been tolerated and even welcomed by a studio chief who had the internal security to feed his ego on the knowledge of his own worth. But Mayer was plainly a person who needed his share of praise, too, who demanded some positive recognition of what a great man he was.

A clue to his itch for admiration was evident in his playing the role of exalted master of the once-a-year picnics he early established for studio personnel, and at the famous Sunday "brunches" he gave for company executives and selected guests at his Santa Monica home. On these supposedly social occasions he took the limelight in sometimes boorish ways and left no doubt that he expected obeisance as the boss of Metro-Gold-wyn-Mayer.

The fact that he was responsible, in some large measure, for the quality of the films, for the constant accumulation of talent and the energetic operation of the studio, was something that, in all fairness, could not be overlooked. Mayer generally backed Thalberg's inspirations—and he had a few of his own.

He was a strong advocate of Marie Dressler and Wallace Beery, two older stars who were restored to phenomenal popularity in such sentimental dramas as *Emma, Tugboat Annie* and *Min and Bill.* And he was all for Jackie Cooper, a newly discovered child star, whom he took great pride in casting most successfully with Beery in *The Champ.*

But the preëminence which Thalberg enjoyed in his own studio was no intramural secret. It was known all over town, and this inevitably unsettled the vanity of Mayer. The nibbling away at his own prestige that Thalberg cultists did was matched in irritation only by assaults that Thalberg continued to make on the Mayer pocketbook.

The campaign of attrition that innocently started in 1925 was becoming extremely vexatious by 1932. And, in the latter year, other circumstances made it even more galling on Mayer.

For one thing Thalberg was tiring. He had heedlessly driven himself to near exhaustion in trying to maintain some sort of watch over virtually the entire output of the studio. Although this was extremely conscientious it was also unreasonable, and it rendered Thalberg testy and demanding in his relations with Mayer.

In April of that year—three years after he had received a substantial lift in his share of the bonus paid to members of the "Mayer group"—he forced Mayer to give him another six and a half percent of the swag, so as to make an equal division of thirty-six and a half percent to each of them. Robert Rubin would continue to get his original twenty-seven percent. This was another damaging blow to Mayer's pride and his pocket-book. He acceded, again in the knowledge that he would be hard put without Thalberg.

The equanimity of the "genius" was badly unsettled again as the result of a sad occurrence on Labor Day, 1932. Paul Bern, Thalberg's most amusing and probably most stimulating friend, was found dead under circumstances that suggested scandal and mystery.

Bern had been married for only a few months to Jean Harlow, a voluptuous blond star who was then the most recent sensation on the contract list at Metro-Goldwyn-Mayer. Their marriage had caused a twitter, since Miss Harlow was known to have had "romances" with several men and Bern was also regarded as one of the more mysterious males in Hollywood. He paid conspicuous attention to many beautiful and popular female stars but had never been married, so far as anyone knew.

Then, on that Labor Day morning, he was found shot to death on the floor of his home, with a pistol beside him. His small, delicate body was nude. Miss Harlow was not on the premises, having spent the weekend at her mother's house. A note to her in Bern's handwriting mentioned the "frightful wrong" he had done her and that "this is the only way . . . to wipe out my abject humiliation." She must understand, he concluded, that "last night was only a comedy."

The body was found by Bern's butler, who immediately called the studio, which reached Mayer and then Thalberg's residence. Mayer was the first outsider on the scene. He arrived and looked over the situation before notifying police. This was an ugly problem in his studio "family"; he took the foolish precaution of pocketing the suicide note.

When the police arrived, he departed. On his way down the drive he encountered Howard Strickling, head of studio publicity, who was racing to the scene. Mayer gave Strickling the details and then confided that he had the note. Strickling was stunned; he appreciated the enormity of Mayer's offense. He urged his boss to go back to the Bern house and turn the note over to the police. Mayer did so, with some misgiving. He would have preferred to keep the whole business a strictly private affair.

The Bern-Harlow case became another Hollywood sensation. And in this one, Mayer, the lofty moralist, played a powerful behind-the-scenes role. He appeared to give testimony (which wasn't entirely consistent) at the coroner's inquest, and later worked toward discouraging a threatened indictment of Miss Harlow on a murder charge. There were those who had strong suspicions that she had been involved in a plot of some sort against her husband with his former common-law wife! The death of this woman of mystery dramatically occurred in northern California a few days after that of Bern.

The case was the first open scandal to disturb the dignity of Metro-Goldwyn-Mayer, and for this reason Mayer found it distressing. He also didn't want his valuable new star upset. But to Thalberg the affair meant the loss of a dear and stimulating associate. Bern's death shook him severely, his own mortality was exposed.

Tired, depressed, and still unhappy about the money he was being paid, Thalberg rebelled a few days after the death of Bern. He as much as told Mayer he was quitting. Mayer, alarmed, called Schenck. The latter came to the Coast with Robert Rubin, and a series of conversations ensued in which Thalberg scorched the ears of everybody and made exorbitant demands.

Those vituperative conversations, which took place in Schenck's suite at the Biltmore Hotel, were probably as violent and ugly as any that ever occurred among the frequently uncontrolled people of the motion picture industry. Thalberg demanded more money, on threat of throwing up his job. Schenck reminded him he had a contract. Thalberg said to hell with that. Schenck coolly and darkly threatened to see that he was barred from any other studio if he didn't fulfill his contract. Thalberg laughed. What a ridiculous threat, he realized, to make to one as valuable as he!

Mayer and Rubin, although interested, left the battle to Thalberg and Schenck. Even Mayer, who was accustomed to temper, was amazed at the heat of the two men. "It was hell!" he later reported. Finally he and Rubin left the room. For awhile it appeared a rupture of unbridgeable width had been made.

However, Joe Schenck, a friend of Thalberg, of Mayer, and most of Hollywood, was prevailed upon by his brother to talk to Thalberg. Eventually a plan was devised whereby Thalberg would be granted options to buy private issues of Loew's stock at a figure well below the current market price.

When this plan was broached Mayer and Rubin were naturally disposed to feel that they, too, should enjoy some perquisites equal to those that Thalberg might receive. Schenck battled against this suggestion and then Mayer threatened to quit. The problem of pacifying the studio leaders was hard and discouraging for Schenck.

Since this bickering over money was happening right in the time of the Great Depression, it is all the more shocking to realize that these Hollywood people had the gall to be so mercenary. It was evident that they lived in a world of their own.

The crisis was eventually dissipated by an arrangement whereby men of the "Mayer group" were given options to buy large blocks of Loew's stock over a period of six years at ten dollars a share. This device of stock options was familiar in American industry. It was a way of arranging for an executive to pick up stock and resell it, if he wished, at a considerable profit to himself, always gambling on the rise and fall of the stock. Thalberg was given an option to buy a hundred thousand shares; Mayer was given options on eighty thousand and Rubin fifty thousand shares. Loew's stock was selling around twenty at the time.

Of course, the stock option arrangement had to be approved by the board of directors of Loew's, Inc., a rugged hard-bitten group on which sat three men representing the trustees that were administering the large block of William Fox stock. Schenck had to go for approval to Winthrop Aldrich, president of the Chase Bank, who was chairman of the trustees. The arrangement was permitted, since it was made clear by Schenck that the very heart's blood of Loew's, Inc., was pumped into its veins by the studio.

But the irony was that the tempest and turmoil that Thalberg aroused—and the deal that was made to keep him—were soon rendered vain by the physical frailty that helped to bring them on.

Homeward bound from the studio Christmas party that winter (1932) Thalberg became ill. When he arrived home he was in real misery and went to bed with a violent chill. His wife, Norma, called the family doctor, fearing the worst, which was heart disease. Mayer was told and had immediate forebodings. He called at the Thalberg home, then telephoned Schenck.

"Irving is very ill," he warned. "I think you had better come out here right away."

Schenck arrived on the Coast after Christmas and went into huddles with Mayer. It was evident that they would have to devise measures to assure the continued operation of the studio without the presence of Thalberg. They could no longer depend upon one man to be the creative inspiration and overseer of the entire program. In the more then eight years since the merger the studio had expanded so much that it was truly a mass-producing factory—a great hive of motion picture manufacturing. Schenck and Mayer could no longer permit themselves the indulgence of relying upon "the indispensable man."

When Schenck went to call on Thalberg, he was not permitted to see the sick man. It was clear that the bitterness developed in those nightmare sessions in September was not yet gone. Schenck took the rebuff as ominous. He and Mayer, now compelled to close ranks, sat down to plan carefully a whole new program of studio policy.

Mayer felt the organization well supplied with secondary personnel, and even a few reliable supervisors, such as Hunt Stromberg and Harry Rapf. Thalberg's little group of favorites was likewise there to carry on. What was wanting was sufficient top-rank manpower in production to insure a steady flow of first-class films.

Mayer's understanding and foresight of the growth of the industry and of Loew's operation in particular was that of the merchandiser. He knew that New York was demanding pictures to keep the theaters supplied with twice-weekly changes of program—a system which had been going on with little alteration since nickelodeon days.

Faced with this critical requirement Mayer made a bold suggestion. He urged the employment of David Selznick, his aggressive son-in-law to whom he had objected so strongly two years previously. But in that brief time the stubborn Selznick had advanced phenomenally. He had promoted himself into the position of head of the Radio-Keith-Orpheum studio. Under his supervision a number of good films had been produced. He was a highly potential prospect to step into at least one of Thalberg's shoes.

Schenck accepted the suggestion and Mayer approached his son-in-law. Selznick was cautious and cagey about jumping for the job. He wasn't at all certain that he wanted to work for Mayer. He knew that he would be under pressure at the Culver City studio. What's more, he and Thalberg were now close personal friends. It was fairly obvious that the latter might be resentful of his taking the job.

However, a tempting offer of four thousand dollars a week on a two-year contract, along with Mayer's guarantee that he could have his pick of stories, stars, and studio personnel was enough to sway the mind of Selznick. While he was deciding, his own father died. On the way back from the funeral, his mother told him that one of old Lewis J.'s last remarks was "Tell Davey to stick with his own people. They're the only ones you can trust."

Selznick took this as counsel that he should let bygones be bygones and work for Mayer.

When Mayer went to tell Thalberg about it, at his home where he was still confined, there was a terrible battle. Thalberg was infuriated to think that a whole new policy had been formulated and Selznick hired without consulting him. He and Mayer had another furious, abusive fight. Again it looked as though they'd reached a parting. Thalberg all but ordered Mayer out of his home.

Then came an arrangement for Thalberg to take a long leave; his doctors advised that he have a complete and lengthy rest. While his illness was publicly stated to have been an influenza attack it was accompanied by a "mild coronary," according to the doctors' reports. It was agreed that he and Norma and their children—they now had a little boy and a baby girl—should go to Bad Nauheim in Germany, where there was a famous heart specialist. Plans were made for them to leave Los Angeles by ship for New York.

A few days before their departure a long letter arrived from Mayer. It was extraordinary and surprising for two reasons. First, Mayer rarely wrote letters to anyone—even office memoranda. He did not commit himself comfortably to written words. He did most of his communicating by face to face conversations or by telephone.

The second reason this letter was extraordinary—probably unique—was because it contained an apology—a *written* apology—from a man who never apologized.

The composition of this letter must have been the most humble act that Mayer ever performed—at least in his business dealings.

This is how it read:

February 23, 1933

Dear Irving:

I cannot permit you to go away to Europe without expressing to you my regret that our last conference had to end in a loss of temper, particularly on my part. It has always been my desire to make things as comfortable and pleasant for you as I knew how, and I stayed away from you while you were ill because I knew if I saw you it was inevitable that we would touch on business, and this I did not want to do until you were strong again. In fact I told Norma to discourage my coming to see you until you felt quite well.

It is unfortunate that the so-called friends of yours and mine should be only too glad to create ill feeling, and attempt to disrupt a friendship and association that has existed for about ten years. Up to this time they have been unsuccessful, but they have always been envious of our close contact and regard for each other.

If you will stop and think, you cannot mention a single motive or reason why I should cease to love you or entertain anything but a feeling of real sincerity and friendship for you. During your absence from the Studio, I was confronted with what seems to me to be a Herculean task, but the old saying still goes—"The show must go on." Certainly we could not permit the Company to go out of existence just because the active head of production was taken ill and likely to be away from the business for a considerable length of time. I, being your partner, it fell to my lot, and I considered it my duty and legal obligation under our contract, to take up the burden anew where you left off, and to carry on to the best of my ability. I believe I have done so, without prejudice or partiality to anyone in the Studio. My only concern has been to organize things so that we will make the very best pictures possible.

I have felt your absence from the Studio very keenly, and have never consciously done anything that might reflect on you, and this I repeat regardless of what anyone may tell you. Of course, I cannot guard myself every moment as to what I say, and which remarks may be misconstrued by malicious scandalmongers and gossipers who thrive on other people's unhappiness.

I regret very much that when I last went to see you to talk things over I did not find you in a receptive mood to treat me as your loyal partner and friend. I felt an air of suspicion on your part towards me, and want you to know if I was correct in my interpretation of your feeling, that it was entirely undeserved. When I went to see you I was wearied down with the problems I have been carrying, which problems have been multiplied because of the fact that the partner who has borne the major portion of them on his shoulders, was not here. Instead of appreciating the fact that I have cheerfully taken on your work, as well as my own, and have carried on to the best of my ability, you chose to bitingly and sarcastically accuse me of many things, by innuendo, which I am supposed to have done to you and your friends. Being a man of temperament, I could not restrain myself any longer, and lost my temper. Even when I did so I regretted it, because I thought it might hurt you physically.

Regardless of how I felt, or what my nervous condition was, I am big enough to apologize to you, for you were ill and I should have controlled my feelings.

I am doing everything possible for the best interests of yourself, Bob, myself, and the Company, and I want you to know just how I feel towards you; and, if possible, I want you to divest yourself of all suspicion, and believe me to be your real friend, and to know that when I tell you I have the greatest possible affection and sincere friendship for you, I am telling the truth.

I hope this trip you are about to make will restore you to even greater vigor than you have ever before enjoyed, and will bring you back so that we may work together as we have done for the past ten years.

And now let me philosophize for a moment. Anyone who has said that I have a feeling of wrong towards you will eventually have cause to regret their treachery, because that is exactly what it would be, and what it would be on my part if I had any feeling other than what I have expressed in this letter towards you. I assure you I will go on loving you to the end.

I am going to take the liberty of quoting a bit of philosophy from Lincoln. This is a quotation I have on my desk, and one which I value highly:

"I do the very best I know how, and the very best I can, and I mean to keep doing so until the end. If the end brings me out right, what is said against me won't amount to anything. If the end brings me out wrong, ten angels swearing I was right, will make no difference."

I assure you, Irving, you will never have the opportunity of looking me in the eye and justly accusing me of disloyalty or of doing anything but what a good friend and an earnest associate would do for your interest, and for your comfort.

If this letter makes the impression on you that I hope it does, I should be awfully glad to see you before you go and to bid you Bon Voyage. If it does not, I shall be sorry, and will pray for your speedy recovery to strength and good health.

With love and regards, believe me

Faithfully yours,

Louis

Thalberg, being a gentleman and also given to philosophizing, replied in similar vein:

February 25, 1933

Mr. Louis B. Mayer
Metro-Goldwyn-Mayer Studios,
Culver City, California

Dear Louis:

I was deeply and sincerely appreciative of the fact that you wrote me a letter, as I should have been very unhappy to have left the city without seeing you. I was inded sorry that the words between us should have caused on your part a desire not to see me, as I assure you frankly and honestly they did not have that effect on me. We have debated and disagreed many times before, and I hope we shall many times again. For any words that I may have used that aroused bitterness in you, I am truly sorry and I apologize.

I'm very sorry that I have been unable to make clear that it has not been the actions or the words of any—as you so properly call them—so-called friends, whose libelous statements were bound to occur, that have in any way influenced me. If our friendship and association could be severed by so weak a force, I am sure it would long ago have been ruptured by that source.

There are, however, loyalties that are greater than the loyalties of friendship. There are the loyalties to ideals, the loyalties to principles without which friendship loses character and real meaning —for a friend who deliberately permits the other to go wrong without sacrificing all—even friendship—has not reached the truest sense of that ideal. Furthermore, the ideals and principles were ones that we had all agreed upon again and again in our association, and every partner shared equally in the success that attended the carrying out of those principles.

I had hoped that the defense of those principles would be made by my three closest friends. I say this not in criticism, but in explanation of the depths of the emotions aroused in me, and in the hopes that you will understand.

I realize with deep appreciation the effort you have been making for the company and in my behalf, and no one more than myself understands the strain to which you are subjected.

Believe me, you have my sympathy, understanding and good wishes in the task you are undertaking; and no one more than myself would enjoy your success, for your own sake even more than for the sake of the company.

Please come to see me as soon as it is convenient for you to do so, as nothing would make me happier than to feel we had parted at least as good personal friends, if not better, than ever before.

As ever,

Irving

Thalberg also spent several days trying to compose a letter to Schenck, explaining his displeasure at the new studio set-up. He finally settled for a brief and formal note.

Mayer did call to say good-bye to Thalberg before he and his family left. It was a simple farewell, without fireworks. The occasion was solemn, indeed, for it wasn't at all certain when Thalberg would return, if ever he did. Mayer had good reason to be unhappy and apprehensive about prospects ahead.

# 11

Thalberg's painful departure hit the Culver City studio about like the removal of Napoleon to Elba hit the people of France. The man practically worshiped as a creative leader was gone; the man looked upon as guardian for tough business interests remained. How much Mayer would exercise authority in creative realms was unknown. Who would continue in the studio was open to question, too. The whisperers, gossipers, and know-alls—the ones labeled "so-called friends" —who had charged the atmosphere with rumors after Thalberg took to his bed were now in peril. The rupture with Mayer was known, as was the latter's tendency to vengeance. There were few secrets in that studio.

That Mayer took control with little friction, kept Thalberg's friends in their jobs, maintained effective production, and actually stepped up the output of films was all to his credit as a person and as an executive. He honestly maintained faith with Thalberg.

Looking back now it is apparent that the next few years, after the illness of Thalberg removed him from production command, were the stormiest and perhaps the most strenuous period in the experience of Metro-Goldwyn-Mayer, up to the point, some years later, when it all but split at the seams. And plainly this critical period was the toughest and most taxing for Mayer. He went through the valley of the shadow, in more ways than one, in these years.

The onset was clouded with disaster. Barely had the word got around that Thalberg was taking a "leave of absence" from which he might never return than a seemingly calamitous occurrence all but paralyzed Hollywood.

The American film industry had done surprisingly well through most of the national depression that began in 1929. The attraction of the new talking pictures and the peculiarly melancholy fact that jobless people sought sanctuary in dark and comforting theaters (until they were completely out of funds) kept the business going nicely into the black year of 1932. Then, as it came on to winter, attendance at movies plunged.

Some larger chains of theaters lost revenue so fast that they couldn't keep up their mortgage payments and moved toward bankruptcy courts. Some small chains and independent theaters simply quit. The consequent shrinkage in earnings was soon felt in Hollywood.

Then came the crowning misfortune—the stunning "bank holiday" that President Roosevelt ordered right after his inauguration in March, 1933. To many motion picture executives this represented The End. In a matter of days, they figured, the public's cash would be spent, there would be no more theater going, and the movie business would be dead. At best, they could envision a long, painful lay-off ahead.

In this crisis all the courage and tenacity of Mayer, his eternal optimism and his belief in miracles, were exercised to the fullest in attempting to rally Hollywood. And a tougher side of his nature was glaringly revealed—his disposition to ride herd on studio employees.

He was now president of the powerful Association of Motion Picture Producers, the Hollywood arm of the so-called "Hays Office" (Motion Picture Producers and Distributors of America). He had been chosen for this office in 1931, succeeding the somewhat monumental Cecil B. De Mille. So it became his responsibility to marshal the producers and direct them on a common course of action that would presumably save their hides.

This was indeed a challenge, for no sooner had the "holiday" been declared than chaos began to develop in the studios. Universal suspended all its contracts on the claim of a "national emergency." Fox informed its people that it could not pay salaries. Several studios considered immediate closing. Metro-Goldwyn-Mayer had been foresighted: it paid all its people in cash a few hours before the President ordered the banks closed.

Now, in this perilous moment, Mayer had the opportunity to call for the help of an organization that he had nurtured against just such a day. That organization was the Academy of Motion Picture Arts and Sciences, the organization which, today, is mainly devoted to bestowing "Oscars" and keeping track of techniques. Its reason for being valuable in 1933 was because it then had a more significant function which is interesting to trace.

Back in 1927, when the Actors Equity Association was trying hard to organize completely disunited acting personnel in Hollywood, Mayer had a cunning idea which he broached at a dinner in his home to Fred Niblo, the *Ben-Hur* director, and Conrad Nagel, a leading actor in the studio. Why shouldn't there be an organization of the creative elite of Hollywood—the actors, writers, directors, technicians (primarily the cameramen) and, of course, producers—an organization which would serve as a Hollywood bureau of standards and, if need ever arose, a convenient mediator and harmonizer in any disputes involving the crafts?

The idea seemed exciting, not to mention flattering, and the gentlemen proceeded to spread it among important friends. A joint meeting of representatives of the five creative groups was held at the Ambassador Hotel on January 11, 1927. Mayer paid for the dinner and was made chairman of the Committee on Plan and Scope. His lawyer, Edwin Loeb, was commissioned to draw the by-laws. Out of the designs of Mayer's committee the Academy was born.

Its board of directors was composed of representatives of each of the five groups, and membership was by invitation, assuring the Academy of pure cream. Even so, it soon succeeded in obstructing the unionizing of Actors Equity by becoming itself the group spokesman for actors in Hollywood. It also preëmpted the functions of an incipient Screen Writers Guild. Although its numerous mediation services were helpful over the next five years, it was fairly evident that it was oriented to the interests of the producers' group. It was labeled a "company union," on a nice, refined, dignified plane —which, of course, is precisely what the gentleman who conceived it intended it to be.

Thus it was to the Academy that Mayer and the producers turned in a moment of major crisis, when it appeared the film industry was on the verge of disaster because of the depression and "bank holiday." Did it have a suggestion how everybody could get together and save the industry? It did. It immediately recommended that all employees of the studios, from top to bottom, accept a reduction of fifty percent in their salaries for eight weeks. Thus, it said, it would be possible for all studios to continue without shutting down.

This seemed a brilliant suggestion—one that dramatically allowed for a great, sweeping gesture of sacrifice on the part of *everyone* in Hollywood. Mayer immediately called a mass meeting of his studio's employees and put it up to them in an eloquent and tearful oration. They "unanimously" agreed to accept the cut. At least that is how Mayer interpreted their response to his ardent plea. The next day he told newspapers that "ninety-seven percent of the contract film players" in the community had indicated their willingness to go along with the Academy plan.

But it wasn't to be quite that simple. A couple of days went by, then the stagehands, the one group of workers with a union, refused to accept the cut. Resentment and resistance also broke out among low-salaried personnel. They felt that their desperate situation had been overlooked by the Academy, that Mayer and other producers had sold it a bill of goods. It was one thing for a producer or an actor earning four thousand dollars a week to take a reduction to two thousand dollars a week. But for a person earning sixty dollars to be cut to thirty dollars was a terrible blow, and there were plenty of people in the studios earning no more than that.

What was more, many employees did not believe that all the studios were in such dire straits that an across-the-board cut was essential—especially at Metro-Goldwyn-Mayer.

The issue reached a deadlock when stagehands said they would strike. On Monday, March 13, 1933, every studio in Hollywood was closed. The producers rushed into anxious conference with their friends of the Academy, and late that day came up with a formula which proved acceptable. It provided that anyone earning fifty dollars a week or less would not take a cut. Those earning above fifty dollars a week would waive a percentage of their salaries, on a sliding scale, up to fifty percent. Each studio's books would be examined, and wherever justified by evidence of financial capacity cuts would be restored or reduced.

Except for some isolated trouble this formula was made to work. The studios continued in business and full salaries were eventually resumed. But the sudden panic at the outset of the crisis and the Academy's willingness to endorse so quickly a program that would have meant a great saving for producing companies exposed its domination. Conrad Nagel, Academy president, resigned midst loud recriminations. Within a month the Screen Writers Guild was revived as an organiza-

tion apart from the Academy. And, in October, a formidable
phalanx of top performers got together to form the separate
Screen Actors Guild.

Actually the consequence of Mayer's maneuvering during
the crisis of the "bank holiday" was a spirit of rebellion toward the Academy that led to the genesis and strengthening
of the Hollywood craft guilds. And these operations brought
on other ugly battles in which he was involved. The long
post-depression period was one of great labor strife in Hollywood. The collapse of Mayer's "company union" was but the
prelude to his troubles all around.

To be sure, the results of this crisis cannot be blamed
wholly on him. Forces much stronger than the will of one
man were moving the film industry. But certainly Mayer's
cute maneuver to raise the Academy as a device for controlling actors and writers and his encouragement to it to play a
hand in the obvious interests of producers contributed to the
end result. Mayer, in his strategic calculations, was sometimes
shortsighted and naïve.

He frequently underrated the smartness of those with
whom he dealt, possibly because he overrated his own fertile
ingenuity. There was the incident, during this period, when
he had Mendl Silberberg, a Hollywood lawyer, in his office
to convince him that a young star whom the lawyer represented
should take the fifty percent cut.

"These are terrible times, Mendl," he started. "When I
think what terrible times these are, I wonder how anybody
who earns two thousand a week can object to taking a thousand, that's all.

"Let me tell you how hard times are, Mendl. I heard a story
the other day about a collector for the gas company going to
the home of some people to try to get them to pay their bill.
When he got there he found a poor, skinny woman in ragged
clothes and a couple of skinny kids hanging onto her. She
told him she was sorry, she just didn't have any money to pay
the bill.

"Then he smelled something cooking in the kitchen. "You can't pay your bill,' he said, 'but I see you've got money to buy food.'

"With that the poor woman started crying. 'I have to tell you,' she sobbed. 'We're so poor and hungry, this morning we killed our little dog. That's what you smell cooking.'

"Imagine, Mendl, they have to eat their little dog! And we have people in this business who kick about earning a thousand dollars a week!"

Silberberg didn't bat an eyelash. He said he'd send his client to talk to Mayer. But before he dispatched her to the office he told her the extravagant story Mayer had told and advised her to be on the alert, that Mayer might try to wring her heart, too.

Sure enough, she was no sooner in his office and in conversation with him than he started to tell the story of the people who ate their dog. The actress burst out laughing.

Mayer was horrified. "What's so funny?" he indignantly demanded. "How can you laugh at such a thing?"

"I've heard that one," she scoffed.

Mayer was outraged. "That Mendl Silberberg!" he grumbled. "Somebody should cook him!"

He was not amused.

Naturally, for a Republican as tough and tenacious as Mayer, who had seen his friend, Herbert Hoover, routed in the elections the previous fall, the presence of Roosevelt in the White House was a reality that did not ease his mind. He had a sense of being personally affronted by the troubles of the times. And the fact that his friend Hearst had actually deserted Hoover to support this Roosevelt, much against his arguments and urgings, sat heavily on his mind. Thus a studio confusion that came to a head at this juncture further aggravated his annoyance and piled another burden on him.

A new supervisor hired by Thalberg shortly before he became ill was Walter Wanger, a bright young fellow who had been a supervisor at Columbia Pictures. He was something of an oddity in the community. He was a college man, and he didn't mind having people know it. He was also a Democrat. These facts might have aroused Mayer's suspicions and objections, but with Thalberg out he was grateful for whatever manpower the blessing of fortune had bestowed.

Wanger, foreseeing possible trouble, had said to Thalberg when he took the job, "You know the sort of person I am. What do I do about Mayer?"

Thalberg answered blithely, "Don't pay any attention to him."

That seemed a bit disrespectful, but Wanger took the advice. He joined the studio, picked out a story, and proceeded with the preparation of a script. The story was called *Gabriel Over the White House* and, interestingly, had to do with a contemporary American president—a fictitious one, to be sure—who didn't take his office too seriously, who was a bit of a rascal, indeed, until he was hurt in an automobile accident. Then, in a coma, at death's door, he heard Gabriel's horn and had a vision of the sort of president he should be. By the time he recovered, he was a changed man, a sort of Lincolnesque character, determined to help all people and improve the lot of the world. He was regarded as crazy, of course, and efforts were made to impeach him.

Wanger secured Carey Wilson as his script writer. Wilson was one of Thalberg's boys. And when the script was ready Wanger did a sly thing: he took it to Hearst. Hearst was delighted with the story. It appealed to his sense of irony. He arranged for it to be scheduled as a Cosmopolitan production and even wrote some dialogue for it.

On sheets of orange paper he scratched in longhand a remarkably prophetic speech to be delivered by the messianic president in a meeting of peoples from all the world, a sort of League of Nations (which, oddly enough, only a few years previous, Hearst had done everything he could to wreck). The sheets of paper, preserved by Wilson, contain these interesting lines, which bear quotation, if for no other reason than as an example of Hearst's occasionally-enjoyed writing for the screen:

The next war will be a terrible story of the terrible failure of antiquated machinery and antiquated methods and of the horrifying destructiveness of modern agencies of war. Navies and armies will be destroyed from the air, and as these airplanes destroy navies and armies, they will destroy cities, they will destroy populations. Peace and faith are necessary among men, not merely for the welfare of nations but for the very existence of nations. The next war will depopulate the earth. Invisible poison gases, inconceivably devastating explosives, annihilating death rays will sweep to utter destruction not only the men but the children who would constitute another generation and the mothers who would bear them. Unless man's God-given faculty for utilizing the forces of nature for beneficent purposes shall surpass their vicious genius for destruction, the race of man shall perish from the earth and the world will be left to the less destructive, less cruel and less stupid wild animals.

Gregory La Cava was got to direct the picture and Walter Huston played the president. The shooting was completed in eighteen days at a cost of only $180,000. (Another $30,000 was spent for retakes later on.)

So excited was Wanger about the picture that he began talking hopefully of a scheme to have it open simultaneously in four big cities, including New York and Washington, on Inauguration Day.

Then the picture was previewed in Glendale, according to regular routine for all the studio's new films, and Mayer was there with his retinue to see it (and, really, to find out what it was about for the first time). When it was over he strode from the theater like an onrushing thundercloud, grabbed hold of Eddie Mannix, and shouted loud enough for people to hear, "Put that picture in its can, take it back to the studio, and lock it up!"

Wanger was struck with consternation. What was wrong with the film? The audience had seemed to like it. Why did it so annoy Mayer?

The reason was rumored the next day. He considered it a calculated slap at recent Republican presidents—Hoover and Harding, especially. Now, for the first time, he realized why Hearst was so interested in it! The whole thing was a piece of propaganda for the incoming president!

However, Mayer was in a dilemma. He had allowed the picture to be made without really knowing precisely what it was all about. (This was not uncommon with him, especially at that time when he was trying to keep the studio going without Thalberg's guiding hand.) He could not afford to scrap the whole thing. So he ordered a print sent to New York, where it was privately viewed by Nick Schenck and Will Hays, another firm Republican. Word drifted back that they were huddling with "experts" on the international implications of the film. Guarded messages to the studio suggested that changes should be made, that particularly the president's enthusiasm for a world tribunal would have to be toned down.

Wanger resisted these suggestions and urged that the picture be released. Mayer backed and filled with his orders and maintained an air of mystery. People were called to his office and whisperingly told that "he" insists on such-and-such changes. Nobody knew who "he" was. Finally, after much confusion, some cuts were made, some scenes reshot, and prints were sent to distributors a month after Inauguration Day. The public's reaction was normal. The nation had more immediate things to worry about at that particular moment than Hearst's ghostly forecasts of doom. President Roosevelt liked the picture; he had it shown at the White House several times.

As for Hearst's concern about the fuss and bother he had caused by originally sponsoring the film, there is no clear recollection of what it amounted to, but he probably got a

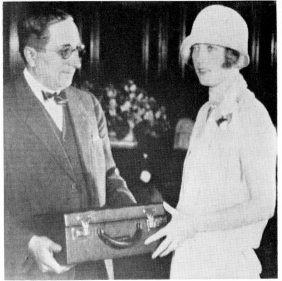

*United Press International*

This photo of Mayer presenting a make-up box to Marion Davies was the first telegraph-transmitted photo sent across the continent by International (1925).

A famous quartet outside the Davies bungalow: Mayer, Charles A. Lindbergh, Edgar B. Hatrick, executive head of Hearst's motion picture interests, and W.R. Hearst.

United Press International

In a fireman's cap, during nationwide tour to promote *The Fire Brigade* (1925).

In the baseball uniform of his favorite institution.

Choosing up sides with his then friendly rival, Irving Thalberg, at a studio picnic.

Culver Service

The beginning of a beautiful friendship. Mayer greets Herbert Hoover, Secretary of Commerce in the Coolidge Cabinet, on his first visit to a motion picture studio.

Former President Coolidge and his wife are shown the Metro-Goldwyn-Mayer lot by Will H. Hays, Mary Pickford, and Mayer.

Culver Service

# THE LADIES, GOD
BLESS THEM!

*Museum of Modern Art Film Library*

Mayer entering the Academy dinner with Jeanette MacDonald (1936).

The lovely Jean Howard, as a Universal starlet.

Ginny Simms.

Mayer with the blond bombshell, Jean Harlow.

Mayer dancing with child actress Judy Garland at studio picnic (1936).

Mayer at his birthday party with Elizabeth Taylor (1944).

Same party, Mayer and Margaret O'Brien.

Proud Grandpa with Judith Goetz, child of daughter Edith (1937).

*Culver Service*

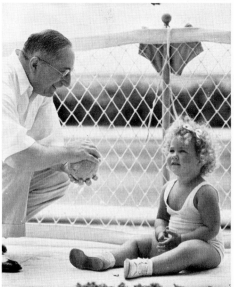

United Press International

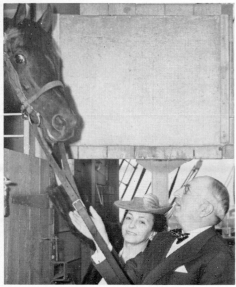

The budding horseman greeting his famous sire, Beau Pere, after the Australian stallion arrived in San Francisco in 1941. Mrs. Mayer looks on.

The lion and the lamb. Mayer escorts the wife of his most hated political enemy around the Culver City lot.

Four men on a bicycle: Edsel Ford, Henry Ford, Mickey Rooney, and Mayer during a visit to Detroit for the opening of *Young Tom Edison*.

Dore Schary with Mayer at the time Schary signed his contract to head up production at M-G-M (1948).

The arch rivals. Mayer at left, Nicholas Schenck at right, with Greer Garson and Mrs. Schenck in between (1947).

*United Press International*

*United Press International*

Dancing with his new wife, Lorena, at the Stork Club in New York (1948).

Mayer received an LL.D. from the University of New Brunswick in 1939. Here, the honorary Doctor Mayer stands with University President C.C. Jones and Mary Kingsley Tibbett, prominent Boston educator.

great deal of amusement out of the upset and embarrassment of Mayer. This was just one further episode in the parting of their political ways.

One thing is certain: the experience did not endear Wanger to Mayer. He sensed that this "intellectual" was deliberately aggravating him.

Thalberg's return from Europe in the summer of 1933 presented the delicate question of his return to the studio. During his long rest in Europe he had conceived the idea of getting back into production with his own independent company. This would do more than free him from the burden of running a large studio; it would make it possible for his accountants to save him a lot of money on his income tax.

He and his family landed in New York in July, and now feeling fit and amiable he went into conferences with Schenck. (It is notable that they studiously avoided summoning Mayer to these conferences.) Thalberg remained under contract to the studio, of course, and it obviously was unlikely that Schenck would release him from that. In the end he was graciously persuaded to return to Culver City as the head of his own producing unit, committed to make some six pictures a year, with the assurance that he might use whatever of the talent and personnel of the studio he chose. He was not to bother himself at all with the rest of the films being made.

"As far as the company is concerned," Schenck told him, "we will be better off, because we will get more money out of that than we would when you spend a great deal of your time on things you don't really have to."

There was to be no change in Thalberg's salary or in his participation in the bonuses of the "Mayer group."

The peril in this arrangement was that Thalberg would run afoul of the competition and ambitions of other producers on the lot. During his eight-months absence Mayer had reorganized the system of production operations along lines that Thalberg had opposed. He had given his supervisors the title of "producer" and had made each one entirely

responsible for the pictures he supervised. Thus David Selznick, Hunt Stromberg, Walter Wanger, Lucien Hubbard,
Harry Rapf, and two or three others of lesser stature possessed an autonomy and prestige that had not been accorded
anybody except Thalberg, and possibly Stromberg, under the
old regime.

This creation of a peerage of producers, a classification of
dukes on a level above directors or any of the other creative
elements in the studio, reflected Mayer's basic inclination
to rely on executives. It also put him in the position of acting
the role of a rajah. He was, in practice, the ultimate ruler,
the court of last resort in matters of story selection, assignment of stars, and budgeting of films. It was he who now
made the decisions that he and Thalberg together had previously made. This inevitably made him the focus of pressures, pleadings, and flatteries.

Sure enough, even though Thalberg was given the guarantee of free choice in the stories he wished to do and in the
writers, stars, and directors he wanted for his films he found
himself having to fight for people from the start and depend
for creative elements upon the willingness of Mayer. At first
this was irritating and mildly discouraging to him. Later, as
he felt himself obstructed, he became indignant.

As early as October he took recourse in writing to Schenck,
voicing guarded resentment against the way he felt he was being treated by Mayer. Down in the body of a long letter
which he termed a "progress report" ("I haven't telephoned
you because I haven't desired to annoy you with any of the
petty difficulties that beset my path," he said), there was this
ominous murmur:

I made a request of Louis, inasmuch as Franchot Tone was dis-
satisfied with the treatment he had been receiving and was insisting on abrogating his contract, that I be permitted to take him
over for a certain length of time. Since he's been with us, he has
been used only in bits and means nothing, and I believed I would
be rendering the company a great service in taking over this man,

meaning nothing, and making him into a star—which I felt I could do.

Louis couldn't see it—and rather than press the matter any further, I dropped it completely.

Thalberg also indicated a sense of shock and dismay at the change in attitudes of the creative people and conditions as a whole in the studio.

"I have never found the men in this institution so completely demoralized and uninspired," he wrote. "Our standards have slipped, in my mind, tremendously. The pictures that I see, while far from bad and some quite good, are juvenile, immature, uninspired, and lacking that finish that characterized our product for so many years. If, however, they are financially successful I presume that is definite proof that we are on the right path. Personally I believe that unless something stringent is accomplished soon, we will be in very grave danger."

He wrote to Schenck again in December:

"The time has come," the Walrus said,
"To speak of many things;
"Of ships and shoes and sealing wax,
"Of cabbages and kings."

The time has come also, I think, for me to write and tell you a few of the difficulties that I see in store for myself and for the company.

I find it very difficult to tell you these things over the telephone —frankly, because you have either gotten to discount my views so much, or you are so desirous of defending and explaining everything that might occur that I find myself in the position of being antagonistic . . .

I want to say at the outset that I am not worried or critical because a few pictures did not go over. That has happened in the past and will happen many times in the future. I am frankly dismayed at the satisfaction that you have expressed and Louis has expressed with pictures and set-ups for the present and the future.

I am not talking now as a heavily interested partner in the enterprise because my voice, as such, has been too frequently overruled to cause it to be offered again; nor am I offering it as the seasoned opinion of an experienced showman whose policies have brought millions of profit to all of his associates and whose advice is eagerly sought after by every company but the one with which he is connected. I am offering it as the opinion of a producer employed by the company—a producer of some merit who is sincerely trying to make some good pictures.

The bitter, sarcastic tone of Thalberg and his pointed allusion to the fact that he was sought by other companies could not have been lost on Schenck.

To me the enthusiasm expressed for mediocre pictures possessing a certain ingredient of obvious audience entertainment, and the wild cheers that accompany pictures possessing considerable merit are disconcerting to the painstaking effort that, as a producer, I might care to exercise.

The difficulties I encounter, as a producer, are specifically an inability to acquire talent and an inability to make that talent give its best efforts. The first is due to the fact that unless I wish to exercise the rights under my contract I cannot get a first-class person employed on our lot.

He told how he had asked for the use of Gene Fowler as a writer; Fowler was teamed with Ben Hecht on a job for Selznick, he said. "I was told it would be weeks before he might be available; then I heard of his being assigned for some rewrites on a Wanger picture and then reassigned to another story with Wanger."

The run-around was repeated. Mayer offered him Hecht, Thalberg said, and then, "two days later, I was informed Hecht was leaving immediately for New York."

"I should have thought that purely accidental were it not so exact a duplication of what happened with Donald Ogden Stewart wherein I assigned him to work with me—he was pulled off the assignment without my being told of it and suddenly restored, only to advise me that he had to leave within three or four days for New York and couldn't finish or even begin either assignment."

Thalberg further complained that, when he tried to get Robert Leonard to direct *The Green Hat,* a remake of Greta Garbo's silent picture, *A Woman of Affairs,* he was casually told that Leonard was being sent to New York; his efforts to get a writer for a remake of *The Merry Widow* were disregarded and he was "forced to work with and give opportunities to the continuously-availables and out-of-work writers that I can pick up."

In all, Thalberg felt very strongly that he was being deliberately obstructed by Mayer, for whom he was rapidly developing an aversion such as he had never known. The two men were reaching a point where they avoided one another as much as they could. Soon came an understanding that disputes would be decided by Schenck.

On behalf of Mayer it should be noted that he had his problems, too. He had to try to dispose the studio's talent as fairly and effectively as possible. That Thalberg was sometimes unreasonable in his requests could not be denied. There were those who occasionally suspected he was merely trying to vex and trouble Mayer.

The latter had this feeling. He subsequently explained: "Thalberg wanted first call on all and every artist on the lot. I told him, 'I will have to throw up my hands, Irving! You ought to be fair. You are going to place me in a position that I am going to flop . . . I will give you every darned thing you want, as if you were my own son, but I've got to run that plant successfully.' "

In one crisis, however, Mayer backed up Thalberg. That was a difficult contention with Hearst as to who, Norma Shearer or Marion Davies, would be given the enviable assignment of playing the heroine in *The Barretts of Wimpole Street.* The popular play had been acquired for Miss Shearer. Then Hearst got the notion that it would be an appropriate vehicle for Miss Davies. Why he or his blond protégé should

have remotely assumed that she could play the delicate role of
the invalid-poetess, Elizabeth Barrett, is hard to understand.
But they did. Mayer firmly supported Thalberg in his insistence that Miss Shearer should have the role. To do otherwise
would have been folly. Hearst and Miss Davies were deeply
miffed. The name of Miss Shearer disappeared from the
Hearst press for quite a while.

Jealousy was an indulgence of more than one or two people
in Hollywood.

Hollywood Rajah

Withal, there was genuine pathos in the steady deterioration of the one-time happy friendship and collaboration of Thalberg and Mayer. The two men had worked so well together in establishing the studio and in developing a trademark reputation of which each, in his way, could be proud that it was a shame—and quite ironic—that circumstances and their natures now prevented them from being cordial companions in the enjoyment of success. But each had his pride and ambitions, his professional interests and his greed, which were thrown into sharp and shattering conflict by increasing complexities of operations in the studio.

The irony was that Mayer wanted, in his willful fashion, to maintain a serene and affectionate relationship with the younger man. He wanted to continue to be his counselor and his champion, as he was in earlier days when the studio was comparatively small. But he envisioned the character of their relationship to be that of father and son, with himself cast unequivocally in the orthodox Jewish father role. This meant, in his deeply founded concept, that his wisdom was unquestionable, his authority was naturally acknowledged, and his word, if he insisted, was law.

Obviously this yearning to play the father came from his need to be respected, appreciated, and admired. It was a psychological hunger that he attempted to satisfy by pretending to act the beneficent parent to one after another younger man. The disposition was a weakness that could easily be played upon by any one willing to flatter and seemingly condescend to him. Many men did. But not Thalberg. His strength and authority were his own, once he discovered and established his ability and power. Thus his determined independence of the paternalistic posture of Mayer disturbed and unsettled the latter as would the rejection of a father by his son.

The fundamental nature of the conflict was one Mayer never seemed to recognize. Why Thalberg turned away from him was something he could not understand. Years later, in looking back upon it, he was still puzzled and dismayed. "He needed me," Mayer would say, with full conviction. "I was his sounding board and wailing wall."

But the anguish of the rift with Thalberg was salved and compensated in part by the satisfaction of helping David Selznick make a fine showing in the studio. Despite his initial resistance and resentment toward this headstrong son-in-law, Mayer was now delighted and exalted by his prowess. In his first few months at Culver City Selznick did *Dinner at Eight,* for which Mayer let him have a liberal budget and unrestrained call on the studio's stars. He used Marie Dressler, Wallace Beery, Jean Harlow, John and Lionel Barrymore, Lee Tracy, Billie Burke, and several others, and fetched forth an impressive film. Mutterings of rancorous friends of Thalberg who circulated the gag, "the son-in-law also rises," did not disturb Mayer. He chortled, "I told you so!"

Selznick followed that with *Night Flight,* starring Clark Gable, Robert Montgomery, and Helen Hayes; and *Dancing Lady,* with Gable and Joan Crawford, one of the studio's most striking young stars. He also began *Viva Villa!* and *Manhat-*

*tan Melodrama* in his first year. By now Mayer was practically convinced that he had *chosen* this brilliant husband for his daughter Irene.

A further chance to play the father presented itself at this time. It concerned the welfare of his other son-in-law, Bill Goetz. Since the latter's marriage to Edith he had been working at Fox, but the connection was not comfortable because of the tension between Fox and Mayer. When Goetz's contract expired late in 1932 Fox did not pick up the option, and the son-in-law was looking for a job.

Mayer went to his house for breakfast one Sunday morning and asked what he was planning to do. Goetz said he was having conversations with Warners and R-K-O. Mayer made the obvious suggestion: why not come to work for him? Goetz thanked him for the offer but felt compelled to decline.

"Why?" Mayer asked him bluntly.

"One son-in-law's enough," Goetz said, mindful of the derision that was just then being hurled at Selznick's head.

Mayer couldn't understand such scruples. "Let me ask you a question," he said. "Suppose we weren't related; where would you want to work most?"

Goetz acknowledged, without hesitation, it would be Metro-Goldwyn-Mayer.

His father-in-law looked at him sharply and a trace of impatience came into his voice. "So you think because we're related you should let *that* stand in the way of your working for the company you *want* to work for?" Such a thing he could not comprehend.

Anyhow, it was thereupon determined that Mayer must do something about Goetz.

Now it happened that Darryl F. Zanuck, a talented and aggressive young man who had been a spectacular "boy wonder" at the Warner studio, was pulling out of that company because of differences with the brothers, Harry and Jack, and was trying to set up an arrangement to go into production with Joe Schenck.

Mayer attempted to lure him to Culver City. That was one thing about Mayer: he was always on the lookout for good people, whenever they might be obtained. His theory was "grab onto a top man any time you can; maybe you don't need him right that minute, but you can always make use of him." And at that particular moment Mayer needed manpower desperately. However, Zanuck wasn't interested in going to work for him. He was biding his time until financing could be assembled by Schenck.

This being the case and financing being hard to come by at the time, right in the depth of the depression, Mayer saw no reason why they should not work out an arrangement advantageous to all concerned. If Zanuck and Schenck would form a company and take in his son-in-law, Goetz, he would put up half the money. The other half could then be obtained.

Obviously such an arrangement (which was kept very hush-hush, by the way) would put Mayer in the position of supporting a producing company that would manufacture pictures to compete with Metro-Goldwyn-Mayer's. The pictures were to be released by United Artists. Whether this slight indiscretion ever bothered him hardly need be asked. His evident concern was to set up a good business for his son-in-law. And besides, if he had any worries they were soon dispelled. Schenck got the balance of the money to start the new company from his loving brother, Nicholas, the president of Loew's, Inc.! Thus the initial financing for the Twentieth Century Company was a matter of family investment on the part of Mayer and Nicholas Schenck.

Each put up $375,000, for which they received the company's stock. Mayer felt that he should make his investment beneficial to others than Goetz. Through one of his many lawyers, Mabel Walker Willebrandt, he set up the Mayer Family Fund as a repository for the Twentieth Century stock. He himself kept a fifty percent interest. The other fifty percent he spread among his two daughters, Irene and Edith, and the latter's husband, Goetz. Irene and Edith each got a quarter of it, for which they gave their personal notes; Goetz, who had also invested a little of his own money, got the remainder—for which, it should be mentioned, he also gave his note.

Mayer had wanted to split that share between his two sons-in-law, thus bringing all four of his "children" into the Mayer Family Fund. But Selznick declined the offer. He wanted none of Mayer's largess. Thus his share was absorbed by the man most interested, Goetz.

Twentieth Century's first production was *The Bowery,* for which Mayer lent the services of Wallace Beery, one of his studio's most popular stars. It was a legitimate arrangement; loan-outs were often made. But it was rare for him to be so generous with one of his biggest stars, especially since he did not get the usual promise of a comparable star in return. He also lent Clark Gable for a subsequent production, *Call of the Wild,* and he put another sizeable investment into the new company. You might say that Mayer was as helpful in getting Twentieth Century underway as he was in adjusting the problems of his own studio in 1933.

Eventual profits were worth it. Twentieth Century prospered from the start and became a major operation when, three years later, it merged with Fox. Stock in the new corporation, Twentieth Century-Fox, was given on a very liberal basis for that in the Mayer Family Fund. And this stock multiplied in value, so that when it was sold and the fund dissolved all family participants reaped small fortunes.

That's what came of fixing up Goetz with a job.

This touching concern for his family, with a little profit on the side, was interestingly paralleled in this period by a new passion that entered his life.

Up to the time that his daughters got married and started homes of their own—and his strangely domineering old father passed to his just reward—Mayer was regarded by companions as a rigidly circumspect man who carefully maintained the morality he so piously and profitably preached. No

one could touch him in his righteous regard for family pro-
prieties. In a business full of lechers and whoremongers he
maintained his boast of purity.

The first actresses he had in his employ were dutifully
treated as employees. He once said of Anita Stewart, "I never
kissed her on the lips," which was a plausible statement. It
was strictly business with her.

But the death of his father, the departure of his daughters
from home, and the inevitable rise of himself to a man of
position and power tended to develop that strange emotional
change that made him susceptible to the more tempting calls
of his trade.

His wife was now settling into a gentle, matronly state,
content to keep house for her husband and anticipate the
pleasures of grandmotherhood. She was not a glamorous
woman, not a striking looking person in any way—just a
pleasant, softly pretty little lady with a quiet, unassuming
dignity. But her husband was in a state of upswing that called
for him to display in every way the vigor and audacity of his
prowess. He had reached the dangerous age.

Ironically, he felt it in the same way his characters had in
those films which he made so much show in producing with
John Stahl. He did not tumble into promiscuity, as he might
have done in the normal operation of his office and the character of his friends. One of his close companions was Frank
Orsatti, a talent agent known as a particularly capable pursuer of high life in Hollywood. That area of the community's
behavior that Mayer had not officially approved now was
opened to him. Orsatti gave wild parties at his place on the
beach, not far from Mayer's home in Santa Monica. Mayer
took to attending his parties—the more intimate affairs given
for a few exclusive favorites where a lot of dancing was done
by the principal guest.

Another of Mayer's pals and preferred friends was the
eminent Joe Schenck, rightly fabled and famous as one of the

heroic hedonists of Hollywood. Schenck was a gargantuan gambler, a lover of the comforts of life, and a particularly capable and candid connoisseur of the female sex. He, too, gave interesting parties where Mayer could have let his fancy roam. But L.B. was not for such loose didos—not yet anyhow. He fell in love.

The lady who aroused his excitement was an actress named Jean Howard, a gorgeous blond who worked for Universal and got small roles. Miss Howard had come to California in the early 1930's in company with Ethel Borden Harriman, a strikingly mannish type who was the daughter of Mrs. J. Borden Harriman, later United States Minister to Norway.

The two had met when they were both in the *Ziegfeld Follies of 1931*—Miss Harriman as performer in a skit taking off Texas Guinan, Miss Howard as one of the show-girl line. The connection is mentioned only because Mayer could not quite understand why the two were inseparable companions. However, he was aware of Miss Harriman's elegant social background (she was a close friend of the then Mrs. Vincent Astor, too), one of the top Newport set. So when the romance with Miss Howard became lively he obliged by hiring Miss Harriman as a scenarist at Metro-Goldwyn-Mayer. After all, Miss Harriman had written a couple of unproduced plays. Mayer had put people on the pay roll as writers who were less qualified.

His meeting with Miss Howard took place at a party of Joe Schenck's and thereafter he was an ardent and devoted pursuer of her. Precisely what he imagined he could arrange is vague, for his connection with his wife was one he obviously did not intend to break. The pursuit was extended over a long period and was, in the view of one of Mayer's close associates, the "goddamndest, silliest romance that ever happened in Hollywood." Here he was, pushing fifty, while she was barely old enough to vote, and his attitude and behavior in the romance appeared to be that of a panting, bumptious youth. In the manner of the story-book romances he was constantly courting Miss Howard. For the first time in his life he was acting a magnificent romantic role.

The novel and wondrous adventure came to an inevitable end in the summer of 1934. Its conclusion was splattered with the sort of seriocomic intrigue characteristic of Mayer.

He and his wife were going to Europe for one of their now frequent trips, and he arranged for Miss Howard to follow in another ship. As a preliminary precaution, he felt it would be wise to have a private detective watch her, just to make sure that nothing went amiss. When Miss Howard arrived at Cherbourg, Mayer was at the dock, full of the romantic ardor of a fiancé. He was somewhat dashed to discover that Miss Harriman was along, but even more distraught by the information his private eye gave him. It was that Miss Howard had seen a great deal of Charles Feldman, a young and then insignificant artists' agent, before sailing from New York.

When Mayer confronted her with this accusation in his suite at the Paris hotel she frankly admitted it—and, what's more, she told him that she and Feldman intended to be married. This was a blow of vast proportions, and Mayer took it in a way that might have won glowing admiration for a hero in one of his films. He allowed that his heart was broken, that there was no point in his going on. His protestations of anguish made quite a rich dramatic scene. The better part of the night he walked the streets of Paris in a daze, accompanied by a silent companion who was the current regular holder of his hand. A few days later Mayer went to Le Havre to put Miss Howard and Miss Harriman on the ship that would return them to New York and to the wedding. He was properly solemn and stoic on this sad occasion. The parting was not dissimilar to that of Armand bidding farewell to Camille.

Miss Howard and Feldman were married on August 25 in a predawn ceremony at Harrison, New York, after a gay dinner party at the Colony Restaurant in New York City. Walter

Wanger was the best man, and others who made the dash to Gretna Green were Paul Warburg, Clarence Brown, the Metro-Goldwyn-Mayer director, and, of course, Miss Harriman.

With anyone less determined and relentless than Mayer this would have been the conclusion of the affair. In the tradition of the good loser he would have bestowed his congratulations and good wishes, and let it go at that. But Mayer was not a good loser. In this area he could not generate the benevolence of one of his noble characters. Although he manifested no resentment toward the magnificent Miss Howard, he was bitter toward Feldman and thereafter instituted a campaign of excluding him from operating as an agent in the whole of Hollywood. Not only did he keep him from serving clients at Metro-Goldwyn-Mayer, but he used his influence to keep others from doing business with the daring young man. The attempt to annihilate Feldman was notorious in Hollywood and was a cause for subsequent amusing and ironic developments.

Meanwhile, the disappointed suitor was confronted with other woes which seemed now to crowd upon him in this time of emotional strain. Suddenly, and without preindication of weakness, his wife was seized with an illness that might have been regarded as a solemn warning to him. The two were still in Europe when an indisposition required her removal to a hospital in Paris. Her husband was in London at the time. When he heard she was ailing he flew to her. His constant dread of illness swept over him. As Mrs. Mayer seemed to grow worse he summoned the most renowned physicians he could get. From London he dragooned Lord Horder, the Prince of Wales's doctor, so forcefully that the startled peer was compelled to cancel a scheduled radio talk to the nation to fly to Mrs. Mayer. Not content with that attention, Mayer the next day got Lord Dawson of Penn, King George V's physician, to fly to Paris to examine his wife. The battery of royal attendants apparently did well by her. The "double

pneumonia with complications" that was said to be her ail-
ment was pronounced waning the day after Lord Dawson of
Penn arrived.

Apparently the shock was sufficient to cause Mayer to reassess his domestic posture—for a brief while. His wife was
thereafter a semi-invalid.

Now he was due for another and even more disagreeable
shock. This came from his much admired and impressive
friend, William Randolph Hearst. Hearst was also in Europe
that summer, making one of his sultanesque swings with Miss
Davies and an entourage of gay companions through the political and social capitals. Mayer, impressed and troubled by
reports he had received of this new man, Hitler, in Germany,
causing trouble for Jews, wired to Hearst and suggested that
Hearst should visit Hitler and try to dissuade him from such
unpleasant practice. In his estimation Hearst had the persuasiveness and prestige to do this job. Hearst did go to see
Hitler. The anxiety of Mayer was mentioned, but Hitler
pooh-poohed the notion that he wanted to cause the Jews
trouble. This was accepted as sufficient assurance by Hearst.

A week or so later Mayer sent a more urgent message to
Hearst. He had been giving some thought to the presidential
campaign that would be coming in two years, and he was
hopeful that Hearst was now prepared to reassess his consideration of Herbert Hoover as the most likely Republican
candidate. Even though Hearst had supported Roosevelt in
1932, it was Mayer's feeling that he should have been disillusioned by the record of the new President in two years.

Hearst's reply to this bold suggestion was characteristically
blunt. In a telegram sent through Harry Crocker, his secretary on the trip, he made it clear to Mayer precisely where
he stood:

Dear Louis: I am sorry but I cannot conscientiously support that
man. He is selfish and stupid. He injects himself into the present
situation for his own advantage. He will harm his own party,
handicap the whole conservative movement, and strengthen the

hands of the radicals. He has said nothing which has not been said better before and he accomplishes nothing but to make millions of people feel that the present incumbent (Roosevelt) would be immeasurably better than this discredited failure . . . If you don't suppress this hoodoo, your party will lose its chance, too, of electing a Congress as well as a President. His name is an anathema to the American public. W.R.

This slashing denunciation of Hoover, whom Mayer continued to admire with a stubborn bourgeois idolatry similar to that he had for Hearst, came as a saddening disappointment. Mayer was not too surprised at the rejection, but he was deeply hurt at the abuse of his friend. The fizzle of his romance, the ominous illness of his wife, and this renunciation upset him.

And still more aggravations were in store. He and his wife were homeward bound from Europe when word reached him on the ship that the political situation in California was taking an amazing turn. It was a state election year—an election of governor and state legislature that fall—and it was suddenly beginning to look as though the Democratic candidate for governor, the ex-Socialist Upton Sinclair, might win.

This was terrifying to people in the motion picture industry, because Sinclair was frankly campaigning on the promise that he would seek heavier taxes on higher income brackets and special taxes on movie studios.

The horror of this possibility was the sole impression upon most wealthy individuals in the Hollywood community. Sinclair's theme of poverty in California did not impress them. They were living in incongruous wealth in the midst of cruel poverty.

In Los Angeles County, alone, there were some 300,000 unemployed, due to the effects of the depression and the growing deficiencies of productive industry. These were mainly white-collar people of the lower middle class who had been attracted to the area in the 1920's boom and were now stranded.

Sinclair appealed to these elements with the promise of taxes to provide relief. His Republican opponent was Frank Merriam, an ex-Iowan prohibitionist and bluenose who had nothing in common with the motion picture industry. But the horror of higher taxes brought most of the people of the industry into the campaign on his side.

It was to this situation that Mayer was coming home.

In New York he was confronted with another blow. Nicholas Schenck informed him that he had hired a man named Sam Katz to go out to the Culver City studio as an arm of management. Katz had a solid reputation in the industry as a particularly shrewd operator. With Barney Balaban and the latter's brothers he had built a powerful theater chain in the Chicago area, then had sold out his interest shortly before the depression hit hard. He was known as an opportunist. Mayer knew he was someone to watch. And the fact that he had been chosen by Schenck at a time when Mayer himself was having trouble running the studio did not contribute to Mayer's peace of mind. They went out on the train together. Who was watching whom?

The defeat of Sinclair was the first order of business on the agenda of Mayer. He approached it with the headfirst onrush that he gave to such matters. Within a few days after his arrival word went through the studio that everybody earning more than one hundred dollars a week was expected to contribute one day's pay to the Merriam campaign. Mayer was not blessed as the originator of this exceedingly partisan and undemocratic idea. But the fact that he would be able to know who contributed and who did not acted as quite a persuader on behalf of Merriam.

Insidious, too, was another high-handed expedient which was originated in the Culver City studio. This was the production of a pseudo-newsreel, called *The Inquiring Reporter*, which was supposed to give typical responses of average citizens to the candidacy of Sinclair. Housewives "interviewed" told how they feared the loss of their homes if Sinclair was elected, bearded and sneering characters were shown hissing in broken English that they were all for the ex-Socialist, bums were shown riding on freight cars supposedly arriving in California to be on hand for the enjoyment of largess when Sinclair was voted in. The material was photographed honestly, but the production was slanted to give a fearful notion of what would happen. *Inquiring Reporter* reels were given free to theaters and were shown all over the state.

"The industry would not have dared show (these films) unless it had a supreme contempt for the intelligence of its patrons," Douglas Churchill of the New York *Times* later wrote, ". . . a contempt that appears justified, for political leaders attribute Sinclair's defeat to the splendid work on the part of the screen."

The power of graphic persuasion was too much for Sinclair's Epic party. Its candidate was defeated by 1,100,000 to 875,000. However, there is still a suspicion that the election was stolen from him by fraud. Ironically, one of the first acts of Governor Merriam was to pass an income tax law, and again Hollywood nabobs began bleating that they would have to move to Florida. They never did.

It has always been generally believed that *The Inquiring Reporter* was one of the major manifestations of Machiavelian means employed by Mayer. But this piece of mischief was not invented by him. True, the bogus "newsreel" was photographed and edited by a Metro-Goldwyn-Mayer crew, headed by one of the contract writers who was assigned the job on a strictly hush-hush basis, and preparation went through the laboratory at the studio. But the individual who ordered the production and took the responsibility was not Mayer. The latter had not returned from Europe when the reels were begun. The responsible party was Irving Thalberg, himself a stanch Republican. This was his only adventure into the realm of politics. It is odd and significant that credit for one

of the most deceitful maneuvers of the motion picture industry in public affairs should not be placed at the door of the
man who organized it but at the door of Mayer.

The accumulation of problems in this dark year of 1934
was not yet completed. Hearst, who returned from Europe
about the time that Mayer did, was still in a peevish humor
vis-à-vis his friend. And Mayer's disposition toward him was
not pleasant. He had a persistent rankling because of the
Hoover telegram, and he was further aggravated by the fact
that Hearst paid a call on President Roosevelt at the White
House and spent a night there before returning to the Coast.
This was close to treachery, so far as Mayer was concerned.
Hearst was too big for him to punish, but he was not in an
amiable mood.

By a fateful coincidence there came up at this point another incident such as that over *The Barretts of Wimpole
Street*. While Thalberg and Norma Shearer were in Europe
in 1933 Robert Rubin had purchased screen rights to the
Stefan Zweig novel, *Marie Antoinette,* to be made into a vehicle for Miss Shearer. A lot of money had been spent on it and
a great deal of preparation had been made in the course of
one year. Even though the script was not ready and the full
matter of costumes and such had not been completed, the
film was on Thalberg's schedule for Miss Shearer.

But upon the return of Miss Davies in October, she and
Hearst suddenly demanded that this property be made available for her. After visiting many of the palaces in Europe,
they had decided that Miss Davies should play the role of the
famous French queen. It was a highly unlikely role for her,
and suspicion is strong that Hearst, vexed at Mayer and
things in general, merely used this demand as a pretext for
causing trouble.

But this time there was no "give" whatsoever in Mayer. It
wasn't a case of protecting Thalberg and what he desired.
"Pop" was not going to browbeat him. Indeed, he threw a

slight harpoon at Hearst by making a proposal which he knew Hearst would reject.

All this time Cosmopolitan productions were financed by Metro-Goldwyn-Mayer, with Hearst sharing in profits and Miss Davies receiving her salary to boot. Now Mayer made the bold proposition to let them have *Marie Antoinette, if* Hearst would pay the cost of production. The great publisher flatly declined, as Mayer anticipated, and the titans had reached an impasse.

The Cosmopolitan contract with the studio being about to expire, Hearst made a sudden gesture toward Jack and Harry Warner. There had been frequent rumors that Hearst was contemplating moving to the Warner studio. Now he made a deal. Within a few days it was settled that Cosmopolitan would move. The famous Marion Davies bungalow was disassembled, and in three huge sections was moved all the way across Hollywood to Burbank and the Warner studios. The passage of this strange caravan through the heart of the colony was somewhat like an historic parade—the visible token of a high-level change involving not only picture making but social prestige and politics. Anyone of an analytic nature might have sensed a transition here.

The commercial association of Mayer and Hearst thus came to an end, although they were not to abandon their friendship. But the old glamour of the 1920's was gone. More than Hollywood had changed in the ten years of their relations. So had Louis B. Mayer.

The incident brought no improvement in the attitude of Thalberg toward Mayer. The two were still antagonistic within the studio. And, on more than one occasion, Thalberg let Mayer know the sharpness of his steel.

A particularly cutting incident was in the experience of the production of *Mutiny on the Bounty*. Film rights to the popular novel by Charles Nordhoff and James Norman Hall had been acquired by Frank Lloyd, a director, and his agent, Edward Small, for the tiny sum of $12,500. They wanted to sell the property to Metro-Goldwyn-Mayer, with the proposal that screen rights would be contributed if Lloyd was hired to direct the film. While Thalberg was in Europe Walter Wanger got interested and begged Mayer to let him make the deal and produce the property with Robert Montgomery in the role of Fletcher Christian. But Mayer was dead against it. He didn't like the idea of a mutineer for a hero. And he said it would be too expensive.

But when Thalberg returned and was resuming, Lloyd and Small took the property to him. He was enthusiastic for it and insisted on making the deal. Mayer waited to see what would happen. What happened was memorable. Thalberg produced an excellent picture that was a huge success. The experience was sometimes privately mentioned as a reflection upon Mayer's judgment.

There was also disagreement over the production that Thalberg wished to make of Shakespeare's *Romeo and Juliet*. Mayer opposed the idea. He said it would cost too much the way Thalberg wanted to make it. And he feared Shakespeare wouldn't please the mob. Thalberg stubbornly insisted. He calculated he could do the picture for $900,000. On the promise that he would bring it in at this unlikely figure he got the approval of Schenck. Again Mayer waited to see what would happen. What happened this time was a film that cost more than $2,000,000 and which, while it made prestige, lost almost $1,000,000 for the studio. This was not the sort of vindication that Mayer felt he could afford. Furthermore he had committed the indiscretion of getting a bit enthusiastic about *Romeo and Juliet* when he saw the finished film.

The hopeless division of the two men was completed in 1935, when Thalberg engineered an arrangement to make himself wholly independent of the studio. Although his contract bound him to the existing regime until December 31, 1938, he manifested his impatience and his long desire to be free by taking legal steps to have his own company after that date. He would release his films through Loew's, Inc., but otherwise he would be entirely separate from any association with Mayer.

By the terms of his arrangement the contracts of several stars, including Norma Shearer and the Four Marx Brothers, would be assigned to his company, "together with the contracts of any other artists, supervisors, directors, and writers who might be engaged" by Thalberg for work in his producing unit prior to January, 1939.

This gave legal sanction for Thalberg to recruit and develop his own personnel during the intervening period. Mayer objected to this, as he naturally would, since it gave Thalberg possession of any new stars or other talents he might develop through the studio. He opposed its exercise in the several contracts that Thalberg wanted to draw. This only added further to friction.

The events of the next few months were hectic, with the cloud of this impending split casting a heavy shadow of unpredictable menace over the future of the studio. Thalberg stayed virtually isolated from the authority of Mayer, pursuing his own production schedule as though he were already on his own. He completed *Mutiny on the Bounty,* and *Romeo and Juliet,* and he started *A Night at the Opera,* with the Marx Brothers, and an ambitious and costly production of *The Good Earth,* based on Pearl Buck's novel. He had projected a production of *Camille,* with Greta Garbo to play the tragic heroine and a new young man, Robert Taylor, to have the role of dashing Armand. Other projects and, of course, *Marie Antoinette* loomed in the offing.

But all of these projects and the turmoil of ugly conflict with Mayer came to an end for Thalberg in September, 1936. He had spent the Labor Day weekend with friends at the Del Monte Club in Monterey—one of his favorite places—and had returned home with a bad cold that was done no good when he went a few nights later to help put on a Jewish festival production in the Hollywood Bowl. The strain and

exhaustion of his energies over the past few years were finally
making their assertions. Pneumonia set in, and in a few days
—on September 14, exactly two weeks after he had contracted the cold—he was dead.

Mayer, with appropriate formality, went to the Thalberg
home as soon as word reached him of Irving's passing. He
spoke his condolences to Norma and shed a few facile tears.
To one of Thalberg's intimates he said he had lost a son.

But that night, a distinguished director whose integrity
and temperance are unimpeachable was shocked to discover
Mayer at the Trocadero, a Hollywood night club, dancing
violently, frenziedly.

"It was almost as though he was performing some barbaric
rite," the observer said.

**13**

After the death of Thalberg there was some speculation in Hollywood whether Metro-Goldwyn-Mayer would continue to try to produce high-quality films. The opinion of sideline observers was that Thalberg had set the sights of the studio on productions with character and class. It was he, they logically reckoned, who had sparked the strong pictures of the past—the Lon Chaney films, the Vidor classics (most notably *The Big Parade*), the Garbo dramas, and, more recently, *The Barretts of Wimpole Street*, *Mutiny on the Bounty*, and *The Good Earth*. With him gone, the expectation was that pressure from New York would prevail—that the studio would be devoted to grinding out a mass of routine, low-grade "popular" fare.

Almost at once the handwriting seemed to be creeping across walls. The well-organized Thalberg unit was deliberately dismantled by Mayer. Bernie Hyman, the Pythias to Thalberg's Damon, was detached to complete the *Camille* that was being made with Garbo and Robert Taylor and to proceed with another Garbo picture, *Beloved* (which was never made). Hyman also got the assignment to put finishing touches on *The Good Earth,* the last Thalberg "Oscar" winner (Luise Rainer's performance as the Chinese woman) and his final memorial.

Hunt Stromberg was set to finishing *Maytime,* an ambitious musical with Jeanette MacDonald and Nelson Eddy. Promptly, Edmund Goulding, Thalberg's choice as director, was pulled off, indicating another disagreement now settled as Mayer wanted it to be. The Marx Brothers' *A Day at the Races* was left to director Sam Wood, with Lawrence Weingarten as producer. Weingarten, who had been married to Thalberg's sister, Sylvia, and was originally a "Thalberg man," was later divorced from Sylvia and had become a Mayer partisan. He was, as a consequence of this conversion, a subsequent favorite of the studio head.

Most significantly, Albert Lewin, who had been Thalberg's loyal slave as chief production assistant, was not assigned. Since circumstances made it obvious that he was being snubbed by Mayer, he resigned, and everyone calculated that he was the victim of the well-known revenge. (Peculiarly, a few years later Mayer made peace with Lewin and brought him back to the studio to produce, citing specifically his loyalty to Thalberg as a good reason for respecting and rewarding him. The ways of Mayer were as inscrutable as are the ways of God!)

But those who assumed from the break-up of the Thalberg unit that the studio would drop the "Thalberg type" of picture did not reckon Mayer's own love of "class," a persistent enthusiasm he had had from the time he began producing films. He may not have had the intuition or taste that Thalberg possessed; certainly he wasn't as creative as Thalberg was. But he wanted to make "first-class" pictures with good material and distinguished casts, and he was willing to spend studio money for what he considered—or hoped—was good. His one philosophy as head of production was to seek out and hire potential talents and give them opportunities to prove themselves.

Also Schenck was no less determined to have top quality films sent along to his salesmen and theaters by his big Culver City studio. He backed Mayer's wholesale hiring program, so long as he was satisfied the company was getting worthwhile pictures and was showing a sizeable profit every year. His constant caution, which was not too insistent, was against what he called "extravagance."

One project of unmistakable costliness that he insisted Mayer now justify was Thalberg's and Rubin's investment in *Marie Antoinette*. Close to four hundred thousand dollars had been spent on screen rights, script, and the furnishings and costumes to be used in the French historical film. Ed Willis, head of the property department, had been sent to France to ransack the shops of antique dealers. He came back with a veritable treasure of furniture. Further, both script and production were custom tailored to suit the person of Norma Shearer, slotted to play the French queen. But after the death of her husband, Miss Shearer announced that she intended to retire.

No doubt the pretty actress was deeply stricken by her husband's death. They had been rightfully regarded as one of the happiest couples in Hollywood—well-adjusted, with two nice children and compatibly successful careers. And, of course, there was no question that Thalberg had done much to give his wife the special opportunities and attentions that helped to make her one of Hollywood's top stars. She well might have reckoned that, without him, she would have a tougher time, particularly if Mayer was disposed to exercise his lust for vengeance.

There was also a ticklish legal question of what share the Thalberg estate would have in future disbursement of profits that accrued to the "Mayer group." Miss Shearer and her attorneys, brought in to replace Edwin Loeb who had been local attorney for Thalberg as well as for the studio, maintained the estate was entitled to receive the full share that Thalberg would have got had he lived and continued to fulfill his contract. Mayer and Rubin held it shouldn't receive anything. This really did not stand to reason or justice, since the films Thalberg was making when he died would be returning profits, presumably for a number of years. Thus the old bickering over money was resumed, even with Thalberg in his grave. Until this matter was settled, Miss Shearer was obviously not going back to work.

The contention was long-drawn and bitter. Mayer's attorneys were adamant and Miss Shearer's were equally stubborn. Finally Schenck got disturbed, being concerned for the morale of studio people and for the fate of *Marie Antoinette*. He issued orders to settle the matter when he learned that many of Thalberg's friends, producers and key executives, were disgusted with what was going on. Mayer was compelled to accept a settlement whereby the Thalberg estate would receive his full share of profits paid the "Mayer group" up to the conclusion of its contract at the end of 1938. Thereafter the Thalberg estate would receive four percent of net profits earned by the pictures more than half completed in the period from April, 1924, through December, 1938. (By this arrangement the Thalberg estate is still receiving money from Metro-Goldwyn-Mayer on films leased to television.)

A further and major condition of the settlement was that Miss Shearer would return to the studio on an exclusive contract to make six pictures at a salary of $150,000 each, which was what she was getting for her services at the time Thalberg died. Her first film, by common agreement, was to be *Marie Antoinette*, which justly turned out to be a "classy" and profitable enterprise.

By now Mayer had worked a transformation of a sort not improbable for him. He had made himself accomplish a change in attitude, not only toward his associates but even toward enemies. Where he had previously been violent, stubborn, arrogant, and unmercifully rude, he softened and was considerate of others. Indeed there were those who felt he was trying to cast himself in the mold of the courteous and contemplative executive Thalberg was at the peak of his popularity.

Perhaps he was. Perhaps the realization that a part of Thalberg's success lay in his way of treating people, pleasantly and considerately (except when he, too, was cold and ruthless), had worked into Mayer's tough brain. Perhaps a twinge of conscience was secretly troubling him.

A share of credit for this transformation was taken by Al Lichtman, whom Schenck had sent to the studio as a sort of observer and trouble shooter in the summer of 1936. Lichtman, one-time promoter of Alco out of which Metro was born, had a background of varied experience and a long familiarity with Mayer. He was also respected by the latter— at least, a little more than was Sam Katz, who was looked upon with dark suspicion as a self-serving spy for Schenck.

In a few months of observation before and after Thalberg's death, Lichtman concluded that Mayer was much to be criticized. He reported to Schenck in private that although Mayer was no doubt a brilliant man, with vision and understanding in the business of manufacturing films as well as a fervor for investing in talent in every phase of production, to the point of extravagance, he was also a careless manager, a favorer with stubborn likes and dislikes, and a braggart who wasted his time and the time of others telling them what a great man he was. This was Lichtman's opinion, dutifully transmitted to Schenck. It is doubtful that it included anything the latter didn't know.

Anyhow, Schenck requested that Lichtman try to have a talk with Mayer, to see if he couldn't persuade him to change his ways a bit. Lichtman made a date to have breakfast with Mayer and came directly to the point.

"Louie," he said, "I am requested to speak frankly to you. Now don't get mad. You have a violent temper and so do I.

So it won't do any good if either of us loses his temper. But there are facts we must face."

Whereupon he proceeded, without pulling punches, to tell Mayer that he was in a precarious situation, that things were in grave disorder, that morale was low, and that Mayer's associates, even some he thought his closest, were seriously put out with him.

Mayer became livid with anger and refused to believe what Lichtman said.

"You mean the men I work with hate me?"

"That's what I mean," Lichtman said.

Mayer raged at Lichtman's indictment. "I am going to find out!" he said.

"You do that," Lichtman told him.

Apparently Mayer did. And apparently some of his associates indicated that Lichtman was right. A noticeable change in deportment did come over Mayer, and for a short time— but time enough to matter—he was elaborately considerate and polite.

His major operational maneuver after Thalberg's death was to strengthen the executive-producer system that he and Schenck had evolved when Thalberg was taken ill. Now he further organized the studio into larger executive units, each responsible for a block of films per year. These larger units, with their corps of producers, writers and directors, were placed under an executive board which met once or twice a week to discuss stories and pass on production plans. This board was composed of studio executives. Its head was the omnipotent Mayer.

Sam Katz was in charge of one unit, responsible mainly for musical films. Lucien Hubbard and Joe Cohn had another which correlated production of low-budget pictures. Al Lichtman, Hunt Stromberg, and Sidney Franklin were commissioned to handle top-quality dramatic films, with the latter elevated from director to producer of *Marie Antoinette*.

This arrangement and the designation of a power of decision to the executive board appeared to be a surrender of a certain amount of authority by Mayer. It presumably gave his associates more voice in studio output. Their considered opinions and decisions theoretically became the long-range and over-all determinants of studio policy. But the board's approvals and disapprovals never departed far from the wishes of Mayer. And when he chose to be noncommittal on certain projects, he was conveniently fortified with excuses in case those certain projects did not pan out successfully.

Also some individuals firmly and silently believed that "production by committee" was discouraging to artistry in films. They held that the need of obtaining majority approval of a group of men who were more or less cautious or condescending to the apparent moods of Mayer had the effect of nullifying inspiration and audacity and tended to introduce monotony into the studio product.

There was, in truth, a certain sameness to the pictures of Metro-Goldwyn-Mayer in the decade of executive-board influence following Thalberg's death. They acquired a consistent slickness, a plush and expensive look, but possessed not many fresh or daring ideas. They were big, melodious, magnificent, but usually romantic and predictable. Someone described their common quality as "expensive vulgarity." This comment was undoubtedly a reflection of the conventional and cautious attitudes of the executive committee, taking its cue from the well-known tastes of Mayer.

Under the circumstances he was now able to enjoy the full satisfaction of feeling himself the benevolent studio head. Although he shared authority for decisions he was the recognized boss, absolute and unquestioned, and he conducted himself as one. His appearances on the lot, when he descended from his office in the executive wing, were precipitate and commanding, as befitted a busy, important man. He always seemed absorbed in some problem. He rarely spoke to anyone in studio streets. As one employee put it, he usually proceeded with "the air of a man on his way to give somebody hell."

And yet he was generally looked up to and even admired by lesser employees, who were glad to have a man of evident confidence and authority as the head of the studio. In such an uncertain business as the manufacture of films it was comforting to feel that a definite mogul controlled the company's destinies.

Mayer himself got great enjoyment from exercise of power and from feeling himself responsible for advancement of someone's career. "I've taken this boy and I have made a great actor (or director or producer) out of him!" That was one of his favorite and oft repeated remarks. He felt he needed to make people grateful and beholden to him. He literally bathed in the sunshine of his own self-esteem.

One of the famous beneficiaries of his good offices was Mervyn Le Roy, whom he hired as a high-priced producer in 1937—the year that Mayer made a memorable trip abroad. Le Roy had been working at Warner Brothers and was married to Harry Warner's daughter when Mayer pulled him away with an offer of $300,000 a year. The figure was so stupendous that it was officially announced at $150,000, so other producers on the lot would not yell.

Le Roy had made a reputation with such bold and hard-hitting Warner films as *Little Caesar, I Am a Fugitive from a Chain Gang, Anthony Adverse,* and *Oil For the Lamps of China*. His first job at Culver City was a feeble item called *Dramatic School,* which helped to tumble its star, Luise Rainer, from the brief eminence she had obtained. After that he did the charming but fanciful and escapist *Wizard of Oz,* which was a perfect example of the sort of film Mayer adored. Le Roy was inevitably regarded as a favorite of the studio head.

Mayer's trip to Europe in the summer of 1937 was primarily aimed to permit him to conduct an inspection of a new producing facility that Loew's, Inc., had leased near London at the Denham studios. But it was also a fitting opportunity for him to go on a talent-buying spree and a particularly appropriate occasion for him to spread himself royally.

This was significantly a "stag" trip. Mrs. Mayer was left at home. His Number 1 traveling companion was his sultanesque friend, Joe Schenck. They sailed in the *Rex,* which was appropriate, accompanied by a retinue of assistants and court attendants, which included Benny Thau, the head of the studio's talent department; Howard Strickling, the publicity chief who was Mayer's inseparable companion on trips abroad; and Lou Wertheim, an operator of gambling casinos and a particular pal of Joe Schenck. Whatever melancholy memories Mayer may have had of his previous trip abroad, when his romance with Jean Howard was blighted, would be canceled in this company.

First item on the agenda was to see a famous blood specialist, Dr. Isidore Snapper, in Amsterdam. Joe Schenck was suffering from arthritis and his brother's physician in New York, Dr. George Baehr, recommended that he see Dr. Snapper. So a message was fired to Laudy Lawrence, the Loew's, Inc., manager on the Continent, to make an appointment with the famous specialist.

Potentate powders were working. Dr. Snapper was in Norway on a fishing trip. This word was sent back to Mayer, who replied that Snapper was to be got or somebody would be sorry. Lawrence called the doctor's daughter to plead with her. Now it just so happened that the daughter had a friend, a musician, who she hoped might get a chance to go to America. When she learned that two such important motion picture men as Louis B. Mayer and Joseph Schenck wanted to see her father, she arranged to get him back to Amsterdam.

Going over on the ship Mayer had decided that he should have a check-up, too. If his friend was to have that attention so would he. Dr. Snapper found Mayer in rather run-down condition and prone to certain cardiovascular complaints, which, considering his strenuous business responsibilities and his extensive social activities, was not surprising.

Among the amazing things the doctor discovered was that Mayer played golf occasionally—but not as normal people play it. Mayer played golf with five balls going at one time and three or four caddies out spotting or trailing along with his clubs. He saw no point in playing with just one ball. If you were going to take all that time and do all that walking you might as well make it worth-while. As a consequence, when he played nine holes he took as many strokes as the normal player would take on forty-five. Dr. Snapper thought this too strenuous exertion for a man of his age and body build and warned Mayer against it. Mayer said to heck with one-ball golf.

Dr. Snapper then advised him that he was pushing himself too hard and suggested that he develop an outside interest which would permit him to relax. The sport of kings was casually mentioned—the breeding and racing of horses, that is. "Many wealthy men find it fascinating," said the doctor. "For instance, the Aga Khan." The association was graceful. Mayer said he would give it some thought.

Checked out as reasonably healthy, the traveling companions and their retinue went to London, where all was in readiness to receive them at the Denham studio. The Metro-Goldwyn-Mayer unit was set up with Ben Goetz, brother of Mayer's son-in-law, in charge of operations and Michael Balcon, a courteous Englishman, engaged to produce the first picture, *A Yank at Oxford,* with Robert Taylor as star.

Immediately, it was apparent that Mayer and Balcon would not get along. Mayer, in his wish to let everyone know who was boss, put on quite a show. He charged around the studio being very critical and severe, and took exception to Balcon's hiring an unfamiliar English actress to play the second female lead. (She was Vivien Leigh.) He completed the break with the producer by standing in an open window, where he could be clearly seen and heard, and bawling out Balcon. That gentleman, disgusted, resigned.

For the visiting Hollywood rajah, an elaborate luncheon at the Savoy in London was arranged. The honor of having Mayer among them was duly impressed upon the British literary set. That luncheon was brilliantly reported by the novelist, Graham Greene, who dared risk the wrath of the mighty by putting his observations in writing. With his permission, here they are in part:

### Film Lunch*

"If ever there was a Christ-like man in human form, it was Marcus Lowe."

Under the huge Union Jack, the Stars and Stripes, the massed chandeliers, the little level Jewish voice softly intones. It is Mr. Louis B. Mayer, head of Metro-Goldwyn-Mayer, and the lunch is being held to celebrate the American company's decision to produce films in this country. Money, one can't help seeing it written on the literary faces, money for jam. But Mr. Mayer's words fall on the mercenary gathering with apostolic seriousness.

At the high table, Sir Hugh Walpole leans back, a great bald forehead, a rather softened and popular Henry James, like a bishop before the laying-on of hands—but oddly with a long cigar. Miss Maureen O'Sullivan waits under her halo hat . . . and Mr. Robert Taylor—is there, one wonders, a woman underneath the table? Certainly there are few sitting anywhere else, not many, at any rate, whom you would recognize as women among the tough massed faces of the film-reviewers . . .

. . . The bright Very lights of Mr. Mayer's eloquence soar up: "Thank God, I say to you, that it's the greatest year of net results and that's because I have men like Eddie Sankatz" (can that have been the name? It sounded like it after the Chablis Superior 1929,

* From *The Lost Childhood and Other Essays* by Graham Greene.

the Chateau Pontet Canet (Pauillac) 1933, G.H. Mumm Cordon Rouge 1928 and the Gautier Freres Fine Champagne 20 ans).

One can't help missing things, and when the mind comes back to the small dapper men under the massed banners, Mr. Mayer is talking about his family and God again. "I've got another daughter and I hope to God . . ." But the hope fumes out of sight in the cigar smoke of the key men. "She thought she'd like a poet or a painter but I held on until I landed Selznick. 'No, Irene,' I'd say, 'I'm watching and waiting.' So David Selznick, he's performing independent now."

. . . It's exactly 3:30 and Mr. Mayer is working up for his peroration: "It's midday. It's getting late. I shall pray silently that I shall be guided in the right channels . . . I want to say what's in my heart . . . In all these years of production, callous of adulation and praise . . . I hope the Lord will be kind to you. We are sending over a lovely cast."

He has spoken for forty minutes. For forty minutes, we have listened to the voice of American capital itself; a touch of religion, a touch of the family, the mixture goes down smoothly. Let the literary men sneer . . . the whip cracks . . . past the glass doors and the sentries, past the ashen-blonde sitting in the lounge out of earshot (only the word "God" reached her ears three times), the great muted chromium studios wait . . . the novelist's Irish Sweep: money for no thought, for the banal situation and the inhuman romance: money for forgetting how people live: money for "Siddown, won't yer" and "I love, I love, I love," endlessly repeated. Inside the voice goes on, "God . . . I pray," and the writers, a little stuffed and a little boozed, lean back and dream of the hundred pounds a week—and all that's asked in return is the dried imagination and the dead pen.

It was on this trip to London that Mayer by chance happened upon an actress who was to become one of the brightest jewels in his crown. He was in his hotel suite one evening, reading the papers, when he let out a yell which caused his companions, Ben Goetz and Howard Strickling, to jump as though struck.

"What's the matter with you guys?" he shouted. "Why can't you tell me what's going on?"

Goetz and Strickling assumed some dire disaster had occurred.

"Here's a show at the Saint James called *Old Music* and you don't even tell me it's in town!"

Now all of Mayer's associates knew that music was one of the things he dearly loved—particularly *old* music, which to him meant Viennese waltzes and traditional Hebrew songs. He knew nothing of classical music or the technical differences between, say, the melodies of Victor Herbert and George Gershwin. But he definitely knew what he liked.

Whenever the music department wanted to impress him with a musical score particular emphasis was placed upon the phrases of violins. Once an associate was moving to get a job for an obliging girl friend, whose one dubious and incongruous talent was a slight ability to perform on the viola. So for her screen test, which Mayer was to pass on, it was arranged that she should merely sit and play an arrangement of the Hebrew chant, *Kol Nidre*. Mayer entirely approved.

Goetz was aware that *Old Music* was a straight dramatic play, nothing that he would have commended to the attention of the boss. But the latter would not hear his explanation. Goetz was crazy, he didn't know what he was talking about! Any show called *Old Music* must have a lot of old music in it. Nothing would do but they must go to it that night.

Sure enough, it was as Goetz told him: *Old Music* was a straight dramatic play—and, what's more, a not very good one. They were about to leave before the end of the first act when onto the stage came an actress who caused Mayer's eyes to bug. She was a tallish slender beauty, with lustrous strawberry blond hair. Mayer grabbed Goetz's arm with violence.

"Who's that?" he barked.

Goetz glanced quickly at his program. "That's Greer Garson," he said.

Now there was no thought of leaving! Mayer was there for the rest of the play, and he was fidgety and impatient when the redhead wasn't on the stage. Goetz was dispatched to her dressing room to tell her that Louis B. Mayer was in the audience and would like her to have supper with him. The actress accepted graciously. When they met in the supper room of the Savoy she was wearing a stunning gown. She had rushed home, changed, and fetched her mother. A proper lady, she was.

Mayer was all charm that evening. He overflowed with magniloquence, directed not only at the actress but at the mother, too. He insisted that Miss Garson do a screen test the next day. She modestly protested she couldn't be ready but nevertheless did not decline. Mayer was so steamed up and excited he couldn't sleep that night. He paced the floor, raving to poor Howard Strickling about the magnificence of his find. The next day an elaborate screen test, with the best facilities possible, was made. Before Mayer departed from London Miss Garson was signed to come to Hollywood.

She was not the only talent Mayer recruited that trip. He and Thau were like millionaire collectors rounding up a mammoth horde of objets d'art. In Vienna they found Rosa Stradner, a statuesque German girl who was quickly dispatched to Culver City to learn English and take a small role in *The Last Gangster,* with Edward G. Robinson. It was her only film for Metro-Goldwyn-Mayer.

On to Carlsbad to take the waters and whatever else they could find, the Mayer retinue put up in royal splendor at the Imperial Hotel. And there they found a lovely blond Hungarian, Ilona Hajmassy, whose cool and delicate beauty captivated Mayer. Miss Hajmassy was by way of being a particular protégée of the director of the Vienna Statsoper. She immediately became Mayer's favorite dancing partner during his stay at the resort.

Everyone there that year remembered, or heard about, one charming episode that occurred during a lively rhumba session. Miss Hajmassy was wearing an evening gown of conspicuously fragile construction, and in the middle of a strenuous dance with Mayer a shoulder strap broke, thus permitting the exposure of a great deal more than was normally intended of the actress' smooth *poitrine*. After a moment of hesitation, she rushed off to seek repairs.

Mayer immediately recognized in Miss Hajmassy a likely performer for a role in *Rosalie,* a Cole Porter musical being readied at the studio. She was quickly signed and sent to Culver City, where her name (which means "garlic") was changed to Massey and her fortunate acquisition to replace Della Lind was announced. (After a small part in *Rosalie,* it was two years before Miss Massey appeared in another film.)

The presence of Mayer and Schenck in Carlsbad was broadcast as news through middle Europe, and agents with little German and Czechoslovakian actresses came flocking into the resort. Some of them, coming down from Berlin and Munich, discreetly removed their Nazi identifications before approaching the Hollywood tycoons.

In the evenings, after dancing and gambling, Mayer would often get the orchestra to stay and play sentimental music for him—just for him and his circle of friends. Touched by the old waltzes, he would frankly give way to tears. Viennese and Berlin music publishers quickly got wind of his taste and sent song pluggers in with sheafs of music that they easily sold to him. The Metro-Goldwyn-Mayer music department had thereafter the largest stock of Viennese waltzes in Hollywood.

To a sensible, middle-aged Hungarian lady he met that summer at the spa, Mayer happily told his life story, with a great deal of emphasis upon his impoverished youth and young manhood. The lady reminded him that he was not, after all, the only emigrant from Russia who had got ahead in the New World, and that his rather gaudy self-indulgence was not uniquely justified. Mayer nodded and gave her a sly wink. "There's no fool like an old fool," he said.

On that trip to Europe Mayer accumulated some seventeen artists. Among them were Victor Saville, a British producer; Julien Duvivier, a French director whom Mayer intended to have direct *The Great Waltz,* a Viennese operetta with which he was vastly in love; Reinhold Schunzel, a German writer and actor; Leo Reuss, a Viennese character actor; Arthur Guttman, a composer; and two French actresses, Mirelle Balin and Jacquelin Laurent.

In London a dark-haired Czech beauty, Hedy Keisler, who had appeared in a picture called *Ecstasy,* which featured her in a sensational nude scene, was called to Mayer's attention. He had not completed arrangements to sign her when he left for home. But Miss Keisler made it convenient for him. She booked passage in the same ship, ostensibly traveling as a sort of governess for a boy violinist, Grisha Goluboff. Mayer had signed not only Hedy but Grisha by the time the ship reached New York.

Altogether he considered that trip a great success.

Mayer returned to Hollywood in October. Affairs were not too happy at the studio. Some promising films had been started during his absence, but he felt there should have been more. The word got around that he was trying to get David Selznick to return to Culver City as a producer, and he was questioned on this point.

"If Dave Selznick comes to my studio I promise to get drunk and stay drunk for twenty-four hours," he told reporters. "And that will be the first time in my life, I assure you."

(Mayer was not being altogether truthful, in fact. He had been soused a few times, but he wasn't what you'd call a drinker. Alcohol did not agree with him.)

"If there is anybody in this business who can take Irving Thalberg's place," he said, "Dave Selznick is the one. Did you see what he did with *A Star Is Born?* He took that story—if it came to me, I'd say 'Make it or don't make it, what do I care; it's been done forty times before, anyway'—he took that story and made a tremendous picture out of it. That's what I mean. And only David Selznick could do it."

This was, of course, a far cry from his original attitude toward his son-in-law. But then Selznick had moved into top ranks since he married Irene Mayer, and at this moment he was making preparations to produce the film of *Gone With the Wind*. Wanting to borrow Clark Gable for it, he had approached Metro-Goldwyn-Mayer and had been told that Gable would be available only if the film were released through Loew's, Inc. So it was by this negotiation that Mayer was hopeful his son-in-law might be brought back to work for him. As it turned out, he was not. The deal was made for Gable, and *Gone With the Wind* was released by Loew's. But Selznick stayed clear of Culver City and his predatory father-in-law.

After his return from Europe Mayer began to complain of the problems of running the studio and his own aggravations in the job.

"Everybody around us is being enticed by other organizations," he told Nicholas Schenck, in one of their frequent conversations via long-distance telephone. "Everybody is jealous of us. It makes it very hard to function and do as good a job as we are doing. I feel it best for me not to go ahead."

Schenck recognized the symptoms of Mayer's alleged distress. The old "Mayer group" contract would be expiring at the end of 1938, and he was suffering the familiar distemper that preceded the negotiation of a new deal. Percentage terms of the old contract that were highly favorable to Mayer would undoubtedly be brought into question. His opening move was to play hard to get.

He was in a good position to do so. The output of Metro-Goldwyn-Mayer and the profits being earned by its pictures were highly propitious that year. Indeed, counting salary and bonus on 1937 returns, Mayer received $1,300,000, which indicates just how good they were. That was the highest income he ever received in one year, and it placed him—when the 1937 report of the Treasury Department was issued—as the highest salaried man in the United States.

Judging a successfully managed studio by its profits, which was what Schenck and the board of directors naturally did, it was clear that Mayer was an executive they did not want to lose.

Schenck came out to Culver City in December and summoned Lichtman, Mannix, and Thau. "Mr. Mayer is talking about leaving and I have to reorganize this studio," he said. The three indicated grave misgivings, and warned Schenck that without Mayer it would be difficult, if not impossible, to keep the producing organization intact. This was not encouraging information for the president of Loew's, Inc.

Mayer's next move was plainly calculated to confuse and agitate Schenck. On no particular pretext he stayed away from his office for several days. When he returned, Schenck went to see him.

"I owe you a duty," he said. "I want to tell you that you are absolutely wrong. You are making a mistake in resigning. You are going to regret it. I don't think you will live six months or a year."

This was an unexpected prophecy that inevitably startled Mayer, because it touched a most sensitive area. He wanted to know what it meant.

"You had this wonderful position and you had wonderful power," Schenck explained. "You love that kind of thing. Maybe *I* could do without it, because I know how to live outside of work. But not you. All you live for is work. That is what you love. That is what you need and that is what your nature demands, and I assure you that you are wrong. You are mistaken."

Mayer argued with him, but an impression filtered through to Schenck that he was a little upset and disappointed because some of the others didn't join in his threat.

"You had better think it over again," Schenck told him.

"Possibly I will talk to the boys. They have all regretted that you have resigned."

Mayer said no and offered to settle the balance of his contract if Schenck thought he was in the way.

"I think that is what we will have to do," Schenck countered. "We have to get ourselves organized without you, so if you really intend to stay out, I think that will be the proper thing to do."

This was as far as the parleys went that day.

The next day Schenck was happy to find Mayer somewhat more tractable.

"Do you really think the boys want me? Do you think they want to work with me and continue to make my work easier?" he asked.

"Yes I am sure of it," Schenck told him. "And you'll never have a complaint when I'm through with this. You will find these boys are happy. They are going to work as they have never worked before, and your work won't be half as hard. We have got as fine an organization as you could possibly build."

Mayer perceptibly softened. He had obviously worked Schenck around to giving assurance not only of a favorable new contract for himself but of concrete inducements to insure the support of his key executives. This was the best guarantee of his own position he could get.

"I want to talk to my daughter and son-in-law," he told Schenck.

The next morning he returned, a man of purpose. "Well, if they want me I'll go back," he said.

Schenck was relieved and delighted. He passed the word to Lichtman, Mannix, and Thau that Mayer had reconsidered and a new five-year contract with him would be drawn.

Consequently, Mayer's salary was increased to $3,000 a week and he was given an annual bonus of 6.77 percent of the profits of Loew's, Inc., after payment of a $2 dividend on the common stock.

By virtue of this liberal bonus and continuing profits of

the company Mayer was, for nine years thereafter, the highest salaried man in the United States—receiving more than the president of General Motors, more than Nicholas Schenck.

The promised inducements to key executives also came in the form of bonuses, with Schenck judiciously deciding upon whom they should be bestowed. J. Robert Rubin, whose contract with the "Mayer group" would expire at the end of 1938, was given a weekly salary of $2,000 and a bonus of 1.4 percent. This was a somewhat smaller share than he had received with the "Mayer group," but his original participation in production was acknowledged to be considerably curtailed.

Others who received bonus arrangements were Sam Katz, Eddie Mannix, Benny Thau, Al Lichtman, Harry Rapf, Bernie Hyman, Larry Weingarten, and Hunt Stromberg. The amounts varied, with Stromberg, Mannix, and Lichtman receiving the largest—1.5 percent each. Stromberg was virtually shanghaied into signing a new contract by Schenck and Mayer.

It is notable that no actors or directors were cut in on the bonus deals. Mayer and Schenck were consistently opposed to giving them any more than their salaries.

Thus the threatened breakdown of the executive ranks of the huge studio was prevented by a generous application of grease to the most favored "wheels."

Or as Al Lichtman sweetly put it, "Mr. Schenck is like a father with a lot of children and a piece of bread to divide. He divides it to the best of his ability to appease the appetites of each."

However, a mere stockholder of Loew's, Inc., might well have been appalled at the immensity of the hunger of these "children," particularly Louis B. Mayer.

# 14

The persuasiveness of money in promoting power and prestige is not a peculiarity found only in Hollywood. Wealth often renders people potent wherever they happen to be. But the knowledge that Mayer was the highest salaried man in the United States—a piece of vital information annually announced through public prints by the obliging Treasury Department over a period of several years—made him loom ever so much larger than he already loomed in his realm.

Associates and competitors who had known him as a hardy executive and a dynamic mover and shaker in group concerns of the producing industry now came to look upon him as something more than a local force. He assumed the impressive proportions of a national phenomenon. He was, in terms of salary, more productive and important than the presidents of big steel companies and captains of industry. This transmitted a certain grandeur to the business of making films and further elevated the level of Mayer's impressiveness and power.

He would have been a rare person if he had not canted a

bit to the additional weight of importance that this evidence
of money put on him. He was only human; he canted perceptibly. He was fully aware of the distinction of being the
highest salaried man in the United States. And though he did
not boast of it or use it to compel acquiescence to his desires,
he did not discourage its being noticed as the proof of his
Success.

Actually the secret of his income and the reason for his
power in Hollywood was the fact that he controlled and ad-
ministered the largest pool of creative talent in the industry.
He had more actors, writers, directors, and other craftsmen
under contract at Metro-Goldwyn-Mayer—more of the top
ones in all categories—than were assembled in any other
studio. And he had an uncanny shrewdness in manipulating
this pool for the use of his own producers and for loan-outs
and reciprocal deals from other studios.

In effect Mayer was in a position to dispense elements for
the production of star-value pictures not only by his own
company, but to a large extent by others. For, so often, others
needed the stars or the writers or directors that were to be
had only at Metro-Goldwyn-Mayer. At least they *felt* they
needed them, as David Selznick felt he must have Clark Gable
to play Rhett Butler, a key role, in *Gone With the Wind*.
And it was Mayer's sharp skill in sensing the urgency of these
needs and in cleverly trading upon them that gave him his
overwhelming power. The heads of other studios might
hate him. He was ruthless and tyrannical. But they respected
his skill, and they admired him because they knew he was
good.

An example of Mayer's influence was his deliberately im-
posing a boycott on Charles Feldman as an agent after the
latter married Jean Howard. Not only did he give explicit
orders that Feldman and his clients be kept off the Metro-
Goldwyn-Mayer lot, but he let it be known at other studios
that he wanted the agent ostracized. In most quarters this
had the nature of an ultimatum, coming from Mayer, so un-

forgiving and vindictive could he be if his wishes were not obeyed.

He frequently crucified people. Francis X. Bushman was one who had early known the bitterness of his vengeance and the effectiveness of his Hollywood pull. Even though the distinguished actor had done a splendid job in *Ben-Hur,* he found himself strangely unwanted shortly after that film was released. On various illogical pretexts studio doors were closed to him and he was compelled to give up movies and seek his living on the stage.

Years later he learned the reason. Mayer had brought his family to see him in a play in Los Angeles at the time that *Ben-Hur* was showing. After the performance Mayer took his family backstage to greet the actor, and an inexperienced valet had refused to admit them to the star's dressing room. Mayer thought he was deliberately slighted. The boycott resulted.

The attempt to ostracize Feldman was carried to a further extreme. Mayer tried to lure his best clients—Claudette Colbert, Joan Bennett, and Paul Lukas—away from him by having his pal, Frank Orsatti, offer them higher salaries at Metro-Goldwyn-Mayer. Fortunately for Feldman, Joseph P. Kennedy was just then acting as receiver and administrator at Paramount and was not submissive to the ultimatum of Mayer. He offered Miss Colbert a considerable advance in salary to put her under contract to his studio, and this providential benefaction by the Boston financier saved the audacious agent's hide.

Also, Feldman was rugged—and he had some considerate friends. Harry Cohn, head of Columbia, was one of them. He took the agent to see Mayer one day and proposed a truce. Mayer was full of bombast, but Feldman got him to agree to call off his boycott at studios other than Metro-Goldwyn-Mayer. This would have been satisfactory had Mayer kept faith with it, for all agents who did business at Culver City were compelled to split their fees with Orsatti anyhow.

That was Mayer's way of dispensing largess to his friend. But Feldman soon discovered he was still having trouble making deals.

Mayer's revenge upon the agent probably would have carried through had it not been for a coincidence that propitiously occurred. Being made ready for production at Metro-Goldwyn-Mayer was a picture about Madame Walewska and Napoleon, in which Greta Garbo was to star. Despite the studio's pool of talent, the only actor Miss Garbo would accept to appear opposite her as Napoleon was the Frenchman, Charles Boyer, and he was under contract to Walter Wanger, who was now an independent producer, following his short stint at Metro-Goldwyn-Mayer.

Feldman got wind of the development and besought Wanger, who had been best man at his wedding to Jean Howard, to allow him to negotiate the deal. Wanger agreed, with pleasure; he had no love for Mayer. Boyer was also agreeable, since Feldman promised to get him a good bit more than the twenty-five thousand dollars a picture that was then his established fee.

With that, they went out to Culver City and had a talk with Mayer. The latter was incensed at Feldman's presence, but there was nothing he could do.

"How much is this Boyer fellow getting?" he testily inquired.

"Walter is paying him twenty-five thousand dollars a picture," Feldman replied. Boyer had previously completed his memorable *Algiers*.

Mayer was cool to the figure. "That's a lot of money for an actor to expect when he has this great chance to play Napoleon opposite Garbo," he said.

"I didn't say that is what we expect *you* to pay," Feldman said. "We expect you to pay a *hundred* and twenty-five thousand. After all, there's only one Charles Boyer."

Mayer was infuriated, but he knew Feldman had him over a barrel. The deal was made for Boyer to receive one hundred and twenty-five thousand dollars for eight weeks work and further mounting compensation for any time over that. As it turned out, they took so long shooting and reshooting the film, *Conquest,* that the actor collected something in the neighborhood of four hundred and fifty thousand dollars for the job. It was a glorious triumph for Feldman and a galling defeat for Mayer.

His rancor was manifested a short time after, when Wanger went to him and asked for the loan of Myrna Loy, one of Metro-Goldwyn-Mayer's most active stars.

"Why should I loan *you* Myrna Loy?" Mayer pugnaciously inquired.

"Because I loaned you Boyer when you needed him," Wanger politely replied.

That did it! Mayer howled with anger and leaped for Wanger, who tried to fend him off. The two fell to the floor in a thrashing tangle, Wanger puffing and Mayer bellowing, "Get out! Get out!"

People rushed in and parted the combatants. Wanger did not get Myrna Loy.

With his own people Mayer had a curiously ambiguous attitude. He would graciously play the father to them, and then con and outwit them. Sentiment often oozed from him in displays of consideration and concern, but behind his appearance of fatherly interest usually lurked a trick. He was particularly clever at handling the demands and requests of his stars, playing upon their emotions and vanities with skill. He thoroughly understood actors and their abnormal psychology, probably because he had the qualities of an actor himself. It was a standing gag that the L.B. in his name stood for Lionel Barrymore. And he occasionally acknowledged to intimates, "I've got a lot of ham in me."

His adroitness in manipulating Joan Crawford and her manifold wishes and complaints by flattery, threats, and entreaties was famous around the studio. He would solemnly counsel and cajole her; if need be, he would cry a little bit,

then drop a few hints of his disfavor and what the consequences might be. It took a long time for Miss Crawford
first to get wise to him and then to summon up the courage
to tell him where he could go.

He used similar tactics with Marie Dressler, whom he liked
as an actress because of her motherly characteristics and
her elementary comedy style. His favorite trick with her, however, was to threaten her with William Randolph Hearst,
whom Miss Dressler considered an ogre. Mayer had only to
mention Hearst's name and the availability of his coöperation
to get Miss Dressler to do what he wished.

And yet, when the aging actress became ill it was Mayer
who took command, as though he were concerned with his
own mother. He made her go to a hospital and be examined
by expert physicians. And when they reported privately to
him that she had cancer and could live only a few months, he
hovered and clucked over her so assiduously and authorita-
tively that she finally beefed, "That man is trying to run my
life!" During her last few months in a hospital he visited her
regularly.

This kind of protective interest, this loyalty to those who
were dutiful to his authority and organization was frequently
evidenced by Mayer. Once Howard Strickling went to him
with an utterly despairing complaint about difficulties with
Wallace Beery, who was anything but the lovable old scamp
he was made to appear in his pictures. He was petty, testy,
and mean. Strickling indicated he was ready and eager to
give good old Wally the harpoon.

Mayer sternly denied approval. "Don't forget, he is one of
us," he said. The point was that, outside the family circle,
there was no question about the people of Metro-Goldwyn-
Mayer.

His constant enthusiasm for company camaraderie led to
frequent studio parties and annual picnics, which were virtually obligatory for all personnel, from stars and executives

to stagehands. Mayer danced with the girls and made speeches full of fervor and professional platitudes.

He also went for mass meetings. Two or three times a year, when he was putting stress on organization, he would summon the entire studio force and give out with long harangues on diligence, loyalty, and economy. These orotund orations were full of heavy sarcasm, threats, occasional congratulations, and encouragement of pep. They may have amused more sophisticated people, but they impressed the run of personnel. Mayer was generally respected as a stabilizing force in his studio.

Of course, he made mistakes with certain people and misjudged situations frequently. Some of his miscalculations were expensive and embarrassing. A year or so after Robert Montgomery had come to the studio and had been launched as a star-in-the-making he went to Mayer to talk with him about an increase in salary. He reminded Mayer that when he had been signed to a contract by Robert Rubin in New York he had been promised verbally they would tear up that contract and write a new one as soon as he demonstrated his competence in films.

"If any official of this company told you that," Mayer replied, "you will get a new contract. Come back to see me tomorrow."

Montgomery returned the next day. Mayer was seated at his desk when the actor came in. Without looking up he bluntly said, "You're a goddamn liar."

Montgomery was stunned. He thought Mayer was speaking to someone standing behind him. He glanced around to make sure. Then he addressed the executive. "Will you repeat that, Mr. Mayer."

Still without looking at the actor Mayer again called him a liar and added, "You were not promised a new contract."

Montgomery moved closer and looked down at him. "If you were a younger man, Mr. Mayer, I'd give you a beating," he said. "But since you're not, I just want to tell you, you're going to pay a quarter of a million dollars for that remark."

He turned and walked out of the office. And a quarter of a million dollars is what was paid. For when the time came to draw a new contract with Montgomery, who was now a top-ranking star, the actor added twenty-five thousand dollars a year to the salary he demanded—and received—for the next ten years.

Another incident of negotiation over a matter of salary reveals the curious complexity and sometimes cruelty in the methods of Mayer. Gottfried Reinhardt, the son of Max Reinhardt, famous German stage director, had a job as a reader at the studio in the 1930's. He and his father and their families were refugees from the terror of Hitler and had come to Hollywood where the younger Reinhardt was given employment at Metro-Goldwyn-Mayer. Naturally Mayer knew of the arrangement with the son of the director, whom he had met and visited on two or three occasions at his castle in Germany.

After a few months in his new job young Reinhardt went to Benny Thau and said he would have to have more salary in order to support his family. "If I don't get more money," he told him, "I'll have to go someplace else."

Thau was sympathetic. "What you have just said I didn't hear—I mean that stuff about if you don't get more money you'll quit. I suggest you talk to Mr. Mayer."

Reinhardt asked for an audience, and a few days later was granted one. That would have been unlikely if he had not been Max Reinhardt's son. When he was shown into Mayer's outer office, who should be sitting there but Nicholas Schenck and Eddie Mannix. Mayer was in another room.

Schenck, out from New York for conferences with the head of the studio, gave Reinhardt a cordial greeting and began talking casually with him, mostly about "conditions" and how he had been compelled to let off two or three servants from his Long Island estate. Then Mayer bustled in and Schenck said to him, "I didn't want to discuss anything before you came, Louis." Reinhardt had the sudden feeling this gathering was prearranged.

"Thank you, Nick," Mayer said with fine formality, then turned to Reinhardt and said, "Now I've talked to Thau about you, Reinhardt, and he assured me that you had said nothing to him about quitting our company if you did not receive a raise in pay. Had you made any such remark I wouldn't see you. But since you didn't I'll talk with you. So tell me, Reinhardt, why do you think you should have a raise in pay?"

Reinhardt told him frankly he thought he was underpaid for the work he did.

"You're absolutely right," Mayer assured him with astonishing alacrity. "You are right! But in a big organization such as this one, you must realize that, while some of the people are underpaid, there are some who are overpaid, too. Now, if everyone was overpaid we'd soon be bankrupt. Look at . . ." And he thereupon named a list of certain executives. "Do you think they are overpaid?"

Reinhardt had to acknowledge that, so far as he could see, they probably were.

"That's exactly the point!" Mayer hollered. "So some people have to be underpaid!"

Still on his feet he went into a long and graphic account of how, at the end of a hard day, he would get into his car and be driven home (he acted this out in pantomime), and how he would think to himself about the people who were being overpaid.

"When I think about those people I get angry," he said, and for a few moments he gave an imitation of an angry man. "Then I say to myself, 'What people are being underpaid?' And right away I say, 'Reinhardt!' Then I think about him. 'Reinhardt,' I say to myself, 'Reinhardt. There's a nice fellow. I like him. He's underpaid, but I like him.' " He patted the young man on the shoulders. "Let's keep it that way," he said.

Reinhardt, jolted out of the image of himself as Mayer's intimate concern, hastened to add that his request was motivated by something more than a sense of justice and pride.

"I *need* more money. I'm the sole support of my family— my father," he said.

Mayer looked at him softly. "You're supporting your father? That's wonderful! That's fine!" Then he lowered his voice confidentially, "But take my advice: don't spoil him. Don't try to give him too much."

The end of the story is that Reinhardt finally walked out of the extraordinary meeting with a raise that amounted to about half of what he asked for—or substantially what he hoped he would get. Mayer, having run through his performance, bestowed it handsomely. Reinhardt was convinced that the exhibition was staged solely for the benefit of Schenck.

The sometime mention of Mayer as a "producer" in these top years of his career was an inaccuracy that offended both the word and his own self-esteem. He was far above anything so limited and demanding of concentration, indeed, as the day-to-day tasks of overseeing the actual production of films. He maintained himself on the level of inspirational boss of the whole works, the sage of motion picture commerce and the kingpin in contact with New York.

He never read scripts or story treatments. He had them told to him by a staff of expert storytellers who knew precisely how to play up to him. Kate Corbaley, Edwin Knopf, and others would narrate and even declaim in ways calculated to stir his emotions as they would presumably be stirred by seeing the film. If aroused, he would frequently pick up the story idea himself and proceed to elaborate it and act it according to his whims. The job of inscribing his ideas or trying to fit them into a script would then be turned over to writers who would sometimes have to tussle hard with them.

Mayer was rough on storytellers. A person who couldn't convey a story idea to him in a graphic fashion usually got short shrift. One time a pompous story editor was giving a dreary account of the contents of a new novel before the executive board. Mayer tried to listen. Then he fidgeted and fumed. Suddenly he jumped up and ordered the story editor and a couple of key executives to follow him into another room. Inside, and with the door shut, he seized the story editor by the throat and was angrily proceeding to choke him when the others pulled them apart.

Generally Mayer's taste in stories still ran to romance and sentiment, with emphasis upon the beautiful and the pure. Gangster pictures and realistic dramas or so-called sophisticated comedies were entirely outside his range of interest. "I don't know anything about gangsters," he regularly said, whenever a picture involving them was suggested, and thereupon he would walk away.

He had a particular fondness for stories in which children appeared, and he was responsible for collecting and maintaining the largest roster of child actors in any studio. After the success of Jackie Cooper with Wallace Beery in *The Champ*, he was constantly on the lookout for likely youngsters and encouraged his producers to be alert for them. This was more than a personal indulgence of fatherly interest and sentiment; Mayer figured the development of child actors was an excellent way of training future adult stars.

The intelligence of his theory is thoroughly supported by the number of popular players that started young at Metro-Goldwyn-Mayer. Judy Garland, Elizabeth Taylor, Mickey Rooney, Freddie Bartholomew, Lana Turner, Peter Lawford, Ann Rutherford, Kathryn Grayson, and many more were fledged as teen-age tyros under the cozy contemplation of Mayer.

Inevitably, one of his favorite production enterprises and boasts was a famous group of low-budget pictures which emphasized the element of youth. This was the Andy Hardy series, also known as the Hardy Family films, of which there were fourteen, turned out between 1937 and 1943.

The series originated far beneath the notice of Mayer, in a little picture of the Hubbard-Cohn B-unit, entitled *A Family Affair*. It had to do with a family named Hardy, living in the fictitious town of Carvel, Idaho, where the father was a judge. A minor member, at the outset, was a mischievous high-school-age son.

Cast as the latter was Mickey Rooney, whose career at Metro-Goldwyn-Mayer had begun when David Selznick signed him for child roles in 1933. Master Rooney won himself a reputation of some proportions in the next five years, especially as the youth in *Ah, Wilderness!* and as the Gloucester fisherman's son in *Captains Courageous,* with Spencer Tracy and young Master Bartholomew. He was definitely a leading child actor when cast in *A Family Affair*.

The little picture was nothing sensational, but a few months after its release, William Rodgers, sales manager for Loew's, Inc., was at the studio and remarked that a lot of favorable comment on it had come in from theater men. "Why don't you make a few more pictures with the same characters?" he asked. The suggestion seemed a good one, and the B-unit went ahead.

The second effort was called *You're Only Young Once,* and in this one more emphasis was placed upon the companionship of the son, Andy, and the judge, now played by Lewis Stone. This led to a third, *Judge Hardy's Children*. It was just about at this point that Mayer began to take an interest in the series and approved its being given a little more push.

Thus, for the fourth in the series, *Love Finds Andy Hardy,* two teen-age girls who were regarded as promising in the studio's training program were cast to vie for Andy's regard. They were Judy Garland and Lana Turner, both of whom had attracted note in small roles.

At the preview of *Love Finds Andy Hardy* all studio executives conspicuously appeared. The word had gone out that Mayer was interested in this uncommonly loaded little film. And results justified anticipation. *Love Finds Andy Hardy* turned out to be a most engaging and successful little picture and, of course, a minor classic of the screen because of the combination of youngsters whose careers were advanced by it.

Mayer's enthusiasm for the series, which was positive and persistent from here on, was something that might have fascinated an inquisitive psychologist. For it reflected more than his interest in a solid commercial success. It embraced his elaborate affection for the family and the home. In his counsels and dictates on pictures he often and poignantly revealed his wishful notions of American home life and the difficulties of his youth.

In a way he became the Hardys' mentor, and worked harder than anyone to maintain the character of the series and hold it to a form. He transmitted his thoughts through Carey Wilson, who was the primary idea man and general factotum on the productions. Wilson had to bear the brunt of Mayer's frequent objections and ultimatums on how Andy should behave.

One of the earlier pictures had Andy in a football uniform rushing to the home of his steady high school sweetheart, Polly Benedict, shouting, "We won! We won!" He was obviously elated and expecting to be admired, but when he reached Polly's house he found her with a handsome naval lieutenant who towered over him, making him feel boyish and small.

That night at the supper table Andy was plainly depressed, keeping extraordinarily silent and toying with the food on his plate. "You're not eating, Andy," his mother noticed. "I'm not hungry, Mom," he replied. Mrs. Hardy looked at him anxiously. "I think it's his liver," she mused. "If what's ailing Andrew is his liver, a lot of boys are suffering liver trouble," the judge remarked.

Nobody laughed at the preview. Mayer yanked violently

on Wilson's arm. (He attended all the previews with Wilson, and pulled and punched him throughout the shows.) Going home after the preview Mayer took the writer to task. "Don't you know a boy of sixteen is hungry *all* the time?" he charged. "You tell me you were brought up in a good American home —in the kitchen! You lied to me! You've let Andy insult his mother! No boy would tell his mother he wasn't hungry! Change that line!"

Mayer then told him how to write it. "Have Andy say, 'Thanks, Mom, your cooking is fine, but I don't feel like eating.' Then Mrs. Hardy says, 'I think it's his liver,' and the judge gets off his remark." The change was made, and sure enough at the next showing the judge's line got a good laugh.

Andy's feeling for his mother was formulated by Mayer again in a critical situation that was presented in *Judge Hardy and Son*. Mrs. Hardy was ill, and for a short while it was feared she might not live. Wilson wrote a scene in which Andy said a lengthy and tearful prayer for her. When it was told to Mayer, he was sarcastic. "Who the hell wrote *that* prayer?" he stormed.

"I did," said Wilson and then endeavored to explain why he thought it would be good.

"You see, you're now a Hollywood character," Mayer shot back at him. "You've forgotten your simple, honest boyhood. You don't remember how a real boy would pray. This is how a boy would do it. . . ." Mayer fell on his knees beside his chair, clasped his hands, and raised his eyes to heaven. "Dear God," he said solemnly, "please don't let my mom die, because she's the best mom in the world. Thank you, God." With that, he jumped to his feet and confronted Wilson. "Let me see you beat that for a prayer!"

Wilson wrote the prayer as Mayer dictated. It was spoken by Mickey Rooney reverently. It became the stock prayer for apt occasions in subsequent films from Metro-Goldwyn-Mayer.

It was early recognized that audiences were almost as sympathetic to Judge Hardy as they were to Andy. In his man-to-man talks with his son, the father's comments and reactions were found as amusing and meaningful as the boy's. Mayer was entirely in agreement. He liked the judge to be human and wise. This was entirely consistent with his notions of what a father should be. He made them see to it that Andy —or Andrew, as the judge called him—should be respectful of his father at all times. Conversations with the father had to be liberally sprinkled with "sirs." And once Mayer said to Wilson a very revealing thing: "A boy may hate his father, but he always *respects* him. Remember that!"

In matters of manners and deportment, Mayer was punctilious, too. He became angry if he detected what he considered a breach of etiquette. There was once a scene in which Andy came into the house and failed to remove his hat. Mayer yanked Wilson's arm at the preview. "Where are your manners?" he growled. The scene was reshot with Andy coming in, forgetting his hat, then suddenly remembering and taking it off with a fine gesture, and tossing it on to the hatrack.

Sex was another subject that Mayer insisted be handled gingerly. "If you let Andy get too crazy about girls you'll lose your audience," he warned.

In *Love Finds Andy Hardy* the gosling hero wanted twelve dollars to buy a jalopy to take a girl to a high school dance. Also, as part of the ensemble, he needed a girl to take. "The thing to remember," Mayer counseled, "is that he wants the jalopy more than he wants the girl." The implication was that the possession was most important to a boy.

Too much kissing was strictly forbidden. Ever after the scene in *You're Only Young Once,* where Andy said to his father, "I like to kiss Polly Benedict; do you suppose there's something wrong with me?" Mayer was constantly insisting they keep the kissing and petting to a minimum.

"It isn't good when a fellow is kissing a girl all the time," he said. "You know girls. They don't like too much kissing. It has to be something special, a surprise."

As the series was extended, Rooney took to mugging, and sometimes Director George Seitz let him get away with too much of it. Once, after kissing Polly, who was always played by Ann Rutherford, he threw his feet up and emitted a wolf-ish "woo, woo, Woo!"

Mayer saw the scene and was disgusted. He took Seitz aside. "George," he said with mock commiseration, "if you want a sex laugh I would like to suggest a better one. After Andy kisses Polly, just have him jump up and unzip his fly. That'll get you a wow."

Seitz got the point. He lectured Rooney, then reshot the scene. After Mayer saw it he said to him, "I hope you noticed Mr. Mayer, Andy didn't even *reach* for his fly."

Naturally, wits in the studio could not resist making jokes about the Hardy pictures. One that amused them very much was a suggestion for combining this series with the later Dr. Kildare films, a new series that was inaugurated by the Cohn unit after the Hardys had caught on so well. The suggestion was that Andy should be made to contract a venereal disease from one of the girls at Carvel High School and should go to Dr. Kildare to be cured.

When someone made the mistake of telling this joke to Mayer, he was outraged at such irreverence and let it be understood that he would tolerate no more levity of that sort among his employees. The Kildare pictures were also favorites of his, partly because they had to do with the practice of medicine, which was of obsessive interest to him, but also because Lionel Barrymore, one of his most respected people, played old Dr. Gillespie in the series.

Along about the fifth Hardy picture Mayer passed the unbelievable word: "Don't try to make these films any better. Just keep them the way they are." And to the logical suggestion that the series might be improved by a stronger director than Seitz, he made the curious rejoinder, "If you had a stronger director the films wouldn't be as good."

The Hardy series was finished when Mickey Rooney went off to World War II, and, by that time, Mayer had become so preoccupied with breeding and racing thoroughbred horses that he had all but lost interest in any films. But the nature and success of that series was always one of his proud boasts. It represented his ideal of content and commerce well combined.

He liked to compare the Hardy pictures to *Ninotchka,* a charming comedy starring Greta Garbo which was released in 1939. This next-to-the-last of Garbo's pictures was directed by Ernst Lubitsch and was a satire on communism, a subject hateful to Mayer in any form.

"*Ninotchka* got everything but money," he would say sarcastically. "A Hardy picture cost $25,000 less than Lubitsch was paid alone. But any good Hardy picture made $500,000 more than *Ninotchka* made."

This was his exaggerated way of justifying his preference for the Hardy films.

It was the incongruity of this sentimentality in taste with his hardheaded business methods that was so often remarked and ridiculed by sharp and sophisticated people who came into close contact with him. "Putting canary's eyebrows before the public is like putting a ham that was raised in Buckingham Palace before my father," he once said. It was comments of this sort that made him the butt of much private mockery, since it was evident that his ideas of "canary's eyebrows" were ridiculously naïve.

Once he told the playwright S.N. Behrman, that he had shown a Hardy film to Eddie Mannix, the former amusement park bouncer, and had noticed tears in his eyes. "When you can get a sophisticate like Mannix to cry at a picture," he said, "it must have something in it." Mannix was as sentimental as Mayer.

Late in 1940 the rising producer, Arthur Freed, brought

William Saroyan to meet Mayer. Saroyan was, at that time, the newest genius in the American theater and the *enfant terrible* of the literary world. His short stories of West Coast Armenians (of which he was one) were all the rage, and his play, *The Time of Your Life,* a glittering compound of talk and tempest, had won the 1940 Pulitzer Prize.

Mayer was impressed by Saroyan, who had a great conversational flair and told him stories of Armenians that sounded to Mayer like stories of old Jewish families. "This is a bright fellow; we should have him," he later said to Freed. "But he doesn't want to work in pictures," Freed unhappily replied. This was a disposition that Mayer could not understand, so he suggested they bait Saroyan by offering him three hundred dollars a week just to come to the studio and look around.

The writer accepted the offer, but a few weeks later they found he wasn't picking up his checks, And then they learned he was at his home in Fresno, far from the lure of Hollywood. Freed urged him to write an original story in hopes that would bring him in, and three weeks later Saroyan delivered *The Human Comedy.*

Kate Corbaley, Mayer's favorite reader, reported that her boss wept three times when this little story was read to him. But Saroyan's price of three hundred thousand dollars seemed a little high. He was asked to come to lunch with Mayer to work out a favorable deal. The latter offered fifty thousand dollars. "Tell you what I'll do," Saroyan said. "I'll toss you—a hundred thousand or nothing." "I can't gamble the company's money," Mayer replied.

They finally settled on sixty thousand as a suitable price, with the further provision that Saroyan would come to the studio at fifteen hundred a week with the idea of being groomed for a producer-director job.

"I can make another Thalberg of this boy," Mayer happily said to Freed.

"No Jew can ever cheat an Armenian," cracked Saroyan. "The Armenians have been cheating the Jews for centuries."

The nub of it was that Saroyan was a writer to whom Mayer could talk, the way he could talk to Jerome Kern and Sigmund Romberg as musicians, which was the reason he liked them so much. He didn't know anything about the qualities of Saroyan's literary style or the Pulitzer Prize. Stubbornly, he persisted in scorning such "high brow" things. But he had a feeling for the gusto and the poetry, such as it was, in the conversation of the writer. And that's what attracted him.

The enthusiasm lasted but a short while. Saroyan's stay at the studio was spectacular but disappointing, so far as its producing "another Thalberg" was concerned. He was angry because Mayer would not permit him to direct *The Human Comedy* and spurned Mayer's urgings that he work on an adaptation of *The Rosary*. Mayer had a lasting affection for this heavily sentimental old play. He thought it would be a great vehicle for Clark Gable. But he could never get anyone to agree.

Instead, Saroyan practiced being a Thalberg by producing and directing a short film called *The Good Job*, based on his own short story, "A Number of the Poor." It barely lived up to its title. At the same time he amused hired hands at the studio with his request for a player piano in his office. It had to be brought through the window from outside. It was also amusing when it was discovered that he was using a projection room for hours each day to look at scores of old movies that he had missed as a boy.

The entertainment lasted only three months. Saroyan departed after having his fun and picking up the money that was generously paid to him. *The Human Comedy* was made, with Mickey Rooney playing the autobiographical role of a telegraph messenger boy in Fresno, which must have amused the author very much. Whether it amused Mayer is uncertain.

It was said that his favorite scene of all time was the opening shot in the picture showing a little boy (played by Butch Jenkins) looking raptly at a gopher hole.

Saroyan's reaction to his experience was expressed shortly after he left in a piece published in *Daily Variety,* called "The California Shore-bird in its Native Habitat." In this thinly veiled excoriation of the processes of producing films, he summed up cryptically:

I left the joint also because sooner or later a man gets bored with bores, finaglers and jitney politicians. A man just naturally gets fed up with the baloney. He gets tired of witnessing the continuous and disgraceful crying, trembling and shaking. I made a net profit of one million (sic) at Metro. That is enough for any shore-bird in the world, Orphan or otherwise.

Later he wrote a play which everybody recognized as a reflection of Mayer. It drew a devastating picture of a vicious egoist and was called *Get Away Old Man*. Considering the enthusiasm and high hopes that Mayer had for Saroyan at the start, this must have been extremely mortifying for one who put his trust in an Armenian.

Mayer had about this time a further sad experience with a young man whom he confidently expected to make into "another Thalberg." The young man was Joseph Mankiewicz, whose career as a writer, producer, and director at Culver City began in 1933. Mayer had allowed him opportunities to make pictures which he himself did not approve, and Mankiewicz's surprising success with them added to his prestige.

But in 1942 a situation of pitiful aspect arose that brought a sudden, shocking cleavage in the happy relations of the two men. Judy Garland had been running into trouble in her mental attitude toward her work. She was deeply disturbed and unhappy and was often difficult. Mayer and the child's demanding mother could not understand that a clear psychological complex was the cause of her recalcitrance. Since Mayer considered himself the all-wise "father" as well as the employer of the girl, he felt it only his privilege and duty to advocate that she be handled through elementary discipline.

Now Mankiewicz happened to be a sympathetic friend of the girl. He recognized her mental confusion and privately recommended that she see the distinguished psychologist, Karl Menninger. The latter sent her to see Dr. Ernst Simmel, an equally distinguished German refugee psychologist in Los Angeles.

Judy had been seeing him for only a short while when her mother discovered it and reported this alarming development to Mayer. He was outraged and wrathful. To think that any-one had gone behind his authority and wisdom to help Judy was more than he could endure. He called his ranking hopeful on the carpet and viciously berated him, to the point where Mankiewicz was so indignant that he said he wanted to resign. Mayer would not accept his resignation; Mankiewicz would not work for him. Finally Mayer released him from his contract to go to Twentieth Century-Fox.

Thus, a possible way of helping Judy was scotched at a critical point, and one of Hollywood's most potent young film makers was lost to Metro-Goldwyn-Mayer.

The sentimentalist would die rather than surrender to the sophisticate.

# 15

It's said that every man is entitled to one wild extravagance in his life, one reckless indulgence of fancy that he cannot quite afford. Some go crazy over paintings, some throw their money away on yachts, and a few go in for race horses, about the wildest extravagance of all.

Mayer went for horses. But unlike most people who lose more money than they should in the myth of improving the breed, he could not only afford the indulgence; he succeeded in making it pay and in establishing himself as one of the leading thoroughbred owners in the United States.

This is not an easy business. It is one of the toughest and trickiest there is. And the fact that he was able to beat it in a few years was nigh phenomenal. But, again, he went at horse racing and breeding the way he went at everything, with enthusiasm, energy, boldness, and a ferocious determination to succeed.

The seed of his interest was planted by Dr. Isidore Snapper in Amsterdam in the summer of 1937, when the physician encouraged him to find a diverting hobby and suggested the sport of kings. Little did Dr. Snapper realize what he was counseling or how meaningless was that word "hobby" to a man such as Mayer.

Oddly, the film magnate hitherto had avoided this sport. He never bet on horses or hung around the tracks; that seemed to him a waste of money and especially a waste of time. Nicholas and Joe Schenck were large horse players, and Joe had owned a few racers from time to time, but they had never been able to get Mayer to go for that form of gambling. His only interest in horses was as enjoyable riding machines and as essential adjuncts to actors in certain types of films.

Then, one afternoon in the summer of 1938, Mayer disappeared from his office without leaving word where he was going. Later his secretary and associates were amazed to discover that he had been to the Hollywood Park race track with Leon Gordon, a writer at the studio. Gordon, a sporty Englishman, owned a horse which he stabled at that track, and he had several times tried to persuade Mayer to go out and have a look. Finally Mayer consented. The experience delighted him.

He was struck by the crowds, the color, the drama, and excitement of the place. But he was particularly caught by the attention given the owner of a winning horse. He liked the way the owner was escorted to the winner's circle and photographed. Evidently here was something he had missed about this so-called sport of kings. He decided to buy a few horses and find out what it was all about.

His first purchase was made, appropriately, from his friend, Joe Schenck, who unloaded on him an undistinguished animal named Marine Blue. Then he had an agent buy him several two-year-olds at the Saratoga sales that fall, and shortly after he bought a horse called Main Man from Jerome B. Respess, a California breeder, for seventeen thousand dollars. Main Man was the first horse to carry Mayer's blue-and-pink silks in a race. When he won the San Jose Handicap at Bay

Meadows that winter Mayer was thoroughly taken with the sport.

But though he embraced it as a hobby and presumably meant originally to obtain nothing more than a little relaxation and enjoyment out of it, he indicated from the outset that he was going to buy horses and try to build a racing stable along the same lines he had built a studio. That is, he was going to invest extensively in promising stock, selected on the customary basis of bloodlines, and then expect the "stars" to emerge.

Friends had early warned him that it took time and patience to build a successful racing stable, that aristocratic families in the east, such as the Vanderbilts and Whitneys, had been working on their stables for years, and that it would be vain and possibly disastrous for him to try. They urged him to keep his efforts modest and have a little fun.

But "fun" for Mayer in any area in which competition was involved was to do as much as he could to gain position, to demonstrate "class," and be the best. Anyhow, another Californian who owned horses, Charles S. Howard, assured him that anyone with money, perseverance, and luck could beat the game. Money he had, and perseverance; whether he would have luck remained to be seen.

Also extremely important in the business of horse racing are an intimate knowledge of horses and ability to train the stock. These, of course, were assets which Mayer himself did not personally possess, and his task was to find the people who could provide them adequately. At the outset he had some misfortunes; he bought a lot of "trash." But he later found better counsel and was able to build on that.

Being an irrepressible showman he early made a bid for publicity, if not complete preëminence, in the racing world. Samuel D. Riddle, the distinguished owner of the great Man o' War, was astonished when his manager came to him one day in late 1938 and told him "a man named Mayer from California" had offered a million dollars for the champion sire. A price of $1,000,000 far exceeded any sum ever offered for a race horse on the American or English turf. When the offer was conveyed to Riddle, he indignantly turned it down. "Tell Mr. Mayer that Man o'War is not for sale at any price," he said.

Later, when the humor of it struck him, the old horseman remarked sarcastically, "I don't know what Mr. Mayer wanted with him, but I thought he might want to use him in pictures. And I would not want that. They would not know how to treat this old fellow. He is happy and contented where he is."

Mayer also offered $1,000,000 in late 1939 for the great English sire, Hyperion, owned by Britain's Lord Derby. Again he was coolly rebuffed, even though the enterprise of horse racing was then curtailed in Great Britain by the outbreak of World War II. Lord Derby's reply to the offer was in the current Churchillian vein: "Though England be reduced to ashes, Hyperion will never leave these shores."

Whether Mayer's offers were serious is open to considerable doubt, for those prices were more than double what had ever been paid for a single horse. About the same time he declined an opportunity to make a purchase of much greater scope than the acquisition of either of these great animals for an extremely reasonable price.

When the war broke out, information came to Laudy Lawrence, Continental representative of Metro-Goldwyn-Mayer, that the Aga Khan was willing to sell all his great stock of thoroughbreds then located in France, Ireland, and England for an undisclosed but most attractive sum. Lawrence, who had been requested to be on the lookout for horses for Mayer, talked with the prince and discovered he could get the lot of the horses for a price he knew Mayer could well afford.

The opportunity was fantastic. Several hundred horses were involved and they constituted perhaps the greatest collection of the best blood in the history of the thoroughbred. Had Mayer been willing to make the purchase and could he have got all the stock to the United States, he might well have altered completely and perhaps forever the history of the thoroughbred throughout the world. In the light of the influence these animals and their progency have since had upon European racing it could have been that their removal to this country would have given Mayer world supremacy.

But he turned down the opportunity. Lawrence was greatly surprised.

However, he did purchase one horse from the stable of the Aga Khan which turned out, by a freak of fortune, to be one of the two pillars of the later high-powered Mayer stud farm. This was a colt, by Hyperion, that went by the name of Alibhai. He was purchased by Lawrence for sixteen thousand dollars at the Newmarket sales in England on December 5, 1939.

Sent to this country in a wartime shipment that narrowly escaped German submarines, Alibhai was put into training and pointed for the meeting at Santa Anita in 1941. But the horse went lame in training, before he was tested in a race, and this left the alternatives of sending him to the glue factory or putting him to completely uncertain stud. Considering his promising bloodlines, the latter was decided upon, and he was put to servicing some of the lesser mares then being acquired.

In the meantime Mayer had purchased a famous stallion named Beau Pere from the St. Albans Stud in Australia. This great horse, then thirteen-years-old, he bought for one hundred thousand dollars, a good but not exceptional price for a horse of Beau Pere's proven merits. Getting him to this country posed an international problem, since Australia was then at war, but it was done, and Mayer staged a reception for the horse when he arrived in San Francisco aboard the *Mariposa* on January 28, 1941.

Up to this time he had been keeping his horses at Deepcliffe Farm in Cupertino, California, and at the Kingston Farm in Lexington, Kentucky, both of which he leased. But now he decided to develop his own particular breeding and training plant. He purchased five hundred acres at Perris, California, about seventy miles from downtown Los Angeles, and there he had constructed what was generally regarded as the finest horse farm on the West Coast.

Lying flat on the edge of the Mojave Desert, with black, jagged mountains behind, the layout was as beautiful and efficient as any loving horseman could wish. There were seventy-two paddocks, ranging from two to twenty-four acres in size; and a full mile track, fifty feet wide, with four-stall electric starting gate. There were handsome white stables, barns, and granaries—a foaling barn for the mares, an isolation barn in which newly arrived horses could be tested for disease, a breeding shed, and two thirty-six-stall training barns, with large interior walking rings, set close to the training track.

There was a five-acre plot in which to experiment on the growing of grasses of many kinds. Seven deep wells provided water for irrigating the whole place. There were neat bungalows, a commissary, and a single-men's dormitory set among the trees. Mayer's own bungalow was no larger or more elaborate than the rest.

Visitors who knew compared it to the famous ranches of Leland Stanford and "Lucky" Baldwin in years gone by. Mayer coined no fancy name for it; he called it the Mayer Stock Farm.

And that was consistent with the nature of the operation of the place. Inevitably, to the owner, it became a handsome but businesslike plant for the manufacture of race horses, the same as the Culver City studio was a plant for the manufacture of films. Some seventy to a hundred animals were usually in residence—studs, mares in foal, young horses in training, and racers resting from their tours around the tracks. In less than five years Mayer assembled a major racing stable in the United States.

As the get of Beau Pere and Alibhai began coming of rac-

ing age in 1943 and 1944, it was evident that the latter was a
superior sire. His progeny were generally fine youngsters,
with great speed and staying power. They won ten races and
earned $21,000 in 1944. In 1947 they won eighty-five races
and earned some $835,000 prize money. Horsemen often men-
tioned the peculiar fortune of Mayer, that Alibhai failed in
training and had to be put to stud. Otherwise he might have
flopped as a racer and been eliminated from further use.

A more striking instance of Mayer's good fortune was in an
animal named Busher which was bought for him by Neil
McCarthy from Colonel E.R. Bradley in 1944. Bradley was
then dying and his stable was being dispersed. Busher was a
promising filly, by War Admiral out of Baby League. Mc-
Carthy, a Los Angeles lawyer and brilliantly astute racing
man who became the principal adviser and perhaps the most
important contributor to Mayer's success, saw the horse in
Kentucky. Bradley wanted fifty thousand dollars for her. "I
think we can get her for forty thousand," McCarthy informed
Mayer.

"If Colonel Bradley wants fifty thousand, that's a good
price. Pay it," Mayer replied. A horse of equal quality would
fetch five times that money in the market today.

Busher started going to the races in 1945, and promptly
gave every indication that she was a great thoroughbred. In
that year she won, among others, the Santa Margarita Handicap for a fifty-thousand-dollar stake at Santa Anita, a twenty-
five-thousand-dollar match race with Durazna at Chicago's
Washington Park, the fifty-eight-thousand-dollar Washington
Park Handicap for a track record at a mile and a quarter, and
the fifty-thousand-dollar Hollywood Derby at Hollywood Park.
She won more than three hundred thousand dollars which
made her the greatest money-winning filly of all time and sev-
enth among all-time money winners. She was chosen the horse
of the year, the second filly ever to win that honor. No wonder
Mayer considered it a compliment when he likened Greer
Garson to Busher in one of his studio talks.

There were other excellent racers in the stable. Thumbs Up, a yearling bought for thirty-five hundred dollars at the Saratoga sales in 1940, eventually went on to earn some two hundred and fifty thousand dollars in his racing career. Whirlabout, Hunters Moon IV, and Domingo were big winners on eastern and western tracks. Mayer's horses won more than five hundred thousand dollars in prize money in 1945, which made him second among money winners in the country in that, his best year.

But actually his record as a breeder, which is the more intricate and esoteric phase of the sport, was more impressive and significant. For it was as a breeder that he became the wonder of California and "the man most responsible for the renaissance of blood stock on the West Coast." That was probably because his disposition to make his horses pay, to earn a profit out of the business could be more safely and surely satisfied in this line.

In the eyes of people interested in horse racing and breeding for sport, Mayer was politely regarded as a strictly commercial man. Like some others who have taken up racing after they have made big successes in other lines—people such as John Hertz and Elizabeth Arden, the famous owner of Main Chance Farm—his basic drives for money soon dominated his interest in the sport. If he hadn't been able to make profits he would probably have given up.

As one racing expert put it, "He had his eye on the box office all the time." His gauge of the success of his operation was the amount of money it brought in. For this reason he was tough on trainers. He made constant demands for results and regarded trainers as he did directors. A trainer was only as good as his last race.

Mayer did what he aimed to do, however: he made a phenomenal success in a business that is even more difficult and unpredictable than that of films. He won glory for himself; his early relish at being photographed with a winning horse was satisfied so often that it became a banality. He got great pleasure from being named by the New York Turf Writers as the leading breeder in the country in 1945. And his deepest satisfaction was undoubtedly in the knowledge that he had demonstrated "class."

Within a few years his racing interests became so demanding of his time and so involved with his personal affairs and fortune that he had to divest himself of them. But while he was in, he was happy. He not only improved the breed; he improved himself.

# 16

Plainly the peak of personal triumph and glory for Louie Mayer was reached and maintained in the decade after 1938. For it was in these ten years that he was able to exercise and enjoy the authority, wealth, and personal freedom that he had battled all his life to attain. The deep-seated insecurity that had haunted his early years and had fed the fires of his aggressions, by which he steamed up his mammoth energy, had been sublimated more or less by the achievement of Success. Now he was on top, unchallenged, a Hollywood rajah in every respect.

He had his professional position, his supremacy as an earner of wealth, his increasing status as a national figure, and his mounting triumphs as a breeder of thoroughbreds. He was gaining an ever-widening circle of important and influential friends who were truly impressed by his vitality, expansiveness, and charm. As the most potent representative of the management corps in Hollywood he dazzled less glamorous industrial magnates with his air of possession of the place. Given his nature and background, it is no wonder that he

spread out in these years as a supercolossal show-off and
grandly self-serving egoist.

There was this about Mayer that was unquestioned and unusual among his ilk in Hollywood: he had a pronounced disposition and ability to make "big" friends. Thanks in part to
his initial contact and experience with Hearst and to the
rugged savoir-faire that he developed at functions in the
Davies bungalow, he had a tremendous capacity to get through
to people socially. He was also distressingly pervious to those
who might want to get through to him.

The variety of his friends was mammoth. They ranged
from Cardinal Spellman of New York, who was one of his
finest and closest, to con men and even worse. Mayer and
Spellman met when the prelate, who was then the auxiliary
bishop of Boston, was visiting the studio in the company of
Cardinal Pacelli, the Papal Secretary of State who later became Pope Pius XII. The two were attending a Roman Catholic Congress in Los Angeles in 1936 and included in their
sight-seeing the "must-do" tour of Metro-Goldwyn-Mayer.
With his usual attention to important visitors, Mayer showed
them around and found an immediate kinship with Spellman
because of Boston and the fact that the bishop had been an
avid baseball player in Worcester at the same time Mayer
was a fan in Haverhill. The two men saw each other thereafter and Mayer seldom missed a chance to call on Spellman,
particularly after he became Archbishop and then Cardinal in
New York.

Indeed it was often suspected and rumored in later years
that Mayer would become a Roman Catholic because of his
close association with the cardinal. There was nothing at all
to these rumors. Mayer had deep respect for the Roman faith
and a strong admiration for the organization, the discipline,
and the rituals of the Catholic Church, but he had no wish to
change his religion. And though he hobnobbed a good deal
with priests, it is questionable whether the Church would

have received him, even if he had wished. His domestic and marital record might have proved an embarrassment.

Religion was something that Mayer seemed to treat rather casually, anyhow, once he had pulled out of Boston and passed beyond the orthodoxy of his youth. Although he belonged to a temple, he rarely attended services, except on those days when it was virtually compulsory for an acknowledged Jew. He lived pretty much by his own standards, which were what was convenient at the time. Once he solemnly told a friend, in extenuation of his then rather reckless conduct, "The Talmud says a man is not responsible for a sin committed by any part of his body below the waist."

For a time he was interested in Moral Rearmament. This was in 1939, and he performed as a speaker at a big rally held in the Hollywood Bowl that year. But his sudden enthusiasm soon faded. A mutual pact of nonaggression was negotiated early between Mayer and God.

Another important friendship was struck up with Henry Ford. Here was an American industrialist whom he particularly admired. Mayer had met Edsel Ford and his family when they visited the studio in 1935. Then in February, 1940, he went to Detroit, along with Mickey Rooney and others, to attend the world première of *Young Tom Edison,* and on this occasion was introduced to the old man, who showed him his Dearborn museum and his automobile factories. Mayer made a solid impression on the elder Ford and kept that contact active until the old man died.

K.T. Keller, board chairman of Chrysler Corporation; Louis Johnson, who later became Secretary of Defense in the Truman administration; and, of course, Herbert Hoover and Hearst were among the powerful individuals with whom he continually fraternized.

His loyalty to Hearst, for all the rancor that developed in 1934, was shown when he made a bold endeavor to block release of the film, *Citizen Kane,* a decidedly sensational drama, produced and acted by Orson Welles. It was, without any question, a thinly disguised and devastating picture of Hearst, and this report was soon circulated around Hollywood when the picture was in production at R-K-O in 1941.

Though Welles had assured George Schaefer, the president of R-K-O, that it could just as well be Sam Insull or a couple of other American tycoons, Schaefer feared he was in trouble when the word began getting around. He wasn't surprised when he received a phone call from Nicholas Schenck asking him to come to his New York office to see him. A call from Schenck was a summons, so Schaefer oblingingly complied. But he was surprised at the suggestion that Schenck made to him.

"Louie has asked me to speak to you about this picture. He is prepared to pay you what it cost, which he understands is eight hundred thousand dollars, if you will destroy the negative and all the prints."

Schaefer gulped. "Such an extraordinary suggestion coming from a man in your position must be carefully considered," he replied.

"The request comes from Louie, not from me," Schenck said.

Now Schaefer knew he was in trouble, with such pressure being applied. He dared not go to his board of directors with the proposal for fear he would be told to accept. On his own responsibility he decided to go through with the release. For one thing, he had a special reason for not wanting to be defeated by Mayer. The latter had tried to bulldoze him into hiring one of his friends to run the R-K-O studio when Schaefer became president in 1939. Schaefer had resisted the "suggestion" and Mayer had "been displeased." This was indicated in little irritations. Schaefer had no use for Mayer.

Assured that *Citizen Kane* was free of libel (except for one line that was changed), Schaefer proceeded to endeavor to get bookings for it. Here he ran into curious trouble. No theater seemed to want to show the film. The Music Hall in

New York City declined it—and that was indeed a surprise, for the Music Hall and R-K-O were in alliance by virtue of their both being interests of the Rockefellers and Chase bank. Schaefer was made suspicious when one day he got a call from Nelson Rockefeller saying he had heard "from a Hearst columnist named Parsons" that the picture should not be shown. Schaefer carefully explained that the picture was not libelous, which apparently satisfied Rockefeller. But the Music Hall was out.

Such being the case, Schaefer proceeded to lease independent theaters in New York and Los Angeles to give the film its initial showing and also launched a big national advertising campaign. But even the head of the company that placed the advertising tried to prevail upon him to give up. It just so happened the company also handled the advertising for Loew's, Inc., and Schenck had a financial interest in it.

Even after the openings of the picture in Los Angeles and New York and a fine reception from the critics and from the public generally, Schaefer couldn't swing subsequent bookings, except in the theaters of R-K-O. The large circuits of Loew's, Fox, Warners, and Paramount wished to keep hands off. Finally, one day Schaefer bearded the head of the Warner theaters and said: "Look, Joe, so far you have refused to book *Citizen Kane*. You know the reviews have been the best. I don't have to tell you of its quality. All you have to do is look at its record. Now why aren't you booking it? I'll tell you. You aren't booking it because Louie Mayer has got together with Joe Schenck and Harry Warner and arranged with them to keep it off the screen. So I'm asking you for the last time—are you going to book it or not? Because if you think this conspiracy is going to keep it off the screen, you are mistaken. I'll sue and expose the conspiracy."

Shortly after that Warner theaters booked the picture and resistance quickly dissolved. *Citizen Kane* was a big success and is now regarded as a classic of the screen. Whether it ever did any damage to the reputation of Hearst is doubtful. (His papers did not review it.) But it offended the *amour propre* of Mayer.

Naturally he did not let up on Schaefer. Sometime the following year the latter got word that top stockholders in R-K-O had been informed that the reason the studio was not prospering as much as they wished was because Schaefer was anti-Semitic. Schaefer traced these rumors to Frank Orsatti, and behind him to Mayer, who he sensed, by these maneuvers, was endeavoring to cause dissension at R-K-O. He also strongly suspected that Mayer wanted to buy a large block of R-K-O stock and was trying to frighten a big stockholder into selling to him.

Mayer's friendships were not all on the level of the Spellmans and the Fords, by any means. He was not above playing buddies with some shady and odorous characters. Carter Barron, the able and popular representative of Loew's, Inc., in Washington, went into the dining room of a leading hotel in the capital one day in company with Howard Strickling, who was visiting Washington with Mayer, and saw the latter lunching with a notorious lobbyist and known associate of criminals. Barron, who was a good friend of statesmen and top people in Washington, firmly refused to go over to Mayer's table and speak to him. When he later explained he didn't choose to be seen in the company of a character such as Mayer's friend—and, incidentally, he did not think it politic for the head of Metro-Goldwyn-Mayer to be seen in that character's company in Washington either—Mayer chided him for being stuffy. "You're a damn Baptist," he said. "Don't you know you've got to know all sorts of people. I use him to do things for me that you won't do."

Certainly Mayer's friendship with Frank Orsatti was in a doubtful realm. Orsatti, while acceptable as an agent, so far as agents go, was a questionable individual even by tolerant Hollywood standards. His capacity as an agent is illuminated by the fact that once, when asked to outline a story that he emphatically described as "the best goddamn story ever written," he indifferently replied, "How should I know what it's about! The author can tell you that."

But it was generally suspected among people who had a knowledge of Mayer that he kept close company with the agent because the latter knew a lot of friendly girls. His beach house at Santa Monica was a lively pleasure-dome, and it was there that Mayer did much relaxing during his expansive years.

This aspect of Mayer's behavior in the years of his success was something that might have stayed private had he been in any other walk of life.

But in the business of manufacturing movies contacts of the sexes are so close and men are involved with women to such a considerable extent that whatever private relations may develop among them become considerations of professional importance and even commercial concern. There is more than lecherous humor in the phrase, "the casting couch." Whom a producer or director is sleeping with, as they say, is knowledge that could be as vital as his current interest in a novel or play.

Furthermore, exhibitionism is a primary trait of the run of people engaged in picture making, and one of the favorite areas of exhibitionism is, naturally, sex. Sexual prowess is, by convention, a major boast among males. And an ability to attract masculine interest is an occupational asset with the opposite sex. Success or activity in this department is considered a matter for public report.

To be sure, public interest is mainly in the amours of the stars—in the purposefully glamour-polished people who are directly exposed to the public gaze. The affairs of producers and directors, and particularly executives, are not usually so interesting or beguiling. Who their mistresses are is mainly of note or consideration to insiders in Hollywood. And because of the power of these fellows, the gossip about them is usually more guarded and discreet.

Mayer was one of those people whom the gossipers had to

treat with a prudence and circumspection that approached aphonia. When it came to gossiping about him voices were kept very low. Word of his sex activities inevitably got around—and those activities became more and more aggressive as he got on in years. But the columnists—especially the powerful female writers whom he pretty much held in thrall —seldom, if ever, reported any sexual life in him. He was of regal order, and it didn't pay for cats to look too closely at kings.

The fact was that Mayer could not be slotted among the more wanton types. He preserved a certain loftiness of conduct in approaching the intimacies of sex. He seemed to desire, in his own mind, to endow his urges with *noblesse oblige*. He preferred to think of the women whom he embraced as sacred vessels, potential mothers, rather than as what they obviously were.

Indeed, it was a joke among his playmates that he was so full of romantic fantasies about the nature of females that he obstructed his own success. They meant that he'd waste so much time talking about the magnificence of virtue and motherhood that he'd argue or bore his willing companion into a state of complete frigidity. The lady, ready to be obliging, would suddenly find herself confronted with a middle-aged satyr who was also a full-time moralist. The experience would tend to be distracting. The lady would often be reduced to lachrymose shame or laughter, either of which was discouraging to the business at hand.

On the occasional libidinous forays that he conducted alone, he was prone to be highly decorous. Some of his contemporaries ruefully recall an evening when they were gathered in a luxurious Hollywood establishment ready to make a big night of it, when the madame interrupted and asked, with much embarrassment and many apologies, that they leave immediately.

"Mr. Mayer has just called and wishes to come here incognito," she said. "He doesn't like to be here with strangers." The gentlemen obligingly left.

In his more delicate personal relations with established and aspiring actresses he was naturally careful and decorous, but none the less vigorous in pursuit of those he lusted after, frequently in vain. Any intelligent woman could easily handle Mayer, with a bit of flattering and flirtation, and most of the smart stars did. He once said to Luise Rainer, "Why won't you sit on my lap when we're discussing your contract the way the other girls do?" A little adroit lap-sitting would go a long way, they found.

He was hardy and persistent, however. Tirelessly he laid siege to some of the more formidable actresses, rewarding them with richer roles or disciplining them with poor assignments, in maneuvering to accomplish his private aims. It was long suspected around the studio that he was "after" Jeanette MacDonald and Myrna Loy, both of whom had the experience of being indulged and then disfavored by him. Miss Loy's long strike against the studio in 1935, when she went to Europe because she justifiably claimed she was being overworked, was generally suspected to be her protest against some machinations of Mayer. Her holdout made her grievance public and earned her a better contract and less work.

With some of the ladies who repulsed him Mayer was less generous, especially if they were so ungracious as to add insult to injury. There was the case of a young actress, fresh out from New York on an optional contract to Metro-Goldwyn-Mayer, who was told by the casting department that a script would be sent to her to read. It was the script of a forthcoming production in which she hoped that she might be cast. Imagine her amazement that evening when it was delivered to her, not by a studio messenger, but by the head of the studio himself.

Later that evening she called Robert Montgomery, an old friend from the New York stage, and told him what had happened—how the visitor had arrived and made the most obvious, clumsy, and ludicrous advances to her.

"What did you do?" Montgomery asked her.

"I laughed at him," she said.

"Honey," the actor told her, "you've just laughed yourself right out of Hollywood."

Sure enough, she was not chosen for a role in the new film, and at the end of a year her option was not picked up.

During this phase of Mayer's surrender to the "dangerous age," friends saw the deterioration of ties to his wife and home. Following her illness in Europe, Mrs. Mayer appeared less and less with him. Her taste was for grandparental status and simple domesticity. But not Mayer's. Though well in his fifties, he wanted to act like a young man. He told friends he'd be damned if he was going to "stay home and sit in front of the fire in a smoking jacket and carpet slippers, the way my wife wants me to do!" The end of the road with the helpmate of his years of struggle was in view.

The rift in the traditionally inviolable association with her seemed to unloosen and unsettle the always tenuous ties with his brothers and sisters, too. An early and angry disagreement with his older sister, Yetta, who was married and lived in Los Angeles, brought an estrangement between them that was never even partially healed. He wouldn't see this sister, and she stayed away from him.

His older brother, Rudy, the one who had been involved very briefly and unpropitiously with him in Haverhill, had moved around as a free agent and operator of sorts through the years, making money, living sportily, and occasionally getting into trouble from which Louie bailed him out. Their quarrels, whenever they dared face each other, were vicious and horrible. Mayer once tried to get rid of Rudy by setting him up in a film importing business in Hong Kong. The business failed and Rudy bounced back. He continued a trial to Louie, dunning and damning his rich brother until he obligingly died.

Brother Jerry, who worked for the studio in the purchasing department, remained more or less in Louie's good graces, but they had a few terrible fights which resulted in ugly estrangements. These were patched up when someone would assume the volunteer role of peacemaker and urge Louie to forget and forgive.

One of these unfraternal fall-outs which happened about the time that Mayer was kicking over domestic traces seemed to be the last. Mayer was more bitter and relentless than he had ever been. Months passed, and the brothers did not speak. Then came the day of the Mayer's Yahrzeit, or anniversary of their mother's death, when by Jewish tradition, they were supposed to go to their temples to pray. This would be the day, if any, to appeal to Mayer's sentiment. So his nephew, Jack Cummings, who was the son of sister Ida Mae, former wife of Sam Kominsky, decided to act.

He went to Jerry's home and got him in his car. Then he drove to Louis's place at Santa Monica. With Jerry remaining outside, Cummings went into Uncle Louie's house and opened a conversation about going to the temple to pray.

"You should kneel beside Jerry and send your prayers up to your mother together," he said. "This way, how do you know whose prayers she is hearing, yours or Jerry's? Maybe she's only hearing his."

Mayer pondered this consideration and was moved to say that, if he could get hold of Jerry somehow, he might be willing to kneel down with him.

"He's waiting for you," Cummings answered.

Mayer was surprised. "He's waiting where?"

"Outside in my car," said Cummings. Mayer was trapped, and the brothers were reconciled.

With sister Ida Mae, Mayer was always on close and affectionate terms. She, of all his siblings, managed to stay on the right side of him.

Such was the state of his existence when, in 1942, there entered it a woman who was to have a profound effect on him.

She was, appropriately, a physician, Dr. Jessie Marmorston, whose specialty in the medical profession was the functioning of the endocrine glands.

Through her late husband, a New York physician who knew Irving Thalberg, she had met Lawrence Weingarten and had got acquainted with his friends in Hollywood. On the night that Bernie Hyman died from a heart attack in his home she happened to be there with Weingarten and was trying to straighten out the distorted corpse, before the arrival of the undertaker, when she was aware of a man with piercing eyes gazing at her from a bedroom doorway. She asked him to go away.

"Don't you know who I am?" the man answered. "I am Louie Mayer."

"I don't care who you are," said Jessie. "I think you should permit me to do this disagreeable thing for this poor body, without standing there staring at me."

Mayer went away, and, later, when Jessie returned to the living room he came directly to her and started talking and cultivating her. For three days thereafter he pursued her. He was fascinated. And she, of course, was fascinated and stimulated by him. Mayer found it significant that Jessie had been born in Russia, as had he; that she had come to America as a child without a mother, had known what it was to be "brought up from the street," and had struggled for a medical education, which was most fascinating of all. He immediately made himself her patient, and, when she returned to New York he went on the same train with her. That was the beginning of an intimate communication that continued for the remainder of Mayer's life.

Jessie Marmorston was small, dark, and pretty, a woman with distinct feminine charm, but a forcefulness and resolution that were almost as masculine as Mayer's. Her intelligence and capacity for understanding his strange psychological quirks made her more valuable to him than the medical attention she gave to his glands. She was probably a good deal like his mother in her elemental sympathies for him, and he wallowed luxuriously in the attention and commiseration he got from this woman of superior mentality and energy.

Whether her friendship and counsels finally persuaded him to take the step that had been apparent as logical for several years is not a matter of record. But in 1944, on the eve of their fortieth wedding anniversary, Mayer said to his wife, "I'm leaving," and moved out of his Santa Monica home. He went briefly to live with Howard Strickling at his San Fernando Valley ranch, then rented and took up residence in solitary splendor in the elaborate mansion of Marion Davies in Beverly Hills.

Now he entered upon a period of self-gratification and display that was startling for a man in his position. It gave his associates grave concern. He lived in lordly fashion, as though wanting to convey by the evidence of his independence the extent of his superiority in Hollywood. Although there was no breath of public criticism his more sensible friends were much disturbed and his daughters were desolated that his private life should have come to this.

There was a brief pause for reflection in the fall of 1944 when he suffered a painful accident at his Perris Valley farm. He was spending a weekend there with a group of convivial friends, which included Jessie Marmorston and Larry Weingarten. These two were now keeping company, he being divorced from Sylvia Thalberg.

On Sunday morning Mayer invited everybody to come out to the training track to watch him ride one of the thoroughbreds that had a reputation for being a brute. He had mounted the horse and had ridden a few times around the track, calling his audience's attention to the fact that there was no checkrein on the beast. There wasn't the slightest question that Mayer was showing off.

Suddenly the animal became skittish, reared, and hurled the rider to the ground. Mayer was lying immobile and groaning when his friends rushed to his side. Jessie Marmorston recognized immediately that something was broken inside, and an ambulance was called to transport him to Los Angeles. On the ride into the city Mayer said to Jessie, through gritted teeth, "Well, he did it!" This was his acknowledgment that a horse had finally got the best of him.

At the Cedars of Lebanon Hospital X-rays showed that he had a fracture of the pelvis. At his age of fifty-nine this was not a minor affliction. And, in a few days, it was complicated by the development of pneumonia. His condition was listed as critical, and it appeared that Mayer, by his own exuberance, had at last brought an end to his career.

But again a miracle happened. The pneumonia slowly cleared and it was evident that the broken pelvis would knit satisfactorily. Mayer went through a long recuperation at his luxurious bachelor residence, holding court for executives of the studio who came to consult with him and acting pitiful for the beautiful stars who brought him home-made chicken soup. Within a few months, he was able to get around almost as well as he had before the accident. He felt well-nigh indestructible.

In the next few years he showed amazing physical vitality and was unrestrained in courting several prominent actresses. Ann Miller, a long-legged dancer at Metro-Goldwyn-Mayer, was a frequent decorative companion in his regular night-club hops. It was evident that he chose tall, graceful, lovely and distinctly non-Semitic types to be his partners in public. He was sensitive about his own Semitic looks.

Most notable of the ladies that he briefly but ardently pursued in this Don Juanish period was the singer, Ginny Simms. She had been in several R-K-O pictures with Kay Kyser and his band, and had appeared with Abbott and Costello in a Universal comedy when she was brought to Culver City to be in *Broadway Rhythm*, a musical. Mayer paid elaborate court to her and tried, through her parents and friends, in the memorable manner of Miles Standish, to talk her into agreeing to marry him. He came to New York when she was playing a personal appearance date at the Capitol Theater and caused embarrassment to executives of Loew's, Inc., by carrying courtship to the point of sitting for hours in her dressing room. The undignified incongruity of the head of the largest studio in the world playing Stagedoor Johnny never seemed to occur to Mayer. However, Miss Simms resisted the romantic ardor of a man old enough to be her father. She married a nonprofessional in 1945.

The deaths of his pal, Frank Orsatti, and his brother, Jerry, in 1947 threw brief shadows across his primrose pathway. And, in that same year, his patient wife, despairing of his returning to her, sued to obtain a divorce. These sad events did not repress him, nor did the considerable fact that the court ordered him to settle more than three million dollars on his wife.

To meet this big bite from his large fortune, it had already been recognized that it would be smart for him to dispose of some of his thoroughbreds. An auction sale of his horses was held on February 27 of that year, and it turned out to be what Nelson Dunstan of *The Morning Telegraph* described as "the most spectacular sale of horses in training ever staged anywhere in the world."

That was entirely in character for the Number One showman in Hollywood. The sale was held in the evening at the Santa Anita track and was witnessed by more than seven thousand persons. Part of it was also broadcast nationally by radio. Sixty horses were sold for an all time record of more than $1,500,000; among them Busher, Be Faithful, Stepfather, and the handsome Honeymoon. Stepfather fetched the highest price of any horse in the show. He was knocked down to Harry M. Warner for $200,000. Had Mayer been sentimental about his horses, he might have cringed at this favorite going to another Hollywood nabob with whom he had long carried on a bitter feud. He didn't care; he was only happy that the horse brought such a good price.

After the auction, Humphrey Finney, who managed the sale, asked Mayer if he was satisfied.

Mayer answered crisply, "Satisfied, yes; pleased, no!"

Actually the sale was but the first of three that were held to clear out the entire racing stable. Mayer's lawyers and tax experts found it necessary for him to dispose completely of the investment and enterprise in order to take advantage of the capital gains provision in the income tax law. Furthermore, Nicholas Schenck was complaining that he was spending too much time playing around with horse racing and not enough at the studio. Mayer got rid of all his horses at further sales in 1948 and 1949 and sold his Perris Valley ranch to the Church of the Latter Day Saints.

When the second sale was held he had George Swinebroad, the eminent auctioneer, come out to Hollywood a few days earlier so he could give him a few suggestions on how he should handle West Coast buyers, especially people of the movie colony. He should slow the pace, give the individuals attention and flattery. Mayer himself demonstrated the auctioneering techniques he was advocating. Swinebroad took the suggestions and sold thirty-nine two-year-olds for more than $1,000,000.

When asked how he liked it this time, Mayer replied happily, "Swinebroad, you were diamonds to a nickel!" That was praise, indeed.

While he was shedding his horses Mayer was acquiring a new wife—an adventure fraught with excitement and a shade of absurdity. Through Louella Parsons and others, who assiduously devoted themselves to playing cupid for him, he became acquainted with Lorena Danker, the widow of Danny Danker, an advertising man. She was a tall, pretty, pleasant young matron, who under the name of Lorena Layton had been a dancer and minor player in Warner Brothers films.

Mayer took a strong liking to her and went through his usual routine of plying her with attentions and the glowing endorsements of helpful friends. So frequently did they assure her of his ardor and generosity that she might have suspected the manipulation of a carefully plotted campaign. Lorena had a young daughter and was so obviously more appropriate to a man of Mayer's age and status than some of the girls he had pursued that his own daughters were delighted at this new romantic turn.

However, the romance did not run smoothly. It often flowed hot and then cold. Neither Mayer nor Lorena seemed able to make up their minds. In the midst of one of these cool stretches, Hedda Hopper, gossip columnist and violent rival of Louella, had the temerity to publish a report that Mayer had no intention of marrying Lorena. Shortly after this he and Hedda met at a party at the home of Dolly Walker, a Beverly Hills socialite, and in a rebuke clearly heard by all those present he reduced the powerful columnist to tears.

"Those crocodile tears don't affect me," he was heard to say by Harry Crocker, a writer for Hearst's papers who was an amused observer of this rare scene. "You are frustrated and unhappy, and you take it out on others. If you hurt my life through your malice I will see to it that you pay!"

The threat did not have to be made good, for Mayer and Lorena were wed, during a phase of mutual inclination, in December, 1948. They had planned to fly to Yuma, Arizona, to be secretly married there, away from the prying eyes of Hollywood, then announce their marriage upon their return. But a storm on the day they intended to fly upset plans, and there was some vague suggestion of a postponement by Mayer. Friends say Lorena said "Now or never," so it was arranged for the small wedding party to go to Yuma on the overnight train.

It was an odd party for an elopement. It included Lorena's eleven-year-old daughter, Suzanne, Howard Strickling, and Whitey Hendrey, head of the studio police. They arrived in Yuma at four in the morning, went first to a motor hotel, then had breakfast at a drive-in restaurant to which a court clerk brought application forms.

Meanwhile word had leaked out that Louis B. Mayer was

in town for the purpose of matrimony, and reporters and photographers began to descend. The party hastily fled the drive-in restaurant, went back to the motel, then, pursued by newsmen, skedaddled to the office of Sheriff J.A. Beard. There, in a grubby sheriff's office overlooking the bare yard of the Yuma County jail, and with a justice of the peace performing the ceremony, the wealthy head of the world's largest film studio took unto himself a second wife.

Sheriff Beard, a friend of Hendrey, then lent the party a couple of deputy-driven cars for a mad dash back to California. There ended the Keystone comedy chase.

The Hollywood colony was amused and a little disdainful when the rococo news appeared in the afternoon papers. After all, this sort of thing was a bit immature and old-fashioned, reminiscent of the doings of "silent" stars. That the sixty-three-year-old head of a major studio should choose to elope seemed absurd. It strongly suggested obsolescence in the thinking processes of Mayer.

And, indeed, there were other reasons for suspecting he was falling behind the times. Circumstances were crowding him out of his glory, as events of the next few years were to prove.

# 17

Even while Mayer was whirling through the lavish illusion of a second youth, hard realities were descending upon studios in Hollywood. The motion picture business, which had waxed during World War II and reached the peak of its prosperity in 1946, was hit in 1947 by a ton of accumulated bricks that seemed aimed to demolish this great entertainment industry.

The postwar evolution in patterns of American life, with new families and new homeowners spending their money and time on things more essential than movie going, caught up with the business in this year and had an effect upon attendance that would have done enough damage by itself. But simultaneous with this economic damper there now began to emerge the great new rival, television, that was to knock the movie business in the head.

From a virtually inconsequential forty thousand receiving sets operating in this country at the end of World War II—and most of those forty thousand presumably in saloons—the number rose to four million in the brief passage of four years (and had gone on to forty million by 1958). And as sharply as broadcasting facilities and the number of home-owned sets rose, just as sharply—and even more sharply at the out-set—did attendance at movie theaters fall.

This dizzying decline was indicated by a drop in the gross income of Loew's, Inc., from $18,000,000 in the first twelve months after the end of the war to a little more than $4,000,-000 in the twelve months prior to September 1, 1948. In two years the company's gross income was reduced by more than seventy-five percent. Alarm bells began ringing all over the place.

The hazard in this situation was rendered more ominous for Loew's, Inc., by the recognized fact that its studio was in an obese and inefficient state. The employee list was loaded with high-priced executives, but there were few creative pro-ducers who could be depended on for quality films. The stu-dio, while literally crowded with contract directors and stars, was strangely not winning "Oscars" or placing pictures on "ten best" lists. Mayer had hired plenty of people on his the-ory of buying "strength in depth," and these people were grinding out pictures, but few of these were hits. Something was obviously missing in the operation of the studio.

On Schenck's perturbed insistence, inquiries were started when the ominous manifestations of 1947 began to appear. Mayer, instructed to get busy and prove his administrative skill, cast about and came up with a decision to abandon the executive producer system that had been in effect in the stu-dio for ten years. All of the bonus-fat executives who had been riding the gravy train during prosperous years were put to producing individually, rather than in comfortable groups, or were discreetly shunted into administrative jobs. Mayer named himself, Eddie Mannix, and Benny Thau as an ex-ecutive triumvirate, with individual producers answerable di-rectly to them.

But, of course, this reorganization amounted only to a shuffling of hands. There was no infusion whatsoever of essential creative personnel. Sam Katz and Al Lichtman, for instance, were primarily businessmen, without the imagination it took to compose exceptional films. L.K. Sidney and J.J. Cohn were bookkeepers and were put to bookkeeping jobs. Hunt Stromberg was gone because of illness. Harry Rapf was passé.

Obviously what the studio needed was a powerful production head—"another Thalberg," as Schenck entreated and Mayer continued to try to find.

The quest became desperate when it was made painfully clear that the studio would show a heavy deficit on its operations for 1947-48. Advance indications that the figures would be some $5,000,000 in the red (they were actually $6,500,000) spurred Mayer like nothing else could. He again tried to urge David Selznick to return to the studio, but Selznick, less interested than ever, absolutely refused. Mayer even made advances to Walter Wanger and Joe Mankiewicz, two of his most afflicted victims, which showed just how desperate he was.

Then by a happy coincidence of suggestion and inspiration, he found the man he was seeking in an alumnus of Metro-Goldwyn-Mayer. The man was Dore Schary, head of production at R-K-O and one of the most controversial young executives in Hollywood.

Mayer had known Schary from years back, and Schary certainly knew Mayer. Considering what they knew of each other, their conjunction at this point was odd. But Mayer was in a situation where he could not let his personal whims intrude, and Schary, unhappy at R-K-O, was looking for a job.

The two had first come into close contact in 1941, when Schary was an up-and-coming writer at Metro-Goldwyn-Mayer. Because of two good writing credits on *Boys' Town* and *Young Tom Edison,* he was on friendly terms with the producer of those films, John Considine, and tried to get him to let him write and direct a small-budget picture from a story called *Joe Smith, American*. The story had to do with a factory worker victimized by Nazi spies in the tense and sensitive period before America entered World War II.

Considine said he would be for it, if it had the approval of Mayer, and thereupon took the writer to see the head of the studio. Mayer protested it would be a "little picture," nothing for Considine to do, and was ready to dismiss the idea when Schary put in a word. He said it *should* be a "little picture," that the "little pictures" of the studio could be improved and that the unit producing those pictures should be the studio's most fertile training ground. The pitch was enthusiastic, and Mayer was impressed by it.

The next day he summoned Schary to meet him on the steps of the Irving Thalberg Memorial Building, the handsome white marble edifice that had been erected in 1937 alongside the Culver City lot to house producers, writers, directors, and top executives. There Mayer picked him up and hustled him into his automobile, which immediately took off through traffic with no indication of where they were bound. Mayer began talking to Schary about the B-picture idea, said he thought it was a dandy and that he meant to do something about it.

Before the writer knew it they were at Hollywood Park race track and Mayer was rushing him forward into his special box, still talking enthusiastically about the B-picture idea. And there, with Mayer also conversing with his trainer and other horsey folks, he offered to make Schary the creative head of the B-unit that he said he was about to reorganize.

Schary had never been to a race track and was flabbergasted by it all, but Mayer was completely casual, as though this was the way he did business regularly. He told Schary if he believed in the idea as much as he said he did, he would happily jump at the offer, promising that he would be left alone and that it was his chance to prove himself as a producer, which Schary did not particularly want to be.

"I want to direct," he protested.

"Why direct?" Mayer said. "Anybody can direct. I've watched you, my boy. I've heard you talk. I know you can do this job."

So that's how Schary became head of a new B-unit and fell into the line of observation of Mayer.

The new unit was eminently successful. It turned out such memorable little films as *Joe Smith, American, Journey for Margaret, The War Against Mrs. Hadley,* and *Lassie Come Home,* and provided training for such new young directors as George Sidney, Jules Dassin, and Fred Zinnemann. However, the unit's business manager was the old-timer, Harry Rapf, with whom Schary had previously had some difficulties, and the two soon found they couldn't get along.

Mayer heard of their troubles and called both men to his office one day, demanding an explanation. Rapf was trying to tell his side, when suddenly Mayer burst loose upon him and gave him a tongue-lashing such as Schary had never heard.

It was horrible and shameful to see Rapf standing there, white and trembling, taking vicious abuse from his old boss. Schary was stunned and nauseated. He finally had to leave precipitately and go to the men's room, where he vomited in sheer revulsion at what he had seen and heard.

He went home, told his wife what had happened, then called Mayer that night and said he felt terrible about the difficulty and asked that Rapf not be fired. Mayer told him to come to see him the next day. Schary did, and Mayer was all smiles, chided him for being soft-hearted and called him "a boy scout." Two days later Rapf's discharge was rescinded.

That was Schary's first glimpse of the angry Mayer.

Another aspect of the man was discovered by him at the Christmas luncheon for executives in the dark and depressing December of 1941. The shock of Pearl Harbor and the menace of a Japanese invasion were still heavy on the West Coast, and the film business, along with the whole nation, was faced with uncertainties. It was a somber group of executives that Mayer confronted when he arose to deliver his usual talk at the luncheon. After acknowledging the perilous times and the studio's resolution to go ahead with the rest of the nation in the ordeal of war, he lifted his wine glass and said, "Gentlemen, I think it fitting at this time that we drink a toast to our president . . ." He paused for everyone to rise and lift their glasses, then added solemnly, "To our president, Nicholas M. Schenck."

The conclusion of that first association between Mayer and Schary came when the latter was denied an opportunity to make a picture he very much wanted to do. It was an allegory on Hitler, Mussolini, Nazism, and Fascism, framed within the format of an American western. Mayer didn't like the idea, thought it too "intellectual." So Schary asked release from his contract. Mayer couldn't understand the fervor and the stubbornness of the young man.

"You've got another job!" he challenged.

"No other job," Schary said.

"Then you want more money," Mayer insisted. "If that's it, why don't you say so?"

Schary tried to explain there were other than salary reasons for a man feeling caught in a job, that there are matters of principle and conviction on which a man must stand. Mayer was provoked and baffled. He gave orders for Schary's release.

That was *his* first encounter with a side of Schary he was to come to know too well.

The paths of the two next grazed slightly in 1947 when the motion picture industry was under fire of a Congressional committee out to show that Hollywood was crowded with Communists. Two men, Adrian Scott and Edward Dmytryk, had written and directed a film called *Crossfire* which Schary had started and produced as studio head at R-K-O. At Congressional hearings in Washington, Scott and Dmytryk had refused to say whether they were members of the Communist Party, and Schary was called upon to testify what he intended to do. He took the position that it would be illegal for him, under California law, to discharge the men for political reasons. This caused certain newspapers to scream RKO HEAD SAYS HE WILL HIRE REDS. Schary was obviously embarrassed in Hollywood.

Shortly after this the industry's leaders were called to an extraordinary meeting at the Waldorf-Astoria in New York to consider an all-industry policy of refusing to employ known or suspected Communists. Mayer and Schary were present as heads of studios and were once more in conflict in their points of view. Mayer was entirely in agreement that anyone suspected of political taint should be kept out of studio employment; Schary stubbornly held, with a small minority which included Samuel Goldwyn, that a man's politics should have nothing to do with his getting or holding a job.

While the relations of Mayer and Schary on this occasion were amiable enough, it was evident to both that their conceptions of the democratic principle were opposed. Once, previously, Mayer had told Schary he was suspected of being a "pink." Schary replied that Mayer, conversely, was believed a Fascist of sorts. They did not then pursue the question further, and they did not pursue it further now. But their juxtaposition on the employment issue left no question of where they stood.

As it happened, the Waldorf meeting voted to accept an anti-Communist policy, and the R-K-O board of directors summarily fired the highly sensitive Scott and Dmytryk, taking the matter out of Schary's hands. Some people thought that, on principle, he could do nothing but resign. However, he remained with the studio until the following year, when Howard Hughes obtained possession of it and began making his tenure miserable. This was just at the time that Mayer was seeking a head of production for the Culver City studio.

The first advances to Schary to consider the job were made by Mayer. This fact, which was subsequently disputed, is incontrovertible. He sent a message to Schary to come to see him several days before the latter's resignation from R-K-O was announced. How strongly Mayer was influenced to call him by others who later claimed they were responsible for Schary's employment is not now (and never will be) clear. The important thing is that the decision to seek him was made by Mayer.

How Mayer could have come to this decision, knowing what he did about the man, his "intellectual" disposition and his firmness on matters of principle, is a trifle mystifying, but it can best be explained and understood by recalling the critical situation at the studio. Schary had a favorable record of successful production for R-K-O, and before that for David Selznick's Vanguard company. Anybody who could satisfy Selznick was well recommended to Mayer. And, besides, there was nothing more impressive than a record of successful films.

Furthermore the mere fact that Schary was a veteran of Metro-Goldwyn-Mayer—that he had been "one of ours"—had some significance to the head of the studio. His stubbornness was also respected; Mayer liked people who had "guts." And he was firmly convinced that he could manage, guide, and "do something with this boy." Finally there was this factor: Schary was a sincere and devout Jew and he was deeply attached to his mother, which fact touched and reassured Mayer.

When conversations between the two men reached a point where an agreement loomed, Mayer notified Schenck, who flew to California with Robert Rubin and his man, Charles Moskowitz. Schenck was impressed by Schary, who was gracious and respectful toward him. He pictured "another Thalberg" in the tall, quiet, bespectacled young man.

In secret meetings to negotiate a contract Schary and his agent asked that his position and authority at the studio should be absolutely defined. Mayer and his old associate, Rubin, were inclined to leave that vague, but Schary was aware of the trouble Thalberg had had because of his indefinite relationship to Mayer. So it was specifically stated that Schary would be "vice-president in charge of production" and that his only superiors would be Schenck as president of Loew's, Inc., and Mayer as the head of the studio.

A contract was drawn to give him a salary of six thousand dollars a week—four thousand dollars payable weekly and two thousand dollars deferred. That was to be the extent of his remuneration; no bonus deal for him. The contract was for seven years, to start July 1, 1948.

The night after Schary signed the contract he had dinner with his friend, Joe Mankiewicz, who was candidly doubtful of the prospect and couldn't see much chance of his being able to impose his will upon production and get around the obstruction of Mayer.

"You're like a man setting out to conquer China," he said. "In three years you'll be a Chinaman."

Schary smiled and shrugged his shoulders. "I can get along with L.B.," he said. "After all he's very much like my father." His father was a futile blusterer.

At the outset, it did appear likely that they would get along handsomely. Mayer was proud of his new head of production, and Schary clearly condescended to him. The power of decision was Schary's, with Mayer consulted only on matters of policy.

His eagerness to see Schary happy was shown in the matter of negotiations to buy the screen rights to *Father of the Bride*. Schary had read the story and liked it very much, but Kenneth MacKenna, the story editor, said he feared it would come too high. So Schary discussed with Mayer what they should offer for it and how far they could go in bargaining. "Do you like the story?" Mayer said. "Do you think it will make a wonderful picture? Then what are you bargaining for, my boy? Grab it and make the picture!" That's the way he was.

Schary, in turn, fell in adroitly with the famous optimism of Mayer.

"I believe that essentially this is a good world and I want to make pictures for men of good will," he told a gathering of interviewers in New York a month after he was in the job. "Others can make the so-called 'arty' pictures, most of which are based on sordid themes, but I prefer to be associated with pictures like *Joe Smith, American* . . . I don't think art is four-letter words written on bathroom walls."

The sentiment could not have been more pious had it come from the lips of Mayer.

The first disagreement of the two men came over a property called *Battleground,* which Schary had carefully developed and wanted to produce when he was at R-K-O. It was a hard-hitting, realistic story of the Battle of the Bulge in World War II, and Howard Hughes had forbidden him to make it because he thought it was too grim. So one of Schary's first moves in his new job was to buy the property from Hughes and schedule it for production by Metro-Goldwyn-Mayer. He also bought the script of another favored property scotched by Hughes: *Ivanhoe.*

To the latter, there was no objection. Right away, it was seen as a fine costume-adventure project of a sort favored by the studio. But Mayer was skeptical and uneasy about the prospects for *Battleground.* He thought it too harrowing a story to be making so soon after the war. However, he did not try to stop it. "Go ahead my boy, make it," he said. "This will teach you a lesson." Schary went ahead.

Later he learned there was much muttering among executives at the studio. They felt he was starting on the wrong foot, doing this picture against the wishes of Mayer. The latter undoubtedly thought the same thing but politely refrained from saying so. He was still very much the studio pundit among executives who remained. The veterans, Sam Katz and Al Lichtman, resigned shortly after Schary was hired, detecting in this development that their days of favor were at an end. And another stalwart of Mayer's, James Kevin Mc-Guinness, resigned in protest against the new man.

A second and more serious disagreement between Mayer and Schary occurred while *Battleground* was still in production. It was over the preparation of a film based on the old historical novel, *Quo Vadis?*, about early Christian martyrs in Rome. This property had been owned for years by the studio and attempts had been made to get a script from it, but all had been unsuccessful. Now it was being tried by producer Arthur Hornblow, Jr., and John Huston, who would direct.

Their idea was to make a picture with a strong, modern point of view. The Emperor Nero was to be a sort of Hitler, the Christian martyrs were to be counterparts of German Jews. Schary approved the general idea and he approved the first draft of a script, which, by a piece of studio trickery, was got simultaneously to Mayer. The latter was greatly agitated when the script was read to him. He pictured *Quo Vadis?* on the order of a spectacle done by Cecil B. De Mille. When he heard that Schary liked it, he was indignant and incensed. Schary would not budge from his opinion and made the bold suggestion that they put the decision up to Schenck. This was a direct challenge to the supremacy of Mayer, holding within it the nettle of some of the recalcitrance of Thalberg in his later years. And Mayer was not made to feel any easier when Schenck came back with the word that, since they'd not been able to get a script of *Quo Vadis?* from previous efforts why not let Schary have his way. Obviously Schenck had sided against the head of the studio.

The reminder of a parallel with Thalberg was repeated when *Battleground* was released, for this picture to which Mayer had objected was a surprising box office success. It brought back vivid recollections of the experience with *The Big Parade*, which Thalberg had insisted on making against objections that it would be too grim. Now Schenck was convinced that Schary was the genius of production they required. He had clearly gained a position of strength in relation to Mayer.

The fact that the latter's wishes for *Quo Vadis?* were ultimately achieved when Hornblow and Huston were com-

pelled to abandon the project and Sam Zimbalist and Mervyn
Le Roy took it on, gave Mayer a bitter satisfaction, particularly when that film went on to be highly successful. But battle lines were drawn. Mayer and Schary were tacitly rival
forces within the studio.

They clashed again over a script called *Europa and the
Bull,* a satirical drama by Ben Hecht, which Mayer thought
too sharp and intellectual. Schary acceded to him on that.
But on his wish to do a film of *The Red Badge of Courage,*
the Civil War classic of Stephen Crane, Schary would not
surrender to all the objections and admonitions of Mayer.

Gottfried Reinhardt had been set as its producer and John
Huston was assigned to direct, when Schary ran into a recur-
rence of some old trouble with his back and was laid up in
his home for a few weeks. While he was out of the studio
Mayer got hold of Reinhardt and Huston and argued them
out of wanting to do the film. It was too old-fashioned, he
told them. "How can you make a picture of boys in funny caps
with pop guns, and make people think the war they are fighting is terrible?" He gave a vivid enactment of how absurd it
would look. Huston later told him it was one of the best per-
formances he had ever seen.

When Schary heard of the defection he wrote a long letter
to Mayer in which he said he could not guarantee the film
would be successful or even very good. "I can only tell you
that, in my conscience, I believe that it has a chance of becoming a most important motion picture that will bring honor
to the studio, plus every reasonable chance of ultimately making money," he wrote.

Mayer was touched by the letter. Having meantime sent
the script to New York and again having had Schenck tell him
to let Schary have his way, he got Reinhardt and Huston back
into his office and persuaded them to resume. The situation
was ticklish and uncertain. He wasn't going to get out on a
limb.

As it turned out, *The Red Badge of Courage,* when completed, was a *succès d'estime* which didn't make a nickel of profit, but that was small satisfaction to Mayer.

What had actually happened in the two years that Schary had been at the studio was a gratifying reversal of the operational loss. From a studio deficit of $6,500,000 in the fiscal year before he came, the studio showed a profit of some $300,000 in his first year. In the second year the profits went up to $3,800,000. With pictures such as *The Asphalt Jungle, Father of the Bride, An American in Paris,* and *King Solomon's Mines,* the revenues and the 'Oscars" began coming in again.

Had Mayer been constituted other than he was, he might have derived much satisfaction from this praise for his protégé. After all, it was he who had picked Schary, even though Schenck was prone to take some credit, too. But Mayer was not the sort to step politely to one side and let another man receive the attention and the plaudits which he felt were partly his due.

For all his ferocious devotion to the studio—and that he had in full measure, since actually he conceived the place as his—he burned and squirmed at the deference paid to Schary as the savior of Metro-Goldwyn-Mayer. His tapeworm ego was revolted, and it gnawed inside him.

In a sense his state was as piteous as it was when he felt himself opposed and superseded by Thalberg. His deep insecurities were disturbed, and he was not rendered any more tranquil by the commiseration and needling of his friends. Observing the ascension of Schary, they would mumble dire anxieties to Mayer and ask in tones of lamentation, "Who's boss around here, anyway?"

Inevitably the rancor seething in him was evident to his new wife, and the fact that he might appear impotent in her eyes was aggravating, too. All of his years of transcendence and unquestioned authority were catching up to him. He was now being forced to pay the piper for the long time his ego had danced.

The climax in the tension between Mayer and Schary— and Mayer and Schenck—came as a consequence of a matter of administration that came up in 1951. Renewals on the contracts of several executives were coming up, and Mayer generously recommended that options for the purchase of Loew's stock be given them. He heard nothing more about it. Then one day word came to him that Schenck had announced the bestowal of stock options on six executives, one of whom was Schary. Others were L.K. Sidney, Benny Thau, Arthur Loew, Joseph Vogel, and Charlie Moskowitz. The last three were executives in New York.

This seemed to Mayer a deliberate affront, taking away from him the credit and the pleasure of telling his own subordinates of the benefaction he had got for them. It cruelly curtailed his preëminence as the dispenser of largess. (Schenck later explained that he had tried unsuccessfully to reach Mayer by telephone to give him a chance to spread the tidings before the announcement was made.)

From this point on the situation was clearly beyond repair. The contention passed beyond Mayer and Schary. It was now between Mayer and Schenck. Friends tried to prevail upon Schary to ameliorate the strain by making a show of acquiescence to the ideas and wishes of Mayer. But Schary did not intend to play the weasel and the sycophant with him.

Dark rumors began circulating. Then a story appeared in the New York *Times,* noting the conflict at the studio and indicating that Mayer was going to resign. Schary read the story and asked Mayer if it was so, expressing at the same time a wish to patch up their quarrels.

Mayer snapped at him fiercely, "What are you going to do, save my job for me?"

While they were talking a phone call came from Rubin in New York. He had seen the story and wanted to know if it was true. Mayer replied to him bluntly, "Nick and Dore want the studio. Well, they can have it and choke on it!"

Rubin cried out in distraction, "This is all because of *Battleground!*"

Schary, overhearing this conversation—or the Hollywood end of it—then asked Mayer to tell him precisely what he meant. With that, Mayer lit into him, accused him of being a publicity hound, of neglecting the studio to make speeches, of pretending to have a bad back.

"I never knew a young man who gets tired so quickly!" he cried.

The vituperation continued and Schary recognized that it was reaching the kind he remembered so vividly being spewed up at Rapf.

"I'll talk about my work," he told Mayer. "I'll talk about that as long as you like. But I'm not going to talk about my personal activities."

"You're doing a lousy job!" Mayer shouted.

He was livid and trembling with rage. Schary saw they were getting nowhere. He got up and left the room.

Significantly, on the same day Mayer got Thomas Brady of the New York *Times* into his office and so abused him for reporting that he intended to resign—so foully and viciously cursed him—that Brady walked out on him, too.

In no time the word of the collision between Mayer and Schary got around the studio, with partisans of the former happily chortling that he had finally given the younger man what for. Schary was bewildered. He sensed he was going to be forced to resign. But he was advised that this would force a decision between the two of them upon Schenck.

However, that decision was soon forced by Mayer himself. After another sharp set-to with Schary, he got Schenck on the phone. "It's either me or Schary," he peremptorily stated. "Which?"

Schenck was ready for that question. Knowing what was happening at the studio he had called L.K. Sidney into New York with a full digest of the studio's books—an analysis of the record of the company's product before and after Schary

came. On the basis of that analysis he wrote Mayer a personal
letter which advised him that, all things considered, Schary
was his choice.

The implication was unavoidable: Mayer was being requested to resign. After twenty-seven years as head of the studio he was being told to go.

The realization was overwhelming. Mayer called in his
closest friends, Mannix, Thau, and Sidney, and threw
Schenck's letter in front of them. They shuddered with dis-
belief and anger. It was inconceivable that this most impressive Hollywood rajah would be forced to abdicate his throne.
But there was nothing else for it. Mayer sent his resignation to
Schenck and it was accepted, to be effective on August 31,
1951.

The news of Mayer's resignation, although not surprising to a few in the know, came like the shock of an earthquake to most people in Hollywood and caused amazement and wonder in many quarters all over the world. It was something to ponder that this old monarch had been mysteriously dethroned.

Those who looked up to him, who believed him the unshakable sovereign of a system of motion picture making productive of great wealth through the years, felt in his sudden unseating the rumble of grave and frightening change. The doom of the old luxurious order seemed to be sounded in this move.

Others—younger elements, new and less well-established men who generally sensed the revolution that was happening in the entertainment world—saw in Mayer's forced abdication the inevitable and anticipated split in the ranks of Bourbons of the business, which betokened the end of their regime. Men less powerful in the peerage had been thrown out as hostages to change. That Mayer should now get the treatment was indeed momentous and meaningful.

Some felt the point of resignation need not ever have been

reached had either Mayer or Schary been willing to compromise. If Mayer had simply acceded to the creative judgment of the younger man and allowed him to make the decisions (which Mayer had usually side stepped, anyhow), he might have avoided the showdown that he permitted to develop with Schenck and thus have remained indefinitely as the studio figurehead.

Or had Schary politely listened to the counsels and opinions of Mayer, making a show of acquiescence and respect for the taste of the older man, he might have deluded and cajoled him into thinking his wishes still prevailed. This is what several people in the studio believed and begged Schary to do.

There are those who still say that if Schary had "played it smart" with Mayer and seen to it that the latter remained as the nominal boss, Schary would have kept an effective buffer between himself and the "people in New York," and this would have been most convenient for absorbing the pressures that were later put on *him*. There were also those who figured that, if Mayer had been less obtuse, he could have stayed in his position of balance and held onto his aura of prestige.

But those were speculations that unconsciously revealed the old reliance on faking and finagling that were only too familiar in Hollywood, as well as the ingrained feeling that everything should be done to preserve the status quo. And these speculations were essentially futile because they neglected to recognize not only the natures of the two men but the inexorable demands for economy and new methods within the industry.

No matter how Mayer had played it, his eclipse was inevitable because his ideas of screen entertainment and his ways of operating were obsolete. His authority as a showman relied upon insistence on qualities of sentiment and make-believe that were nothing short of "corny" in the postwar age. To have gone on pushing for these qualities and running a studio with them as the aim would have been commercially dangerous and, physically, too complex.

More fatal for him, however, was the fact that his strength was based upon the maintenence of a large productive capacity that no company could any longer afford. His old system of keeping hordes of talent and spending money to have "strength in depth" was impossible in a day of few pictures and increasing independence of creative personnel. His technique of spending lots of money and time in developing stars to be held under contract to his studio was utterly passé. Thus his power as a manipulator of a pool of talent was curtailed. The abundance of resources and personal daring on which he had long sustained himself in Hollywood were all but evaporating. Only a myth of mightiness remained.

This sad fact of Mayer's obsolescence and his own self-destroying qualities was recognized most realistically by people in his own studio. Romantically, he had a notion that his departure would be the signal for a wholesale display of indignation and rebellion by executives and stars. He even let on that he expected a few key people to resign or give notice that they would join him when their contracts expired.

And perhaps a few might have done so, if he had shown any positive signs of going into independent production, as he vaguely implied he might do. He announced that he owned the screen rights to a couple of properties, one of which was a Biblical story, *Joseph and His Brethren,* and another the old musical comedy, *Blossom Time*. But those were scarcely sufficient to offer encouragement.

There was an exciting rumor, a few months after he resigned, that he might become the head of the Warners studio. His good friend, Louis Lurie, San Francisco real estate man, and Mario Giannini of the California banking tribe attempted to buy a controlling interest in Warner Brothers in 1951, and if they had succeeded they would have made Mayer head of the studio. But the deal fell through and that prospect went aglimmering.

So, quietly and with as little recrimination as possible, people at Metro-Goldwyn-Mayer washed the raw wounds of their recent schism and went about their jobs. Those who had sided with Schary were secretly relieved; the noted partisans of Mayer were naturally nervous that the worst would happen to them. Nothing did. Neither Schenck nor Schary took vengeance on a soul. They permitted the emotional upheaval to expend itself and subside. Schary even waited a discreet time, a matter of a couple of years, before having Mayer's elaborate office redecorated and moving in.

The only disturbing question that remained was how much money Mayer would get in settlement of his contract. He owned a ten percent interest in the residual rights of all pictures produced at the studio since 1924. This posed a large consideration, for already there was talk that these old films might be sold to television for not inconsiderable sums. The dollar value of Mayer's ten percent interest had to be figured and fixed.

There were prolonged negotiations, in the course of which offers were made by David Selznick, Harry Cohn of Columbia Pictures, and the talent agent, Lou Wasserman, to buy Mayer's interest and use it as an investment for later deals. But Serge Semenenko, a Boston banker, who was acting on behalf of Loew's, Inc., finally prevailed upon him to sell to the parent company for $2,750,000 in cash. (Later, $150,000 had to be returned to settle a suit by a stockholder who questioned the legality of the deal.)

As it turned out, the sum which Mayer accepted was a great deal less than one-tenth of the monies the company received when it finally got around to leasing its old films for television use. He realized this was likely, but he wanted to get his money out in 1951. Thus he took a beating in his last negotiation with Loew's, Inc. But in that there was some poetic justice. On balance he came out far ahead.

As a footnote it might be mentioned that he milked every penny he could from that $2,600,000. Through the good offices of a friend, the House of Representatives was persuaded to pass an amendment to the Internal Revenue Code which permitted this rare type of income to be classed as a capital gain rather than current income, and thus subject to much less tax. Mayer's capacity to chase the dollar remained prodigious to the end.

Indeed his enthusiasm for business and the acquisition of money continued to burn with unabated fierceness after he left the studio. Some friends tried to urge him to take it easy, to let up, to live on his sizeable fortune, even to give some of it away. But there were two things he could not fathom, even as he got on in years. One was relaxation and the other was charity. He had occasionally talked of retirement, in a wistful and self-effacing way, particularly when the going was rough in the studio. But no one who knew him ever imagined that he desired such a thing. As Schenck had long since warned him, "If you stop working, Louie, you'll die."

Once, in a mood of sweet contentment, shortly after Schary had arrived at the studio as head of production and all was serene between them, Mayer explained to him that he was thinking about getting ready to retire and asked Schary how he thought this might be accomplished so he could go out gracefully and gloriously.

Schary considered the matter and suggested he might take a cue from the way other wealthy men had done it—men such as John D. Rockefeller and Alfred P. Sloan.

"Take a million dollars from your fortune and set it aside," Schary said. "Then, when you announce your retirement, say you're giving that money to the people of the motion picture industry—to the industry that has been so good and profitable to you."

Mayer followed him with close attention.

"You could give a quarter of a million dollars to the Academy, which you started and which does a valuable work," Schary said. "Then you could give another quarter million to the Motion Picture Home, for the care of old movie people, and a quarter million to the benevolent funds of the guilds and labor unions, and  . . ."

Mayer interrupted him. "That's what you'd do?" he snapped tersely.

"I think that would be great," Schary replied.

"You say that because you're a *kabtzin*," Mayer said sharply. (Kabtzin is the Yiddish word for pauper.) "Only a *kabtzin* would say a thing like that!" Then he indicated the subject was closed.

This reluctance to part with his money for charitable purposes was one of the more irritating characteristics of Mayer, and it was the cause of much private comment among those who knew him well. He had bitter fights with Samuel Goldwyn and Harry Warner because of it, and a few times he caused some embarrassment by not doing what was expected of him.

On a sentimental trip back to his old town of Saint John in 1939, he was graciously made the recipient of an honorary degree by the University of New Brunswick, situated nearby. Such an honor is usually acknowledged by a suitable contribution of funds, and this, it can be said without prejudice, was naturally expected of Mayer. He neglected to make a contribution. Neither did he give anything to the local temple, previously the synagogue that his father had helped to found. Needless to say, this omission was cause for considerable dismay. However, some time later, he did join with Nathan Cummings in giving a small funeral temple for the Jewish cemetery in Saint John, in memory of their respective mothers. The community appreciated that.

His intimates often excused him by saying he didn't like to be pushed, that he preferred to make contributions as his own spirit moved him. And there are cases on record of his being so moved. But a good friend, an eminent lawyer, tells of saying to him one time, "Louie, why don't you give more of your money to charity? You can't take it with you, you know." To which Mayer answered politely, "If I can't take it with me I won't go!"

In the year following his resignation Mayer variously busied himself with a resumed interest in horses and dealing in stocks and real estate. He began buying horses at Keeneland in the summer of 1951 and soon had a good stable going, which he kept at Lexington, Kentucky, on the farm of Leslie Combs. Through good friends he made strong investments and he bought big chunks of real estate in Florida, San Francisco, Los Angeles, and Beverly Hills. With markets generally booming, he was successful all along the line.

But a chance to get back into the movie business in the fall of 1952, under circumstances that seemed to promise new glory, was one he could not resist. It came with an invitation to him to become the chairman of the board of the Cinerama Productions Corporation, which had a spectacular new process for projecting films.

The Cinerama process, which everyone must know is a way of projecting movies on a giant, curving screen, was invented by a man named Fred Waller and was mechanically developed by him in association with an engineer and industrial promoter, Hazard Reeves. Their long and involved negotiations to raise money for the device and finally to make a picture with it were so complicated and grotesque that it would take a small volume to recount them.

Suffice it to say that the first picture, *This Is Cinerama,* that was made by the Cinerama corporation was given its world première at the Broadway Theater in New York on September 30, 1952. Coming as it did amid a flurry of public excitement about "three-dimensional" films, and being an immensely graphic and startlingly eye-filling show, *This Is Cinerama* was a sensational hit. It attracted heavy attendance for every performance at the Broadway Theater.

But there were two serious problems. First, it had cost a great deal to get the new enterprise going and the corporation was heavily in debt. Second, a lot more money was needed to equip more Cinerama theaters in cities around the country and eventually to make more Cinerama films. The task of raising this money, even with the first film a big hit, was much more devious and difficult than an average person would assume.

In casting about to do it, Dudley Roberts and Lowell Thomas, who were officers of the corporation, got the bright idea of inviting Mayer to join them. (The suggestion actually came from Merian C. Cooper, a veteran Hollywood producer who worked on the first Cinerama film.)

The idea was full of promise. Who in the business, they asked, was better known as a man of executive genius and towering successes than Mayer? Who could provide the corporation with wiser counsel or a more impressive front? Who might even dig down in his own pocket and bring up the needed financing?

Mayer was approached by Roberts and Thomas. He agreed to go in to New York to have a look at *This Is Cinerama* and discuss the idea with them. One experience with the picture before an audience and he was completely sold. Here was a great innovation, as important as sound, he said. He was full of enthusiasm and eagerness to get into the show. The promotion of Cinerama was a prospect as pleasing as the selling of *The Birth of a Nation,* he said.

A contract was drawn up with him to serve as chairman of the board of Cinerama Productions Corporation at one thousand dollars a week plus traveling and other expenses, which, with Mayer, could run into a lot. He also received stated options to buy the corporation's stock at a price much below the market, and it was further agreed that the corporation could purchase the screen rights to story properties he then owned. These were *Blossom Time, Joseph and His Brethren,* and *Paint Your Wagon,* a musical comedy.

Mayer returned to California bubbling with excitement and zeal. This latest thing about which everyone was talking —it was his baby now! From the vale of comparative obscurity into which he had settled for the past year, he was now back in the Hollywood limelight and very much the man of the hour.

Shortly before he signed with Cinerama, announcement had been made that he would be the recipient of the annual Milestone Award of the Screen Producers Guild. This was an honor reserved for men who had been distinguished in production. It usually went to a pioneer.

In the light of his new distinction, the awards dinner was a gay affair, studded with famous show-world speakers and Metro-Goldwyn-Mayer stars. Van Johnson, Esther Williams, June Allyson, and Stewart Granger were there. So was Norma Shearer to recall the old Thalberg days, somewhat more sentimentally than the total record justified. Conspicuous by his absence was Dore Schary, whom Eddie Mannix had tried to persuade to attend in the cause of good fellowship. But Schary probably feared that Mayer might take the occasion to say some unkind things, which it was quite within the range of his known indiscretion to do.

As it was, he appeared in fine humor, reminiscing happily, boasting about Cinerama, and predicting that "the film business is not going to die." It was a gathering reminiscent of many previous ones at which he had been the center of attraction. It was the last one of the sort he was to enjoy.

His official function with Cinerama was to counsel and advise, and this was a simple service that he very much liked to perform. In his talks with Roberts and Thomas and others of the Cinerama group, he was ready with bold suggestions and expansive ideas. "The trouble with the movie business today is that nobody has guts," he would cry, and the promoters of Cinerama would hang hopefully on his words. But when it came to the question of whether he was going to invest a sizeable sum of his own money to put Cinerama on the road (and that was the first expectation that prompted his being invited to join the company), he became curiously bashful. Outside of his purchases of bonds and stock of the corporation at option prices that would allow their profitable sale, he did not put a cent of his own money into the Cinerama operation.

However, his services to the corporation were helpful and worth their cost to the extent that he did stand forth as its champion in subsequent tough financial deals. A loan of $1,600,000 was obtained from the Bankers Trust Company early in 1953 largely on the strength of Mayer's presence and reputation, it was believed. Later, when $1,000,000 was needed by Cinerama in a hurry, he got his friend, Louis Lurie to put up the money on his guarantee. That money was repaid without interest, which was a considerable boon. And, finally, when the struggling corporation appeared to be up against the wall, it was through Mayer's extraordinary connections that a salvation deal was arranged.

His good friend, Edwin Weisl, a New York lawyer with the firm of Simpson, Thacher and Bartlett, seeing the plight Cinerama was in and not wishing Mayer to have a black mark against his name, went to some of *his* friends at the head of Stanley-Warner Theaters and got that company to become dominant in the Cinerama corporation. The deal was involved, and at one point, when it looked as though a law suit might be joined, Mayer came in from California and said that he would pay all legal fees himself if it was necessary to fight Stanley-Warner in court. Fortunately that was not necessary, and a satisfactory arrangement was engineered. Mayer then settled his contract with Cinerama in November, 1954.

At the time the corporation owed him some eighty thousand dollars in back pay, and twenty-six thousand dollars in expenses. He agreed to settle for half the pay, the expenses, and thirty thousand dollars for the rights to *Paint Your Wagon,* which the corporation had originally optioned to buy. These monies were eventually paid in full before he died. So with these and several hundred thousand he was believed to have made by dealing in his optioned stock, it appeared that he did right nicely with Cinerama in two years.

How nicely Cinerama actually did with him is still a debatable question. That he helped the corporation over some perilous financial rocks is recognized and accepted. But did he begin to do what might have been done to exploit this new and exciting device that cried for imagination and production know-how to build on its early impetus? In the time that Mayer was with it the Cinerama corporation did start production on two new pictures and opened several theaters in this country and abroad, but realization on its early promise was acknowledged to be lacking.

Mayer's best friends admitted that his work with Cinerama was not what it might have been, had he been younger and not consumed with inner grief and bitterness. Had the operation been centered in California rather than in New York, had his interests been undivided, had his mind been happy and at ease, he might have been able to propel it as he did enterprises in earlier days. But he was old, he had fought his battles, and resentments gnawed viciously at him. All of his voracious chickens were coming home to roost.

His violent Republicanism took a bad blow in 1952 with the nomination and election of General Eisenhower. Mayer was a strong Robert Taft man. He felt that the party's mission lay in the economic and political conservatism represented by the Senator from Ohio. When Taft died of cancer and the young Republican wing got control Mayer began to lose interest in the party and in politics. His status in the state organization also took a dive when he was no longer in a position of power in Hollywood.

Slowly, perhaps inevitably, his interest and enthusiasm turned toward Senator Joseph McCarthy, who was just then swinging into line as the angry and reckless spokesman for a fringe of followers whom Dean Francis Sayre of the Washington National Cathedral described as "the frightened and credulous collaborators of a servile brand of patriotism."

Mayer's admiration for McCarthy mounted, and in April,

1954, he expressed his enthusiasm in clear and positive terms. On a visit to Haverhill, Massachusetts, where he had started his theatrical career, he told a local gathering "the country needs more Joe McCarthys.

"The more McCarthy yells, the better I like him," Mayer said. "He's doing a job to get rid of the 'termites' eating away at our democracy. I don't care how many toes he steps on, including mine, as long as he gets the job done. I hope he drives all the bums back to Moscow. That's the place for them.

"I used to consider myself a liberal years ago," he further said, "but it was the kind of liberalism my father and my friends' fathers taught. That was the liberalism to help others less fortunate than yourself. It's a different kind of liberalism today and a kind I don't like because I am an American."

The eventual discrediting of McCarthy was a bitter pill for him.

And the cumulation of his sorrows came much closer to his heart as the consequence of a battle he had with his daughter Edith in the fall of 1952.

Edith had always been his darling, the daughter whom he had regarded as the ideal of feminine charm and grace. And he also had a strong attachment to her husband, Bill Goetz. Whatever Edith did, he regarded with admiration and pride. His sense of possession of the couple was one of his most rewarding joys. He frankly assumed paternal credit for the advancement of Goetz's career and often referred to his daughter's husband as his own "son."

He had, of course, been instrumental in starting the Twentieth Century Company and making that an enterprise for Goetz. And, ten years later, he helped in negotiations when Goetz left Twentieth Century-Fox and formed an independent producing company, International, with Leo Spitz. At the annual Academy awards function in 1943, Mayer made a public declaration of his pride in his "son" and told him, face to face before the gathering, that "if you keep on going the way you are, you'll soon be a great producer, like me."

This was as innocent and honest a compliment as Mayer could pay.

But then, as Goetz did go on to making one after another successful film and truly establishing his independence, certain nettles began to intrude. When the Motion Picture Alliance was formed in 1944 as an organization for the arch reactionaries and the "100 percent Americans" in Hollywood, Goetz was strongly opposed to it. This irritated Mayer. He charged it against the known fact that his son-in-law—and his daughter, too—was a stalwart Democrat.

Other irritations followed. Mayer was piqued that Goetz would not come to work for him at Culver City when he was seeking a top producer as early as 1945. He felt this a serious neglect of an obligation of loyalty. He was outraged at Goetz for making a percentage deal with James Stewart on a film. This, he said, would ruin the business—giving actors percentage deals! Then, in 1950, there was an ugly quarrel about a horse.

Goetz was the official owner of a thoroughbred named Your Host, in which Mayer felt a proprietary interest. The horse won the Santa Anita Derby that year and was highly regarded as a prospect in the Kentucky Derby, for which he was shipped east. Goetz and his trainer, Harry Daniels, figured the horse needed a tune-up for that race and entered him in the "Derby trials" at Keeneland, two weeks before the big event at Churchill Downs.

"Don't do it," Mayer advised him. "Don't do it, I say!"

However, his advice was not taken, and Your Host went on to win the tune-up at Keeneland in record time. Goetz was pleased but Mayer was still angry.

"You mark what I tell you," he said. "He left his race on that track."

Your Host was now the favorite for the Derby, but the day before the race James Roach of the New York *Times* cautioned, "There may be some surprises in the race tomorrow."

There were. In the Number 1 post position, Your Host,

with Johnny Longden up, broke fast, bounced to the front, and stayed there until, coming into the home stretch, he went to pieces. He crossed the finish line in ninth place.

Mayer was furious. This was the one big chance he had for a horse that was "in the family," as it were, to win the Kentucky crown. He blamed the jockey. He blamed the trainer. But most of all he blamed Goetz. "You should have listened to me!" he ranted.

It took him a long time to get over that.

Then he took to criticizing the tastes and extravagancies of Goetz. The latter was known as a particularly keen and high-bidding collector of fine art, owning many famous modern paintings. This was something Mayer could not understand. He thought it an expensive affectation. And he severely criticized Goetz for owning a private airplane, even though several times he borrowed it himself. "It's dangerous and you can't afford it," he told his son-in-law. The tension over this was so unpleasant that Goetz finally got rid of the plane.

Thus, there was a history of conflicts and emotional flagellations when family relations came to a crisis in the fall of 1952. Goetz and Edith were friends of Dore Schary—close friends, as Mayer well knew, since it had been a matter for discussion when Mayer and Schary reached a parting of the ways. "That's all right," Mayer had said then. "You may still have to do business with that studio. There's no reason why my trouble with Schary should cause you to fall out with him."

Mayer also knew that his daughter and son-in-law were Democrats, and that they, along with Schary, were leading advocates in Hollywood for the presidential candidacy of Adlai Stevenson. His daughter's political disposition was never agreeable to him, but he accepted it philosophically and with an effort at good grace. At parties he would come out boldly and say, with an evident trace of regret, "Look at my daughter, she's a Democrat. But do you think I try to stop her. I don't!

She's entitled to her opinion, just as I am. That's what makes this country great."

However, while Mayer was east in October, 1952, to make his Cinerama connection, an incident occurred which stretched his tolerance to the limit. Adlai Stevenson was scheduled to speak at the Shrine Auditorium in Los Angeles, and Schary felt there should be a cocktail party given for him during his visit so that he could meet leading Democrats in the film industry.

Schary thought the party should be held at the home of Goetz, who was chairman of the Hollywood committee, and suggested this to him. Goetz was agreeable to the party but didn't want it to be in his home. He was willing to halve the cost with Schary, if the latter would have the party at his place. Schary went ahead with arrangements and sent out telegrams inviting the guests. The telegrams began, "William Goetz and I are giving a cocktail party to honor, etc . . ."

Well it wasn't long before word of this telegram got to Mayer, and, for reasons not hard to imagine, it thoroughly infuriated him. The thought of his son-in-law permitting his name to be placed alongside that of Dore Schary inviting people to meet the Democratic candidate for president was too much for him to bear! In his state of wounded pride and anger he could well imagine this to be a deliberate compound of insult and injury, intended by Goetz as a slap at *him*.

When Mayer returned to California he let it be known that he was angry, and this soon got back to Edith and, of course, to Goetz. As a consequence she did not call her father, as she usually did. But in a few days, Mayer's wife, Lorena, sweetly telephoned her and besought her to speak to her father because she understood he was "on the outs with Bill."

Edith well recognized the old gambit—Mayer having a third party act as his intermediary in a delicate affair—and she realized that this foreboded a likely unpleasantness. But she did telephone her father. He was cool at first. Then he broke loose and began berating Goetz for letting his name appear on that telegram.

Initially Edith tried to tell him that her husband did not realize his name was to be used on the invitation. But when her father shouted, "That's a lie! That sunnuvabitch you're married to is the biggest goddamn liar I've ever known! If Jesus Christ was to come down here and tell me to believe this man I wouldn't be able to!" she boiled up herself.

"You can't talk like that!" she stormed. "I've invested many years of my life with Billie. What do you want me to do, get a divorce from him?"

Mayer didn't pause in his vituperation. He continued to vilify Goetz. "You tell him the next time he sees me, he'd better turn his head!" he screamed.

Edith shouted, "Well, if that's what you want of him it goes for me, too!" and slammed down the phone.

That was the last conversation that she and her father had.

It was a mad and piteous disruption, and as word of it got around among Hollywood patricians (as it was bound to do), many well-meaning people attempted to get Mayer and his daughter to make up. But it was an emotional cataclysm that could not be bridged with soft words. Too much of Mayer's weakness and fury had been exposed in that wild storm.

After this terrible estrangement from the daughter whom he so loved—the daughter who was the Cordelia to his groaning Lear—it is small wonder that his frustrations and resentments crowded ever more heavily on him and caused him fits of violent temper and agonized, sleepless nights. His hatred of Schenck and Schary was more viciously and openly expressed, so that it didn't do to get him started on the subject, for fear he would explode.

He took to calling Schenck by the epithet "Mr. Skunk," and he would sometimes say to people, "I've got more brains in my ass than Mr. Skunk has in his head." Schenck's right-hand man, Charles Moskowitz, he lightly and sneeringly termed "Carnation Charlie" because of the flower that Moskowitz always wore in his lapel. So often and so precisely did he repeat his condemnation and contempt for Schenck that the catalogue became almost a ritual, a tasteless and embarrassing cliché.

To friends and interviewers he would insist that his treatment by Schenck was due entirely to the latter's envy and jealousy. Then he would speak like an actor getting off a line in some fustian melodrama: "Jealousy, in the heart of a fool, you are master!" he would declaim.

But to his close friend, Jessie Marmorston, who continued through the years to be his daily attending physician and respectful confidante, he would pour out his heart in anguish, humiliation, and despair at the consequences of his violence and his passion to prove himself. He would tell of his thwarted intentions, his being misunderstood, and she would try to comfort a spirit too volatile and dynamic for rest.

He spent much time with his old friend, Clarence Brown, the former Metro-Goldwyn-Mayer director who was almost as wealthy as was he. Together they would look at television and discuss affairs in the home that he and Lorena now lived in. It was on St. Cloud Drive in Bel-Air. Some dozen or so paintings by Grandma Moses were on the living room walls.

It was there that Mayer did much of the planning for the last dramatic act of his career.

# 19

Had Mayer himself ordered the scenario for what happened in the affairs of Loew's, Inc., in the five years after his removal, it could not have been more punishing for those he considered his persecutors, nor more a brief for his own dire prophecies, than was the denouement dictated by realities. For in those five years the company went inexorably downhill, plagued by executive paralysis and a flow of generally weak films.

The course of its decline was graphed in figures on balance sheets, which showed a continuation of the sickening plunge from the peak of 1946. For instance, net profits of the whole company were $7,800,000 in 1951; they were down to $4,500,000 in 1953. A loss of $1,000,000 in studio operations was marked in the latter year. Earnings on common stock of the company fell below ninety cents a share.

More portentous of further deterioration was the evident unwillingness of Schenck to take drastic steps to save the company by sharp economies and audacious moves. Much of Loew's basic misfortune could be charged to the depressing effects of television on the whole film industry, but it was obvious that Schenck was neglecting many of the things that other companies were doing to protect themselves.

He held out against television and refused to sell or lease old films of his company to the new medium and thus obtain additional revenue. He strangely stuck by the old Mayer practice of maintaining an expensive production plant, and he was loathe to go with the tide then running among major companies to make profit-sharing deals for new pictures with independent producers, directors, and stars.

Also, most vexing to stockholders who were jittering at the decline, he neglected to cut the high salaries of himself and other executives, even when damaging revelations of nepotistic concessions within the company were brought forth against him and his lieutenant, Moskowitz.

Anxiety was further aggravated by the fitful quality of the company's films and by rumors of discord and incompetence within the studio. Some shockingly costly pictures which Schary had strongly endorsed were failing at the box office, and the word was getting around that friction was growing between the "Old Guard" and the new element. Schary himself and such veterans as Mannix, Freed, and Thau maintained polite but painful contacts, yet between those men and such ardent Schary "boys" as Leonard Spiegelgass, Charles Schnee, and Allan Rivkin there was outright enmity. An observer put it neatly: "Schary's office is like Panmunjom."

Eventually the fears of large stockholders who were threatening to start proxy fights to shake up the board of directors and the pressure of large banking firms forced a seeming surrender by Schenck, now seventy-four. He resigned as president of the company in December, 1955, to be succeeded by the son of the founder and long-time chief of the highly successful foreign operations, Arthur Loew. Schenck became chairman of the board, and the new president received the endorsement of the two largest interested banking houses, Lehman Brothers and Lazard Frères.

But the step brought no quick improvement in the affairs of the company, nor did it satisfy those nervous about the influence of Schenck. Indeed, it was strongly suspected that he was still trying to run the company and that Moskowitz, vice-president and treasurer, was supporting him. The embarrassment of such a situation was believed a major reason for Arthur Loew's abruptly resigning in October of the following year.

So sudden and unexpected was the withdrawal by Loew that it caught the board of directors without a new president. Later, his explanation that he had long since besought the chairman to find someone to replace him because he was unhappy and exhausted only pointed up the stagnation and procrastination of Schenck. The resignation also shocked the motion picture industry and the financial world into an awful realization of the sad disorder of Loew's, Inc.

It was this revealing occurrence that finally set the stage for what was to be, in the ten months that followed, one of the most desperate battles for control of a major American corporation that has ever been waged. And, in turn, it was this dramatic battle, more theatrical than a play, which afforded a final field of conflict for the rugged aggressiveness of Mayer.

Following the affairs of the company from his comfortable Bel-Air home and probably getting frequent information on the troubles of Schary from spies, he detected signs of disruption in the ponderous organization he knew so well, and sensed with supreme satisfaction the squirming of "Mr. Skunk."

When the latter ambiguously relinquished the presidency to Arthur Loew, whose secret reluctance to take it was well known by intimates, Mayer shrewdly and unmistakably anticipated what was ahead and began to make ready for action through a young man named Stanley Meyer.

Meyer was a Hollywood figure who, in 1954, had made a minor reputation and a million dollars as the coproducer of the television serial, *Dragnet,* which had Jack Webb as star. He was also a son-in-law of Nate Blumberg, the veteran chairman of the board of Universal Pictures, through whom he became a friend of Mayer.

When he sold out of *Dragnet* in 1955, Meyer began scouting for something attractive and exciting to do, and it was then that Mayer broached the brazen idea of moving in upon Metro-Goldwyn-Mayer. The gambit for this undertaking was to pry his way into Loew's, Inc., by getting the confidence and backing of owners of sizeable blocks of stock. With that as a task for exploration, Mayer sent the young man to New York, to make some discreet inquiries through a certain brokerage firm.

There, in the course of his snoopings, Meyer discovered that Joseph Tomlinson, a big Canadian road builder and operator in securities, owned 180,000 of the 5,300,000 outstanding shares of Loew's common stock and that this was the largest single block held by an individual. Meyer sought out Tomlinson and found him to be a rangy aggressive character with a hearty disgust for the condition and management of Loew's, Inc. He was just what Meyer was seeking in the way of a possible wedge, and he soon had a quiet liaison set up among himself, Tomlinson, and the distant Mayer.

Why Mayer desired, at this point, to get even remotely involved in the troubled affairs of his old company will have to be surmised. Revenge might seem one motive. He could have wished to assist in the ultimate decimation and humiliation of Schenck. Then again he might truly have imagined that he could counsel and direct a revival of the great producing outfit he had guided for so many years. He often told friends that he could do so. "If you want to save this company," he would say, "you go to the man who made it great in the first place." He felt he could manage it through Meyer.

And, of course, it could be suspected that he was only interested in getting a salvager's share of that huge company whose physical assets were figured above $200,000,000. If

so, he was not the only watcher with that voracious idea. Wall
Street was full of raiders who had long since decided that
Loew's was a likely company for a fat financial "spin-off,"
that it was "worth more dead than alive."

Anyhow, Mayer was lurking on the sidelines with Meyer
and Tomlinson, when Arthur Loew's resignation brought on
the crisis that made an occasion for striking for control of
the company most inviting and opportune.

The crisis itself was fantastic. Simultaneous with the resignation of Loew, two directors on the board as agents of Lehman
Brothers and Lazard Frères likewise resigned, giving tacit indication that the 400,000 shares of stock those banking firms
represented were withdrawn from support of the regime.
This made it doubly imperative that a new president quickly
be found before a coalition of disgusted stockholders might be
formed to depose the management.

For ten days Schenck, as board chairman, sweated to find a
man to put in as president. Several outsiders were approached
and he again made a futile endeavor to clinch the job indi-
rectly for Moskowitz. The grave misfortune of this agitation
was the appalling spectacle it gave of the presidency of a
great corporation being virtually put up for grabs.

Finally the job was given to Joseph R. Vogel, who was then
the president of Loew's Theaters, which was being tediously
"divorced" from Loew's, Inc. Vogel had started with the theaters as an usher, some forty years before, and was a man of
quiet assurance and well-known integrity. Often he had been
mentioned as a likely successor to Schenck, but his previous
disqualifier was the fact that he was not a "Schenck man." He
did not have the blind devotion and unquestioning obedience
of Moskowitz. However, in this situation Schenck had to turn
to him. The announcement that he was president of Loew's,
Inc., was made on October 18, 1956.

At the same time it was announced that Arthur Loew
would resume as head of Loew's International, that he would
be chairman of the board, and that Schenck would be "hon-

orary chairman." This was a title, nothing more, and it plainly indicated that the old nabob's days of authority were passed. After fifty years with the company he was finally compelled to withdraw. His complete retirement was announced before the end of the year.

Thus Mayer's most hated nemesis was out, the same as was he.

It was only a matter of a few weeks before Schary was likewise removed. Vogel summoned him to New York and requested that he resign. Schary, sadly realizing that he was without support, complied. He took a hundred thousand dollars in settlement of his contract which had thirteen months to go. (His original seven-year contract had been extended in 1951.) He was also to receive a hundred thousand dollars a year for nine years. This represented accumulation of his deferred salary. (At the time it was inaccurately reported that he was *paid* a million dollars to leave.)

With Schenck and Schary thus ousted in a little more than five years it might have been thought that Mayer's resentment had been satisfied, that he would have no more wish to meddle in the affairs of the shaky company. And, for an interval of a few weeks, it looked as though this might be so.

Vogel was in Culver City in December to confer with Thau, whom he had picked to take over as manager of the studio. Actually he was desperately considering closing up shop for six months, to give himself time to settle his many uncertainties.

Shortly after his arrival he was invited by Mayer to attend a wedding anniversary party in the latter's home. Vogel had never been able to work up much admiration for Mayer; they had once had a bitter disagreement over a picture called *Parnell*. Mayer was in love with the picture and had shown it to Vogel on one of his visits to the Coast. He was outraged when Vogel told him he thought it was no good. For a couple of years thereafter Mayer scorned the New York man.

On this occasion Vogel was suspicious of the invitation of

Mayer, but Thau urged him to accept it as a gesture of courtesy. It was a routine party, at which Mayer made his customary speech. Afterwards Vogel mentioned that he thought the
host rather cool toward him. Thau disagreed, and tactfully
suggested that Mayer might wish to be sought for advice,
that a rapprochement which could be helpful in the present
situation might be made with "L.B." Similar guarded suggestions came from other sides. But Vogel was not interested in
currying favor. He said bluntly, "Tell Mr. Mayer to go to
hell."

In the back-light of future developments Vogel wondered
whether perhaps he might then have made some discreet
obeisance and thus won a truce with Mayer. But obeisance
was not in his nature—especially not to Mayer.

Actually, the latter was suspicious that Vogel was a
"Schenck man"—at least, that he had made some bargain
with him in order to get the presidency. And when Vogel
made no endeavor to disabuse his mind, Mayer developed toward him the same hatred and intransigency that he had toward Schenck. This peculiarly personal feeling was markedly
manifest in the ruthless campaign of opposition that was now
launched on the Vogel regime.

Already Meyer and Tomlinson had been working on the
bankers in New York to support them in getting themselves
and Mayer into the company. They were somewhat surprised to discover that the awesome name of Mayer did not
have the magic in Wall Street that they had been led to suppose. They found that bankers were mindful of Mayer's age
and his past extravagances. He was hardly the man they reckoned to put on economic brakes.

So the cabal of Mayer, Meyer, and Tomlinson, with Mayer
staying well behind the scenes, letting the others do the
talking, took another line. This was to threaten Vogel with a
slam-bang proxy fight to get control of the board of directors
at the annual stockholders meeting in New York on February
28. They waged a campaign of charges that even included

the nepotism of Schenck. Significantly, they neglected to re-call the former nepotism of Mayer.

Under this barrage of accusations, and influenced by the climate of concern that was known to exist among stock-holders, Vogel succumbed to a bluff. He let Meyer and Tomlinson convince him that he could avoid a possible defeat by agreeing in advance to let them place six members on the upcoming thirteen-man board. Six others would be selected by Vogel. The thirteenth candidate would be selected by a joint committee of the two factions. (As it turned out, he was selected by the very much interested bankers, Lehman Broth-ers and Lazard Frères.)

Thus, by a bold maneuver, one stockholder, Tomlinson, who owned a bare two and a half percent of the shares of the company was able to obtain the management's permission to name an almost working majority of the board.

When the candidates of the Tomlinson faction were an-nounced, it was clear to see that Mayer was master-minding the maneuvers, for three of the six were his close friends. They were Louis A. Johnson, a Washington lawyer and former Secretary of Defense; K.T. Keller, former Chairman of the Board of the Chrysler Corporation; and Fred F. Flor-ence, President of the Republic National Bank of Dallas, Texas. Tomlinson and Meyer were also named, as was Ray Lawson, a Canadian banker and friend of Tomlinson.

The candidates picked by Vogel were William Parker, Chairman of the Board of Incorporated Investors, Inc., a large stockholder in Loew's; Frank Pace, Jr., an executive of the General Dynamics Corporation and a former Secretary of the Army; George L. Killion, President of the American President (steamship) Lines; George A. Brownell, a New York lawyer; John L. Sullivan, a Washington lawyer and former Secretary of the Navy; and, of course, Vogel himself.

The thirteenth man, chosen by the bankers, was something of a surprise. He was the youthful publisher of the New York *Herald-Tribune,* Ogden R. Reid.

The stockholders elected this panel, as stockholders are wont to do, at a meeting which was marked by much declaiming and a few pointed references to Mayer. The latter, following his usual tactics, stayed far away on the West Coast. Tomlinson stated at the meeting that he was "very happy to sit with Mr. Vogel," and said, "We have selected what I think is a very fine board." But at a caucus held a few hours after the meeting, he was making an attempt to swing the directors to an immediate resolution to remove Vogel as president and elect Stanley Meyer in his stead! The move was unsuccessful, but it indicated what was in store.

Exercising their privilege as directors, Tomlinson and Meyer now asked for office space in the Loew's Building and were given the board room on the eleventh floor. They moved in with a staff of secretaries and accountants and immediately began demanding the company's books and other documents for investigation, and playing occasional pranks. A piece of statuary in the office was designated "Moskowitz," and they would bow low to it in mock courtesy when they entered the room.

As weeks passed, it was clear that Meyer and Tomlinson were embarked upon a plan to harass and discredit Vogel and his management as much as they possibly could. Their demands for the books and records were unreasonably peremptory, often rude, and they persistently annoyed the President with countless telephone calls. Daily letters were sent to all directors, full of charges that called for quick replies; and through the public relations firm of Tex McCrary, critical stories were released to the press. Meetings of the board were inquisitions at which Vogel had to stand up to barrages of insinuating questions from the six-man opposition group.

Plainly, the aim of Tomlinson was to get control of the executive committee of the board, and he hoped to accomplish this triumph at the monthly directors' meeting on March 28. A few days before that meeting, Louis Johnson and Fred Florence gave a clear indication to Vogel of what was in their minds. As Johnson frankly put it, "The sixty-four dollar question is can Louis B. Mayer come back into the company?" Vogel answered. "No!"

Before the meeting gathered, it was evident that Tomlinson could not get enough votes to command the executive committee, so he withdrew his candidates. The committee elected was Vogel, Pace, Reid, and Killion. After this failure Meyer and Tomlinson moved out of the Loew Building and changed their tack. Now they resorted to what Vogel characterized as a "whispering campaign."

Through the industry and the ranks of large Loew's stockholders seeped persistent reports that Vogel was "a nice guy" but "incompetent" and "not big enough for the job." He found himself the recipient of numerous telephone calls from avowed friends and well-wishers, warning him that he was in peril and advising him that "to save the company" he should make peace with the Tomlinson group.

The peace terms invariably suggested were that he take a subordinate job and permit Meyer or Tomlinson to be named president and Mayer given a position as "studio advisor" and general factotum of the company. Later, other men were suggested for the presidency—Noah Dietrich, who had been financial advisor to Howard Hughes; Samuel Briskin, a former producer at the Paramount studio. But always the name of Mayer was brought up. He was the man whom the whisperers were sure could "save the company."

But, by now, Vogel and his associates knew the nature and purpose of the campaign, thanks to an unusual incident which unmasked the Tomlinson group. Right after the March 28 meeting Stanley Meyer made a secret call on Louis Nizer, who was special counsel for the management of Loew's, Inc., in this entire affair. Meyer sought the sympathy of Nizer and offered to disclose all the facts of "a plot" which he said "had been engineered against Vogel."

The next day, on the telephone, with three lawyers and Vogel listening in and the conversation being tape recorded,

Meyer voluntarily told Nizer that he deeply regretted what he and Tomlinson had done, and specifically acknowledged that Mayer was behind the campaign to obstruct management. He denied that he any longer had ambitions to be president of the company and said he felt he could be of aid as head of the television department or as an assistant to Mayer, if the latter should ever return to the studio.

Meyer's purpose, according to Vogel, who swore to the facts here disclosed in an affidavit later presented to the Delaware Court of Chancery, was to avoid being named as a defendant in a possible conspiracy suit which might have been filed against the Tomlinson directors. "He was attempting to buy his peace by confession," Vogel said. But since no suit was instituted and the alleged "conspiracy" was not revealed to the stockholders at the time, Meyer realized that his fears were unfounded and continued as a partisan of the Tomlinson group.

Meanwhile, the circumstances of the internecine strife became more or less common knowledge among top men in Hollywood, and old friends of Mayer wondered gravely at his sanction of an obstructionist campaign. The feeling throughout the industry was that Vogel should be given a chance, that nothing but harm could come from upsetting and perhaps fatally disrupting Loew's, Inc. What could be the rational reason for this determined assault by Mayer? He had had his revenge. He did not need money. And he was certainly not starting a career.

Perhaps the most kindly explanation was made, in retrospect, by David Selznick, who had come to be one of Mayer's stanchest partisans. "Mayer, without a company to run," said Selznick, "was like Knute Rockne without a football team to coach. Maybe he felt he could not associate with the big men of other industries without a big position of his own."

Less kindly persons put it bluntly: Mayer had a psychopathic need for power.

The futile battle of the factions continued through the spring of 1957, with every meeting of the board of directors degenerating into a tug-of-war. Withal, Vogel was able to accomplish some constructive moves in management. He cleaned out the cells of nepotism. He caused some economies. He initiated plans for bold productions, including a mammoth remake of *Ben-Hur*. And, to the chortling satisfaction of Meyer and Tomlinson, he obtained the resignation of Charlie Moskowitz.

Nonetheless, Ogden Reid, who was chairman of the executive committee, was dismayed at what he termed the "shotgun tactics" of the Tomlinson group. So, in May, with Vogel's acquiescence, he commissioned the management consultant firm of Robert Heller and Associates of Cleveland to make an exhaustive survey of the company. Assigned to direct this survey was C.R. MacBride, who already, unbeknown to most of the Loew's board, had tacitly accepted an offer to go to work later for Frank Pace.

MacBride soon perceived what was obvious, that Vogel had control of management but was having to spend his time "protecting his flanks" with the directors instead of running the company. He saw that the board was split in factions— Tomlinson's "solid six" and the Vogel and "banker" factions, which were flexible.

Invariably, in his talks with many people, he heard the name of Mayer mentioned as the key to the trouble and the possible solution to the woes of the company. So MacBride decided it was essential that he should meet this man.

An appointment was set up through Vogel, and MacBride flew to the Coast to spend a day in the company of Mayer in his home. That visit was of critical importance. Mayer put on an excellent show. He acted the whole plot of *Quo Vadis?* complete to getting down on his knees, praying, crying, and rolling on the floor in a death agony. But he kept full control of his temper and did not curse Schary or Schenck. His only comment on them was that they were "misguided men."

MacBride questioned him on what he thought would be the way to rehabilitate the studio and found he had a positive, albeit rather conventional, plan. It was to go in for production of *big* pictures exclusively—what were then being called "blockbusters"—by independent units that would be tied up on long-term contracts. He would give these independents the most generous profit-participation deals. "You have to spend a dollar to make a dollar and ten cents," he told MacBride, echoing an old Mayer aphorism. Only the profit-participation concession was new.

All in all Mayer impressed MacBride profoundly as a sincere and honest man. "I will move my bed into the studio in Culver City," Mayer repeatedly said. While that seemed beyond the call of duty, or indeed practicality, it conveyed a sense of the enthusiasm of the doughty old man to MacBride. The latter came to the conclusion that Mayer was not suited to administrate, but that he would be most effective as an "elder statesman" and as a magnet for attracting top producers and stars.

However, he found Mayer completely adamant on one point: he would not work with Vogel. Vogel would have to go!

MacBride's report on his survey was scheduled to be presented to the meeting of the directors in July. Then Vogel gave way to a fateful whimsy. He called for that meeting to be held at the Culver City studio. His reasoning was that the directors knew little about the manufacturing of films, had meager acquaintance with producers, and that some of them had never seen a motion picture plant. He thought this would be a good time to impress them with Metro-Goldwyn-Mayer. Little did he reckon on the peril of leading them straight into Mayer's back yard.

When the elements began to gather for this meeting it became evident that there had been talks behind the scenes, that the Vogel and "banker" factions had possibly shifted and that a showdown of some sort was in the wind. Rumors of a dramatic denouement added to the mystery and suspense.

Ogden Reid and his wife went out early and paid a significant call on Mayer, who was uncommonly charming to them. He showed Reid his living room full of Grandma Moses paintings, talked race horses to him, and took Mrs. Reid to the Farmers Market, where he bought her some fine strawberries. (Mayer always maintained a knowledge of where the best foods could be obtained.)

Carefully Reid attempted to probe and find out from Mayer what his aims were and what kind of effort he might be ready to make for the company. He got the pronounced impression that Mayer was eager to "get back" and that he would do anything he could to "help the studio." But would he consider accepting the *presidency* of Loew's, Inc., if it were offered to him? Reid put the question cautiously with no assurance whatsoever that it would be officially proposed.

Here was the ultimate challenge, the critical moment of truth. Was Mayer prepared to let himself be considered for the really important job—the job of making the big decisions—that he insisted had been bungled by other men?

He would not give Reid an immediate answer, said he would like to ponder it. That night he talked to his good friend, Ed Weisl, who happened to be the lawyer for both Lehman Brothers and Lazard Frères. Together they reached the grave conclusion that the job would be too tough for him. The next day Mayer imparted this information to Reid.

That same day Louis Johnson arrived in Los Angeles with a vital piece of speculation that he said he had got from Frank Pace. It was that MacBride's report would probably contain a recommendation that a change be made in the presidency. When informed by Reid and Weisl that Mayer was not interested in the job, it came as a staggering blow to him. He was there to lead a bold assault to get Mayer elected president at the upcoming meeting of the board!

However, Johnson did not despair completely, and the evening before the meeting he and a group of the Tomlinson-faction directors tried hard to get Mayer to change his mind, while they were gathered for an intimate cocktail party in the Mayer home.

Meanwhile, the Vogel forces found themselves in a vastly vulnerable spot. Two of their much-counted-on directors, Pace and Sullivan, could not get to the meeting on the Coast. This reduced their voting strength from six to four. The Tomlinson faction had them outnumbered, even without the vote of Reid!

In the face of the Hollywood rumors of an attempted coup d'état Vogel had good reason to become alarmed. He fearfully telephoned Louis Nizer (who happened to be in New Hampshire at the time), and a lawyer from the Nizer office was hastily flown to the Coast.

Ominous presentments of the crisis were evident on the day before the meeting, which was to take place on July 12. The directors had been invited to spend the day in a tour of the studio and have an informative luncheon with top producers and executives. Tomlinson, Meyer, and Johnson did not show up at all. Lawson and Florence attended the luncheon, but skipped the afternoon tour. It was learned that they had gone to a meeting with Tomlinson. This greatly embarrassed Vogel and caused one of the "Old Guard" executives to plead for a chance to tell the directors that the morale of the studio would be shattered by a return of Mayer.

That evening a cocktail-dinner party for the directors and their wives was given by the company at the Beverly-Hilton Hotel. When it was learned that a rival cocktail party was under way at the Mayer home, there was nervous waiting to see whether any of the Tomlinson directors would attend.

Sure enough, the Beverly-Hilton party was well under way and the Vogel people were beginning to despair, when Fred Florence, the Dallas banker, arrived alone. Florence had been hopefully reported as the least enthusiastic of the rival group. Later, when the guests had sat down to dinner, Tomlinson and Meyer arrived. Vogel's friends breathed a little easier. After dinner all the guests were taken to a preview of the new Metro-Goldwyn-Mayer musical, *High Society*.

However, the mood was far from sociable when the directors gathered the next morning in the big executive conference room of the Irving G. Thalberg Building at the studio. After some preliminary sparring Vogel asked MacBride to give his report, and the latter went into a lengthy examination of the management picture in the areas of finance, publicity, and sales.

Eventually, Johnson, in seeming impatience and with more than an intuitive sense of what to expect, asked MacBride if he had a report on the president. "I think in fairness to him and to the board, we should know that, if you have a conclusion," he said.

MacBride paused for a moment, cleared his throat, and said, "Our opinions on the president are that we have regretfully come to the conclusion that, because of the atmosphere, because of the questions raised by the president's failure to do some things which in our judgment he should have done, that a change should be considered by this board."

The answer dumbfounded Vogel. He expected trouble, yes, but he was not prepared for such a shattering recommendation. For several minutes he sat silent, stunned, while Johnson and K.T. Keller continued to question MacBride on the reasons for his recommendation. They seemed to be preparing a case. Soon a recess was taken, and the directors began caucusing.

During this recess Vogel received another sharp surprise. It was that Tex McCrary was in the building, waiting to release to the press word of results of the meeting. It was evident it had been assumed that important news would be forthcoming. On the previous day McCrary had alerted news-

papermen as far away as New York to be ready for a big announcement. McCrary happened to be not only public relations man for Tomlinson but also for Ogden Reid.

There was no doubt in Vogel's mind, at this point, that he
was faced with a carefully laid plot.

And, in subsequent reflections on this meeting, Johnson
and others have surmised that they might, then and there,
have ousted Vogel and forced the election of Mayer, *if* they
had been able to give assurance to other directors in caucus
that the latter would take the job. But they could not. Mayer
stood by his decision. He had resisted the urgings and pleas
of his determined friends at the cocktail party the evening
before. So, with no other candidate to offer, the Tomlinson
faction was balked. The rallying point for their assault had
evaporated. Right there, the tide of battle turned.

It was not over, by a great deal. That day Johnson stubbornly pressed for immediate action on the MacBride recommendation, and when Vogel would not let the question be
discussed, because it was not on the agenda and the full panel
of directors was not present to permit it being put there,
Johnson arbitrarily took over the meeting from the president
and appointed a committee to prepare a memorandum on the
recommendation. It seemed significant that he appointed Pace,
Reid, Tomlinson, and himself.

Immediately after this explosive meeting, Vogel got together with counsel and several directors who were unswerv-
ingly loyal to him and decided he would have to call a special
stockholders' meeting, wherein he would expose "the plot"
and call for ouster of Tomlinson and Meyer from the board.
"I could no longer deceive myself that I could traffic with
evil," he said.

On July 22, Vogel issued his call for a special stockholders'
meeting and prefaced it with a candid and withering denunciation of the man who had always said he "had made
the company great." He wrote:

Tomlinson and Meyer, with the constant guidance of Louis B. Mayer, have been actively attempting to seize control of this great public company and against the interests of the stockholders. The stockholders and the entire motion picture industry are well aware of Mayer's record when he was in supreme command at the studio. During his tenure of twenty-seven years, he received over $20,000,000 in compensation. In the last three years of Mayer's sole authority as the studio's head in 1947, 1948 and 1949 the pictures released lost about $9,000,000. This is the man who, at the age of 72, is attempting to recapture his position through the Tomlinson-Meyer machinations.

But events leading to a grisly ending were even then under way. The special committee appointed to study the Mac-Bride report had met without coming to any conclusion, and Reid and Pace had suddenly resigned as directors, saying the whole matter should be left to the stockholders.

With the Vogel faction again weakened, Johnson and Tomlinson hastened to call a directors' meeting to be held on July 30 in New York. Vogel naturally refused to sanction this meeting, so it became a "rump" affair, with only Johnson, Tomlinson, Meyer, Lawson, and Keller attending it. Fred Florence had resigned in disagreement with the tactics being pursued.

Mayer went to New York for this "rump" meeting and allowed himself to be named a director, along with Sam Briskin. Vogel had the building full of armed guards, just in case an attempt was made to stage a physical coup d'etat.

To reporters who spoke to Mayer while he was waiting, hat in hand, outside the board room at Loew's he appeared jaunty and answered lightly, "I am here because I am lonely for Leo the Lion." But it seemed a dismal reunion. And it is doubtful, indeed, that Mayer had any real expectation of its being legal or permanent.

Also, on the day of the "rump" meeting, MacBride significantly submitted a written report, amending his former recommendation and saying, in the light of all that had occurred, it appeared evident that it would be better for Vogel to carry on.

Evidently Mayer was just completing what he felt was an obligation to the men whom he had originally encouraged and drawn into this dramatic assault. Certainly he had no taste or intention to be a director, nothing more.

Years before, in giving a deposition in a stockholders' suit against Loew's, Inc., he had made a positive declaration of his feelings on this point. Asked by counsel for the plaintiffs why he did not wish to be a director of the company, he said:

"I don't want to be a director . . . just because of what you fellows are doing in this case. Take the greatest company that was ever built—it is a romance. Take a stockholder with ten or twenty shares compelling you to sit here and have to answer for everything that has been built, after you have built what I have built!"

Q. "You mean you would rather not take the legal responsibility of being a director?"
A. "I don't want to be a director or an officer of a bank or anything else. I don't like directorships in any kind of an institution."

Some people who were very close to him felt that he was severely hurt when he realized that the bankers and others were not falling over themselves to get him back into the company. The necessity of having to battle, to charm, and even to beg for a chance to return to the studio was believed to have shaken him. And when he finally sensed his position as a mere factor in a campaign to grab the company to which he was basically devoted, he was said to have lost all heart.

Louis Johnson has another speculation for his refusal to be a candidate for the presidency. He thinks that Mayer, even then, may have known that he was sick and that his strength was beginning to ebb. Johnson had several times urged him to go to the Mayo Clinic for a check-up, he said, and Mayer had scoffed at the suggestion. Did he fear what a check-up might reveal?

Perhaps so. But only a few days after that flying visit to the Loew's building in New York, Mayer went to San Francisco and checked in at the Stanford University Hospital. He could no longer deny the exhaustion and discomfort he felt. There he remained for seven weeks frequently seeing friends and making a last feeble effort to get George Killion to strike for the presidency of the company. On August 26 Delaware courts ruled the "rump" session illegal. So Mayer was not a director of Loew's, Inc. He was a sick, defeated man.

The official word was that he had a "blood disorder," and that is what he thought he had. They did not tell him he had leukemia, a form of the cancer he had dreaded for so many years. When he was returned to his home in September, he confidently believed he was getting well, but three days later he had to be taken to the Medical Center of the University of California in Los Angeles.

And that was the end of his road.

The last few weeks of his life must have been misery of the cruelest sort for Mayer, for in those weeks he was finally confronted with the realization of his own mortality. When he entered the Medical Center he seemed hopeful and happy enough. Much attention and consideration were shown him by attendants and friends. His daughter, Irene, came on from New York to see him, spent a few days, then returned, giving him the intended illusion that everything was all right and she could safely go home.

But as the days dragged on and he got no better—as the liquid they pumped into his veins was a constantly visible evidence to him that his life was hanging, as it were, by a rubber tube—he sensed the extremity of his condition. He certainly suspected his disease. And his stubborn self-assurance of a recovery was based entirely on his belief in miracles.

One day his nephew, Jack Cummings, was visiting in his

room, when the tube of the intravenous feeder came loose
from the connection with Mayer's arm. A look of dismay and
terror came over the face of the ill man, and he stammered
to his nephew to rush out and fetch a nurse. When the tube
was reconnected, Mayer gave a sigh of relief.

A few weeks later the same thing happened, but the patient, now more wasted and weak, feebly called it to his
nephew's attention. This time, after it was returned, Mayer
sighed, with profound dejection, "It's not going to work. I
can't go on." That indicated to his nephew that he had abandoned hope for a miracle.

In the last days his separation from his daughter, Edith,
apparently haunted him, and he often muttered to Jessie
Marmorston, who stood by firmly, "Has she come yet? Is she
outside?" The anxiety of what would have happened had
Edith entered his room was one of the sad considerations and
reasons that kept her away.

The ultimate dramatic incident in this crisis was enacted
in New York. There, on October 15, the stockholders of
Loew's, Inc., overwhelmingly voted confidence in Joe Vogel
and completed the rout of the Tomlinson group. That was
the final, shattering skirmish in the bitter, destructive, deadly
war.

But the humiliation of it had by now drained out of Mayer.
He was past disappointment, past caring. He had come to
the end of his rope, and he hadn't the physical or moral
strength to tie the knot and hang on.

What was perhaps his conclusive and pathetic summation
of life was said to his loyal friend, Howard Strickling, shortly
before he died. In an effort to make some conversation
Strickling was telling him of the progress and problems at
the studio.

"Don't let them worry you," Mayer muttered. "Nothing
matters, nothing matters."

That was all.

At thirty-five minutes after midnight, on October 29,

1957, Mayer died. His wife and daughter, Irene, were at his bedside, to use the conventional phrase.

The funeral arrangements were handled by Irene, who wished to have Spencer Tracy read the eulogy written by David Selznick, Carey Wilson, and John Lee Mahin. Up to the very minute of the service, there was anxiety whether Tracy would come through, and Wilson was standing by to go on for him. But that was not necessary.

Ironically the temple was not filled for the services. Mayer's funeral was not now the occasion for the great community grief that it might once have been. Daughter Edith attended, but not her husband, Goetz. There were some conspicuous absences in the ranks of the mourners. One was Nicholas Schenck.

However, the studio which the dead man had headed for so long was represented well by all of the "Old Guard" of executives, now loyal to the new regime. Their presence, lined up in a phalanx, provoked a ghoulish joke which became, in the Hollywood tradition, the popular comment on the passing of Mayer.

An observer, viewing the solemn phalanx, was reported to have said to his companion, "Well, I see that M-G-M has got L.B. back at last."

"Yes," his companion was supposed to have answered, "but on its own terms."

# Epilogue

"This is the end of a volume, not a chapter," Rabbi Edgar Magnin said, in speaking his own personal eulogy at the funeral of Louis Mayer. What he meant was that an age had been completed, and *finis* written, with the passing of this man.

The fact was that the age he represented—the age of great expansion in American films, the era of the motion picture mogul—had passed several years before he died. Many and subtle changes in the film business after World War II had rendered obsolete and archaic the kind of monarchial management for which he stood. The stars could no longer be collected and controlled within his own galaxy; the market could not longer be engrossed with a massive output of glittering films.

Vainly Mayer sometimes insisted, "I want to rule by love, not by fear." Incredibly he never realized how passé was his point, "I want to rule."

The pitiful thing was that he pictured himself an endowed

proprietor of the motion picture medium, and resented the preëmptions of younger men. He could not perceive the medium as a great, fluid cultural device, available for anyone to use it, like language or the alphabet. And thus, with others of his generation—or his age in the film industry—he saw change as a personal invasion, not as the promise of better things ahead.

Bitterness putrefied his last years, and the final shock to friends in Hollywood was the revelation of his dead hand making last vengeful slaps through his will, drawn for him in 1954 by a law firm he had not previously used. To his wife he left a modest fortune: $750,000 and their home. To his daughter, Irene, and his adopted daughter, Suzanne, the daughter of Lorena, he left $500,000 each. He also left sums to Irene's two sons, to Howard Strickling, and to his sister, Ida Mae. But he specifically directed that no legacy be given to his once adored Edith or her children. "I have given them extremely substantial assistance during my lifetime," the will sourly said. He likewise neglected to leave a bequest to his friend and doctor, Jessie Marmorston.

Ironically most of his fortune, which was ultimately checked out at some $7,500,000, a great deal less than it was thought to be, was left to the Louis B. Mayer Foundation, a fund for charitable purposes, presumably, but no instructions for its disposition were given the trustees, who were his widow, his business manager, Myron Fox, and his nephew, Gerald Mayer. Possibly he expected them to find some way to send it on to him.

Several relatives and other persons later contested the will. Thus the dismal contentions continued long after Mayer died.

Whether this was, indeed, intended by the violent, relentless man is a tempting speculation. He may have sensed, subconsciously, that he would be best remembered for his turmoils and inconsistencies.

The last time this writer called upon him, he took from

his desk a card on which was printed a poem, and presented
it with pride. The printed title of the poem was "The Man
in the Glass," and these were the first and last stanzas:

> When you get what you want in your struggle for self
> And the world makes you king for a day,
> Just go to a mirror and look at yourself,
> And see what that man has to say . . .
>
> You may fool the whole world down the pathway of years
> And get pats on your back as you pass,
> But your final reward will be heartache and tears
> If you've cheated the man in the glass.

Perhaps he was thoroughly contented with the image he
had of himself. Or that may have been the impression,
the illusion he wanted to give.

# Index

ABIGAIL E. WEEKS MEMORIAL LIBRARY

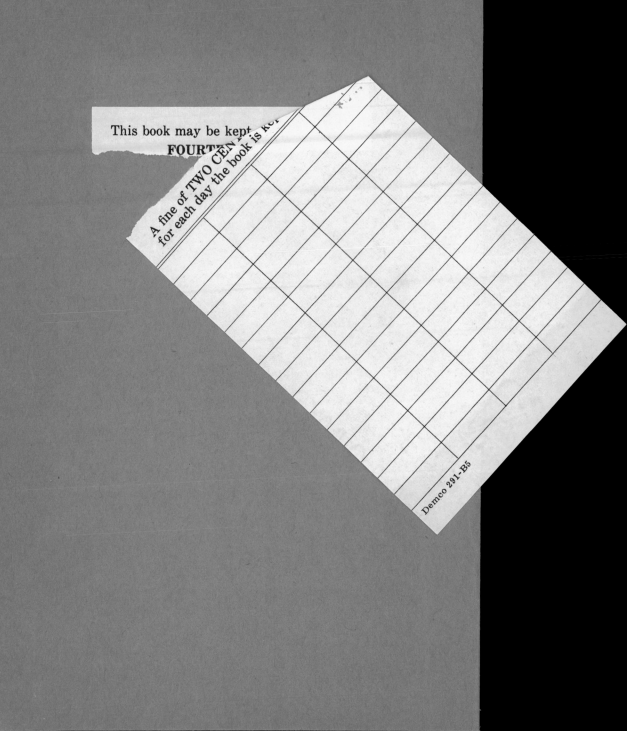

This book may be kept

**FOURTEEN**

A fine of TWO CEN
for each day the book is ke

Demco 291-B5